The Bibliomania

THE BIBLIOMANIA

or

𝕭𝔬𝔬𝔨 𝔐𝔞𝔡𝔫𝔢𝔰𝔰

CONTAINING SOME ACCOUNT OF THE

HISTORY, SYMPTOMS, AND CURE OF
THIS FATAL DISEASE.

In an Epistle addressed to
RICHARD HEBER, Esq.

BY THE
REV. THOMAS FROGNALL DIBDIN, F. S. A.

EDITED BY
PETER DANCKWERTS

Styll am I besy bokes assemblynge,
For to have plenty it is a plesaunt thynge
In my conceyt, and to have them ay in honde:
But what they mene do I nat understonde.
Pynson's Ship of Fools. Edit. 1509.

RICHMOND: TIGER OF THE STRIPE

2007

Paperback first published in 2007 by
TIGER OF THE STRIPE
50 Albert Road
Richmond upon Thames
Surrey TW10 6DP

This edition first published in 2004 by
TIGER OF THE STRIPE

ISBN-10 1-904799-17-5
ISBN-13 978-1-904799-17-7

Typeset in the UK by
TIGER OF THE STRIPE

Printed & bound by Lightning Source
Milton Keynes, UK & LaVergne, TN, USA

Contents

Introduction

Dibdin's *Bibliomania,* first published in 1809, is an
anthem to the printed book, a warning to the unwary
about the perils of obsessive book-collecting, and the
confessions of a rabid book-collector.

THE PURPOSE OF THIS EDITION

While this edition will be of particular interest to
historians of printing and the book, to librarians and
book-collectors, it should also appeal to anyone with
an interest in human nature or the cultural history of
England seen from a distinctive Regency perspective.

As a casual glance will show, Dibdin's footnotes
predominate over text, and it is in the footnotes that
the interest lies. They invite questions as often as they
answer them. What is the supposed similarity between
'Orator' Henley's library and Addison's memoranda
for the *Spectator*? What cutting words did Edward
Gibbon write about Thomas Hearne? Why should we
not be surprised to find a book on American history
by a Spanish admiral in the library of the President of

the Royal Society? Who was Captain Cox who 'could talk as much without book, as any Innholder betwixt Brentford and Bagshot'? Was Polydore Vergil a plagiarist and John Bagford a biblioclast? What is blot-erature? Sometimes Dibdin tells us, sometimes he assumes we know, and sometimes he chooses to tantalise us. The endnotes provide some of the answers and will, I hope, lead readers to discover new books and new writers, or, more often and more pleasurably, *old* books and *old* writers.

BOOK MADNESS

The BIBLIOMANIA, or the collecting [of] an enormous heap of Books, without intelligent curiosity, has, since libraries have existed, been the rage with some, who would fain pass themselves on us as men of erudition. Their motley Libraries have been called the Mad-houses of the human Mind... The BIBLIOMANIA has never raged more violently than in the present age... [D'Israeli 1807, i, p. 10]

Is there really such a thing as THE BIBLIOMANIA? Were John Leland, Thomas Hearne, the Duke of Roxburghe, Earl Spencer and Dibdin himself suffering from some sort of obsessive–compulsive disorder? Certainly, some were driven to spend vast sums on books they could not hope to catalogue, let alone read. Although the texts were of primary importance to many of these collectors, even Dibdin, whose *Intro-*

duction to the classics [Dibdin 1808] lays such emphasis on textual accuracy, cannot ignore the allure of large paper copies, 𝕭𝖑𝖆𝖈𝖐𝖑𝖊𝖙𝖙𝖊𝖗 type, copies on vellum, and luxuriant bindings.

Dibdin's *Bibliomania* is not, of course, a medical text, but a light-hearted and entertaining jaunt through the byways of bibliophilia, only occasionally skirting the sadder aspects of true mania (as in the case of Leland). It is interesting that a certain gloom only descends upon Dibdin's writing in *Bibliophobia* [Dibdin 1832] when book prices are falling. One might have thought that low book prices would be welcomed by the collector but, not only does it devalue his existing collection, it also calls into question his judgement in buying so extravagantly in the first place. In Dibdin's case, one also feels that he regrets that the true worth of some noble volumes is no longer appreciated as it should be.

The first edition of *Bibliomania*, however, was written and published in 1809, in a period of exuberant and extravagant bibliophilia which had lasted for many decades. The eighteenth-century sale catalogues cited by Dibdin bear witness to this. Of course, with few public institutions to remove books from circulation permanently, there must have been greater liquidity in the book market. It might be thought that this, coupled with relatively low literacy rates, would mean that books would be quite cheap in real terms, but we learn in *Bibliomania* (p. 66) that a copy of Somervile's *Chase* illustrated by John and Thomas Bewick fetched £15 4*s* 6*d* in 1804, only eight years after it was printed. At this time, a London compositor, one of the most skilled and highly-paid craftsmen, might expect to earn £1 13*s* per week [Howe 1947, p. 163] and would therefore have had to work for over nine weeks to pay for such a book. Dibdin himself only earned £30 a year for an evening lectureship at Brompton [Dibdin 1836, p. 221]. At the time of writing this Introduction, several copies of this book are available, one in a Rivière binding from Blackwell's Rare Books for £675 and a large paper copy in contemporary full blue morocco with elaborate gilt panelled sides, described as 'a very handsome copy', is available from Thomas Thorp, Fine and Rare Books, for £600. Even at the National Minimum Wage of £4.50 per hour, it would only take about four weeks to pay for a copy, so it can be seen that some very high prices were being paid in the early nineteenth century. Perhaps there really was a bibliomanic miasma in the air. However, it must be admitted that the copy referred to by Dibdin was on vellum, and it is impossible to guess what that would sell for today.

Dibdin was prompted to write *Bibliomania* by the appearance of a poem of the same name (which is included on p. 85) by John Ferriar, a distinguished Manchester physician. Ferriar, who worked with the

mentally ill, would have been better placed to pass a
medical judgement upon the existence of the book
disease than Dibdin, but his poem is no more a medical treatise than Dibdin's book. Nonetheless, the medical associations with *Bibliomania* are not insignificant. Dibdin's pages are peopled not only with wealthy
aristocrats, such as the Duke of Roxburghe and the
Earl of Pembroke, but with physicians, anatomists and
surgeons. We find here references to William Hunter,
the Anatomist, William Heberden, a pioneer of smallpox inoculation, Edward Jenner of smallpox vaccination fame, John Ferriar, whose doctoral dissertation
was on smallpox, and Thomas Sydenham, the 'English
Hippocrates'. Others include John Caius (of College
fame), James Jurin, Richard Mead, Patrick Blair, John
Burges and Charles Chauncey.

Quite why medical men play such a large part in
Bibliomania is unclear. Does it reflect their importance
in book-collecting of the period or a bias on Dibdin's
part? The former seems more likely as Dibdin's early
training was in the law, not medicine. In general, of
course, members of the medical profession were reasonably well educated and reasonably wealthy. Some,
such as William Hunter, became remarkably wealthy.
Their wealth allowed them to collect and their education gave them the desire to do so. Or it may be simply
that the altruism which guided the lives of so many

medical men also prompted them to share their libraries and their literary discoveries freely with others, something which Hulsius describes as essential in a bibliographer (pp. 78–80, note 72).

The many references to medical men point to another aspect of *Bibliomania*. To its intended readership, this little book is full of allusions; it has the power to conjure up images of so much more than printing, books and book-collecting. Almost every person, every book mentioned, sets up sympathetic resonances in the informed reader's mind.

For instance, one can hardly fail to notice the preponderance of Anglicans, Lutherans and Calvinists, for Dibdin's God, if not an Englishman, is certainly of a Protestant complexion. Dibdin's later religious pamphlets show him to be an old-fashioned Anglican, tolerant of other faiths and forms of Christianity, but passionately concerned to keep the Church of England Protestant, a stalwart in the fight against Puseyism and Newmanism. In his pamphlet, *On modern Catholicism,* Dibdin wrote:

> When Ministers and members of the *Church of England* disclaim the designation of *Protestantism,* and call the Reformation 'the rebellion of Henry VIII.' – When Clergymen bow before the altar, and turn from the congregation in the utterance of certain portions of the Liturgy – and when the Cross and Crucifix are introduced where, hitherto, such

introduction was considered 'the outward and visible sign'
of *Papacy* – it is time to call things by their right names, and
to take up a position which the circumstances of the case
clearly and strongly inculcate. [Dibdin 1839, p. 3 f.n.]

At the same time, Dibdin is careful to preach toler-
ance, telling us that 'in this free and happy country, we
quarrel, or *ought* to quarrel, with *no* man for going to
what place of worship he pleases' [Dibdin 1839, p. 10].

Not surprisingly, *Bibliomania* notices pamphlets associated with the Marprelate Controversy, including *A
checke or reproofe of Mr. Howlet's untimely screeching in
Her Majesty's ear* by the Puritan Perceval Wiburn, and
John Lyly's anti-Marprelate tract, *Pappe with an hatchett*. Whether intentionally or not, Dibdin has, by the
mere mention of a few pamphlets, reminded us of one
of the formative moments in the Church of England,
the battle of words between episcopy and the Puritans,
conducted with equal vehemence and wit.

It is natural, also, that Dibdin should favour the old
English historians Leland, Camden, Stowe and Hearne
and the more dubious charms of Fabyan, Hall, Holinshed and Hardyng but it is sad that the old calumnies
are repeated against Polydore Vergil, one of the most
methodical of Tudor historians. His only crimes were to
question the historical accuracy of Arthurian myth and
to have acted for the Vatican as collector of St Peter's
Pence, but the one offends against English patriotism

and the other against Anglicanism (if, indeed, they are divisible). Naturally, Lady Jane Grey, the tragic Protestant pretender to the throne, is also mentioned.

Dibdin's love of 𝕭lackletter is not so much a fondness for 'that very black and rough appearance of the letters' (although that seems to have played a part) but their Englishness or Britishness. Long after the introduction of roman types, English texts tended to be printed in textura, whilst Latin (and other foreign tongues) in the same volume would be set in roman type. When Dibdin praises Sir Walter Scott and Francis Douce for their mastery of 𝕭lackletter texts (pp. 72–3), it is because these texts had been largely ignored by earlier scholars, and because they represent English literature and English history.

It must be said, however, that Dibdin is no Little Englander. On pp. 12–13, he expresses pride in his nation's achievements:

> …if ever there was a country upon the face of the globe… distinguished for the variety, the justness, and magnanimity of its views; if ever there was a nation which really and unceasingly 'felt for another's woe'… if ever there was a country and a set of human beings, pre-eminently distinguished for all the social virtues which soften and animate the soul of man, surely Old England and Englishmen are they!

But he is quick to acknowledge that this may be dismissed as the 'common cant… of all writers in favor of the country where they chance to live'.

Another possible theme in *Bibliomania* – if only in the editor's imagination – is the anti-slavery movement. Gathered in this slender book, published twenty-four years before the passing of the Slavery Abolition Act, we find John Ferriar, William Roscoe, Charles James Fox and Antonio de Ulloa, all in their way opponents of slavery. No doubt this theme is unintended; mention enough contemporaries and near-contemporaries in 1809 and a proportion of them will be anti-slavery activists. But this does not matter; the book offers us an opportunity, and an excuse, to study Regency attitudes and customs.

Whatever the intended or unintended allusions, the main subject of *Bibliomania* is, as it should be, books. Dibdin does not yet display the great familiarity with the book trade of his own day which is evident in his later works but, thanks to what must have been an impressive collection of auction catalogues, he can look back over sixty years and more to tell us who bought what, when, and how much they paid.

Dibdin seems to invite us to share his passion – imagine you had been at the Missenden Abbey sale of 1774 and had been able to buy Wynkyn de Worde's *Orcharde of Syon* for £1 13*s*; or you had attended the sale of John Ratcliffe's library in 1776 and had bought Spenser's *Shephearde's calender* and Whetstone's *Castle of delight* together for £1 2*s*.

Almost all that follows in this section is drawn from Dibdin's *Reminiscences of a literary life* [Dibdin 1836].

Birth and Education

Thomas Frognall Dibdin's father, also Thomas, a former officer in the Royal Navy, moved to India in the 1770s to earn his living as the skipper of a merchantman. Here he carried freight and passengers between Calcutta and Madras. In 1775 he married Elizabeth Compton who had accompanied her brother, another sea-captain, to India. Their marriage license was the first ever issued in British India. Their son, Thomas Frognall Dibdin, was born in Calcutta in 1776.

Captain Dibdin suffered a series of mishaps. He was duped and defrauded by officers of the East India Company several times, his ship foundered and he was injured by lightning.[1] In 1780, he and his wife decided to return to England, taking a Danish vessel to the Cape of Good Hope and a Dutch vessel thence. Sadly, Captain Dibdin died while the ship was off the Cape, and his widow continued the journey, with her three-year-old son, to Middleburg in the Netherlands, where she herself died.

The young orphan was fortunate to be placed under the guardianship of his mother's younger brother,

William Compton, who seems to have discharged his duties well. Although there was not much money, Thomas received a decent education.

His first school was run by a Mr John Man of Hosier's Lane, Reading. He was a kind and clever man who allowed Thomas the free run of his book collection.

Thomas was then sent to school in Stockwell, now a bustling suburb of London, but then a small village in Surrey. During his two years here he learnt French, Latin and drawing.

His final school, situated between Brentford and Isleworth, was run by a Scot, the Reverend Dr Greenlaw. The school was later attended by Percy Bysshe Shelley and one of his biographers gives us this description:

> Sion House Academy was a large, somewhat gloomy brick building, formerly belonging to the Bishop of London; its situation was open and healthy; a garden was attached, and a playground walled in, and possessing a solitary elm, known as the Bell-tree, from its serving as campanile for the harsh summoner whose tongue jangled forth the order to resume lessons. There was certainly no luxury or refinement at Sion House; economy was kept well in view by Mrs. Greenlaw and her sister, Miss Hodgkins. [Dowden 1887, i, p. 13]

In contrast, Dibdin tells us that it had 'both within and without, a most cheerful air' [Dibdin 1836, p. 70]. At any rate, he thrived here and particularly enjoyed rambling through Twickenham Meadows and climbing Richmond Hill.

Having achieved a sufficient mastery of Latin and Greek, Dibdin then went to St John's College, Oxford. From his own account, the University seems to have offered a very poor standard of education. To fill what Dibdin called 'the dull, aching void', he and a number of his colleagues proposed a 'Society for Scientific and Literary Disquisition' which would meet in a hired room of a private house. Unfortunately, this required the consent of the Vice-Chancellor, Dr John Wills, who, in Dibdin's words, 'considered *innovation* and *revolution* as synonymous' and prohibited this arrangement. Undaunted, the undergraduates held meetings in their own rooms and the group, commonly known as 'The Lunatics', was born. It seems to have been during this period that Dibdin developed his abiding interest in English Literature and the 𝔅𝔩𝔞𝔠𝔨𝔩𝔢𝔱𝔱𝔢𝔯, despite rather than because of the University (it must be remembered that Oxford only appointed its first Professor of English Literature in 1904).

A Legal Career

Dibdin took an early interest in the law and often went to the Guildhall to watch cases being pleaded by leading KCs before Lord Kenyon, Chief Justice of the King's Bench. When he left Oxford, it was not surprising that he chose to train for the Bar. He enrolled as a student in Lincoln's Inn, kept the dining terms and was taken on as a pupil by an able bankruptcy lawyer, Basil Montague.

Perhaps a less amiable pupil-master than Montague would have required greater application from the young man, but Dibdin's interest wandered and he spent much of his time at the Royal Academy Summer Exhibition when he should have been learning the law and making contacts. When the time came for him to set up his own chambers in Gray's Inn, he found that no work came in.

In desperation, Dibdin, who was newly married, determined to move to Worcester where he hoped to work as a provincial counsel. This plan also proved unfruitful and he eked out a living from conveyancing.

A Career in the Church

Realising that he was not suited to the law, and being drawn to religion and literature, he decided to become a priest in the Church of England. He was ordained a deacon on 24 December 1804 and a priest less than three months later. He was then appointed to a curacy in Kensington, where he remained for nearly twenty years.

Thanks to the patronage of Earl Spencer, he was appointed vicar of Exning in Suffolk, two miles from Newmarket, in 1823. His next preferment (which Dibdin also credited to the Earl) was to the new church of St Mary's, Bryanstone Square, Marylebone, which was consecrated on 7 January 1824.[2] His other appointments included an evening lectureship at the Brompton Chapel and the position of Preacher at the Swallow Street Chapel. In 1831 he was appointed a Royal Chaplain in Ordinary.

A Writing Career

Dibdin's literary output was substantial and it is beyond the scope of this book to give a full acount of it. For that, the reader should turn to the bibliography by John Windle and Karma Pippin [Windle & Pippin 1999].

Dibdin's first book was a collection of poems [Dibdin 1797]. As *Bibliomania* tells us (p. 11), he ended up destroying half the 500 copies he produced, although the poems compare quite favourably with, for instance, the youthful offerings of Lord Byron in *Hours of idleness*. A more interesting foray into the poetic art may have been his poem 'Vaccinia' promoting vaccination. However, as far as is known, no copy survives. In the same year he published *Whole law relative to the rights of persons*, and (perhaps in 1798) *Law of the poor rate* 'on a very small sheet, price 6*d*' [Dibdin 1836, p. 191]. Neither of these publications seems to have survived.

In 1798 he and some friends launched a weekly arts magazine, *The quiz*, the existence of which was cut short by a fire at the printer's premises.

His first book with a vaguely bibliographical lean-
ing was *Introduction to the classics*, originally published
in 1802. The second edition appeared in 1804, the third
in 1808 and the fourth in 1827. This book, a simple annotated list of available editions with comments on the
quality of the texts, was extremely successful and must
have encouraged Dibdin to turn his hand to more am-
bitious projects.

By the time that Ferriar published his *Bibliomania* in
1809, Dibdin was well into one of his most impressive
works, a new and enlarged edition of Joseph Ames's
Typographical antiquities. It was no doubt thanks to this
preparation, and his work on *Introduction to the classics*,
that Dibdin had the information 'at hiz fingers endz'
for his own *Bibliomania* and could compile it with such
impressive speed – it was written 'within a lunar month'
[Dibdin 1836, p. 272], a remarkable feat when one con-
siders the mass of information it contains.

Typographical antiquities [Ames 1810–19] set the
pattern for most of Dibdin's later output. The quality
of its printing and illustrations (a mixture of wood and
copper engravings) is superb – and the expense must
have been horrific for a man of Dibdin's limited means.
Fortunately, it was a success and Dibdin cleared about
£600 profit [Dibdin 1836, p. 280]. Perhaps the possibil-
ity of large profits, as well as bibliomaniacal zeal, drove
Dibdin to publish more and more books.

In 1811 the second edition of Dibdin's *Bibliomania* appeared, no longer a slender 92 pages, but a stout 796. The second edition of Ferriar's *Bibliomania* was to appear in 1812, but only enlarged by a few lines.

Another of Dibdin's major projects was the *Bibliotheca Spenceriana* [Spencer 1814–15], a massive work which grew larger when Earl Spencer bought the Cassano Library. Dibdin finally added two heavily-illustrated volumes, entitled *Ædes Althorpiana* (1822), on the books and pictures of the Earl's country house. Dibdin calculated that he had spent four years on the Spencer Collection but he looked back on those years 'with unmixed satisfaction' [Dibdin 1836, p. 486].

The next major work, in 1817, was *The bibliographical decameron* in three hefty, heavily-illustrated volumes, a total of 1,748 pages. Dibdin paid almost £2,000 for the copper engravings alone, and the printing and paper for them cost another £350, to mention nothing of the typesetting, the wood engraving, letterpress printing and text paper [Dibdin 1836, pp. 583–5]. In a reckless moment, Dibdin had his friends throw the choicest woodblocks on the fire, unintentionally ensuring that no French edition was practical [ibid., pp. 627–8, 652]. As in the 1811 *Bibliomania*, the *Bibliographical decameron* takes the form of bibliographical discussions between Dibdin and his friends using 'romantic' names. As in *Bibliomania*, the main interest lies in the footnotes.

In 1821 Dibdin published *A bibliographical tour in France and Germany,* another highly-illustrated book in three volumes which cost him £4,740 to produce [Dibdin 1836, p. 654]. This time, he lost £120 on the book, excluding his travelling expenses of £300 [ibid., p. 663].

Dibdin's next major work was *The library companion* in 1824 and the reviews were rather poor, although Dibdin does not tell us what the financial outcome was. For some years, Dibdin contented himself with more modest publications, including *Bibliophobia* in 1832. His *Reminiscences* of 1836, although over a thousand pages, was not extravagantly illustrated. However, in 1838 he published his *Tour in the northern counties of England,* another large and expensive work, full of engravings and lithographs. Once more, some of the reviews were unfavourable.

Decline and Fall

It is not clear that Dibdin was afflicted by true bibliomania, or even that such an ailment exists, but it does seem that he suffered from an addiction to publishing in a manner which was recklessly extravagant. He was like a compulsive gambler who, having won, bets again in the hope of repeating his success; when he loses, he bets again in the hope of recouping his losses.

Had he not outlived most of his friends and acquaintances, his books might have continued to sell well through their continued patronage, but it was not to be. The world had changed and the book market, as he described in *Bibliophobia,* had declined. Moreover, Dibdin's scholarship was rather antiquated. He was a Regency amateur in the harsh new world of Victorian professionalism. His carelessness, especially over names,[3] was less tolerated in this new age.

It is said that in 1819 Dibdin became 'entangled in those pecuniary difficulties for which, for the remainder of his life, he continued to suffer' [*Gentleman's Magazine,* Jan, 1848, i, p. 91].

He died in 1847 after a long illness, having suffered 'paralysis of the brain' (a stroke). It was said that his wife and daughter (his two sons having pre-deceased him) were 'relieved from the pressures of distress which might otherwise have overwhelmed them by the generosity of Earl Spencer' (that is, the the third Earl Spencer, son of Dibdin's patron) who had insured his life for £1,000 [ibid., p. 92].

Dibdin as a Bibliographer/Bibliomaniac

Dibdin can hardly be said to fit the modern conception of a bibliographer. His admiration of books as artefacts often overwhelmed his interest in their contents, to the extent that he craved uncut copies. To any sensible person, a book with uncut bolts is an abomination because it cannot be read, and yet there are still many book collectors who will pay a premium for a book which is thus *virgo intacta*.

Equally foolish to the modern mind is his emphasis on first editions. His references to Homer 'first editions' in *Bibliomania* and *Introduction to the classics* seem to imply that first printed editions are somehow more important, more authoritative, than later editions, without any consideration of the manuscripts from which they are derived.

A yet greater folly is the concept of 'true' editions where press variants which any sensible person would regard as uncorrected errors are elevated to a position of greater importance than texts in corrected states. William Jerdan, in his memoir of Dibdin, wrote:

> Instead of valuing books for the intelligence their authors had committed to them, book-collectors were taught that the sense they contained had nothing at all to do with their market cost, but that, to be uncut, and consequently unread; to be an 'editio princeps,' and therefore without later corrections or improvements; to be 'ymprynted' by William Caxton or Wynkyn de Worde; to be rare, and, in addition to their rarity, to be remarkable for some notable mistake or error; or, above all, to be unique, were the grand recommendations.   [Jerdan 1866, p. 170]

Jerdan and others seem to lay the blame at Dibdin's door, but this is unfair. Dibdin at least acknowledged the folly of his passion for uncut copies (p. 59) and he made the same argument as Jerdan with regard to first editions (p.68). Again, Dibdin is as scathing about 'true' editions as is Jerdan (p. 69). Either Jerdan had not read Dibdin's *Bibliomania* or he had completely misunderstood it.

The characteristics which Jerdan identified with bibliomania are still with us today. Antiquarian books are valued as artefacts and, surely, there is nothing wrong with this; in most cases, their contents are now superseded by more authoritative editions, but one can still admire their presswork, paper, typography and bindings. If this admiration is mingled with a certain amount of greed, ignorance and bad taste, that is simply the nature of modern society – one need only look at the art market to find all three in abundance.

Dibdin may have been associated, to some extent, with dilettantism,[4] but to criticise him as a bibliographer is to miss the point. He was not a bibliographer in the modern sense, using the physical evidence to establish more accurate texts, but a bibliophile, a book-collector and (dare I say it?) a bibliomaniac.

JOHN FERRIAR

John Ferriar was born in 1761 in Oxnam, Roxburgh-shire. He studied medicine at Edinburgh University, writing a dissertation on smallpox, and graduating in 1781. After a spell in practice at Stockton-on-Tees, he moved to Manchester in about 1785 and was appointed Physician at Manchester Royal Infirmary. Between

1792 and 1798 he published *Medical histories and reflec-tions* and, in 1799, *An essay on the medical properties of the Digitalis purpurea, or foxglove.*

Ferriar proved himself an innovative and enthusias-tic campaigner for public health. He made a study of typhus fever during the outbreak of 1788 and advocated improvements in living conditions of the poor. He championed shorter working hours, public baths and the provision of cricket facilities.

Ferriar also supervised the 'Anti-maniac' therapy carried out at the Manchester Lunatic Hospital which contained twenty-two cells for private patients [How-ells 1984, ii, p. 576]. A description of this work appears in the first American edition of *Medical histories* in which he writes 'though I would exclude everything painful and terrible, from a lunatic-house, yet the management of hope and apprehension in the patient, forms the most useful part of discipline' [Ferriar 1816, ii, p. 188].

Remarkably, Ferriar, 'debarr'd of ease and studious hours' (p. 92), still found time for other interests. He was a prominent member of the Manchester Literary and Philosophical Society. Under its ægis, he published many works, including 'Illustrations of Sterne' which pointed out the borrowings in *Tristram Shandy* from Burton's *Anatomy of melancholy* and other sources.

Ferriar also rewrote Southerne's dramatisation of Aphra Behn's *Oroonoko* as *The prince of Angola*

[Ferriar 1788] to give it an even stronger anti-slavery message and dubbed earlier versions 'a grovelling apology of slaveholders' [Aravamudan 1999, p. 63].

A NOTE ON THE TEXT

The text of Dibdin's *Bibliomania* is based on a copy of the 1809 first edition in my possession. Admittedly, there are good arguments for using the text of the 1811 edition which Dibdin himself regarded as 'of an entirely different construction, and more full and satisfactory under every point of view' [Dibdin 1836, p. 272] or, more sensibly, the 1842 edition. However, the 'different construction' to which Dibdin refers expands the text more than eightfold without, it seems to me, adding a commensurate amount of useful information.[5] Instead of the spare text of the first edition, which is really just a framework on which to hang footnotes, later editions consists of a 'romance' in six parts (The Evening Walk, The Cabinet, The Auction Room, The Library, The Drawing Room and The Alcove) with bibliographical conversations between Dibdin (as ROSICRUCIUS) and his friends (all with 'romantic' names). This artificial style of presentation can soon become tedious and seems a poor excuse to add seven hundred pages. Here, therefore, I present the lean, vigorous text of 1809.

Dibdin's text is almost untouched. Where Dibdin used italics, so have I. His capitals, small capitals and spelling have also been retained. His punctuation has only been changed in a few places to make the text more intelligible. A few minor literals, such as '*venez acoupler!l!*' for '*venez acoupler!!!*' (p. 6 f.n.) and '1. THE HISTORY OF THE DISEASE' (p. 14), where a roman numeral is called for, have been silently amended.

Since Dibdin's typesetter used single and double quotation marks inconsistently, and sometimes left out either the opening or closing one (or opened with one sort and closed with the other), I have standardised on single quotation marks (except for quotes-within-quotes) in line with modern British editorial practice, and supplied missing ones. Quotation marks for broken-off quotations in the text were also used inconsistently and have been removed. Full stops after headings such as 'Advertisement' and 'Synopsis' have been removed.

In his haste to publish *Bibliomania*, Dibdin ended up with no footnote (55) or footnote (57) and two footnotes (56). I am fairly certain that the first footnote (56) is intended to be (55) and I have renumbered it accordingly. Dibdin has no reference to footnote (57) in the text. Renumbering the remaining footnotes would have introduced an unnecessary and potentially confusing difference between this edition and the original, so no further renumbering has been undertaken and the reader will find that there is no footnote (57).

Dibdin's spelling of proper names is not always consistent and he does not always use a form which is commonly accepted today. Count Justin de Mac-Carthy Reagh, for instance, is referred to as 'Count Macarty'. The binders Padeloup and Hering are called 'Padaloup' and 'Herring'. However, these and other names were spelt in a variety of ways at the time and it cannot be said that Dibdin's spellings are necessarily 'wrong', so I have made no attempt to change them. Nor have I supplied missing accents to foreign names or words, such as 'Vérard' and 'bibliothèque'.

As William Savage, the printer of the original edition, will have been painfully aware, there is no way to keep two lines of text and thirty lines of footnote in perfect harmony, and this edition, like that of 1809, will sometimes have a footnote on another page than that to which it refers. I apologise for that, but not even the most subtle artifices of the modern compositor can do anything to remedy it. I believe that this edition is slightly better than the original in that respect.

To Dibdin's text, I have added a number of endnotes indicated by superscript numbers (whereas Dibdin's own footnotes are indicated, as they were in the original, by numbers in parentheses). At the risk of upsetting the more learned, I have assumed no great knowledge of printing history or literature among the readers of this volume. This edition is intended to appeal to those with an interest in cultural history, Regency London, general antiquarianism and the foibles of human nature as much as to librarians, book-collectors, bibliographers and historians of printing. I hope (and believe) that the notes contain some useful information for all of them, and for almost anyone who cares to look at them.

The endnotes are not in direct proportion to the importance of their subject matter. On the contrary, as readers will have no difficulty looking up more information on the less obscure subjects, I have often concentrated on more obscure matters which I think may interest, elucidate or entertain.

The text of Ferriar's *Bibliomania* (pp. 85–94) is based on a copy of the 1809 edition in the British Library (shelfmark 78.f.7). The pagination differs from that of the original, so the footnote signs (*, †, ‡, §) have been altered as necessary.

Proper Names, the Index and the Bibliography

Dibdin has been criticised for his carelessness with personal names,[3] but, in truth, they are a minefield in this sort of book. Dibdin favoured Latinised forms – Wolfius rather than Wolf, Turnebus for Turnèbe, Stephanus for Estienne – while I have favoured

vernacular forms, but there are sufficient cross-refer-
ences in the Index that this should not pose a problem.
However, readers should bear this in mind when consulting the Bibliography.

There is an awkward and unavoidable transition between the period in which surnames did not exist and
later times when they did. Medievalists will expect to
find Richard de Bury under Richard rather than Bury,
and so they shall, but by the fifteenth century names
are more formalised. Wynkyn de Worde is commonly indexed as 'Worde, Wynkyn de' so I have adopted
this style. The same applies to William de Machlinia.
Names of French origin are a particular problem. Following normal usage on both sides of the Channel,
D'Orville and du Bellay are to be found under 'D' but
the duc de La Vallière under 'L' and Charles de Sainte-
Maure under 'S'. However, Count Magnus De La
Gardie will be found under 'D'. Frankly, this system
(if it can be dignified with such a description) is rather
absurd, but the reader will find, at least, that it accords
fairly closely with that of the Bibliothèque Nationale,[6]
the British Library and other major libraries. Anyone
who (in pre-computer times) has found Lord Byron
indexed under 'Lord' in the Chancery Rolls or the
Victoria & Albert Museum under 'South Kensington'
in the Bodleian Library will be unsurprised and un-
concerned by such foibles.

The Bibliography has been kept simple. Data which are missing from the publication itself, such as authors, places of publication and dates, have been supplied. Dates in roman numerals have been replaced by arabic numerals and places of publication in Latin have been translated. Following normal practice, book catalogues are indexed under the collectors' names rather than the compilers'. Where books have long and informative titles, I have not sought to abbreviate them unduly. Likewise, much printer and bookseller information has been retained at the expense of consistency.

ACKNOWLEDGEMENTS

I would like to thank the staff of the British Library, the Wellcome Library for the History and Understanding of Medicine and the London Library for their unfailing helpfulness. Emma Marigliano of the Portico Library in Manchester also deserves thanks for letting me have a copy of their *Bibliomania* leaflet at short notice.

I would like to express my gratitude to the technical support staff at Virginia Systems who helped me to iron out some problems (of my own making) with their InFnote software. The people at Sonny Software deserve a mention for their very quick response to queries about their Bookends program.

Anyone compiling British biographical information would be a fool to ignore that wonderful resource, *The dictionary of national biography*. I have consulted it frequently, usually as a starting point for further reading, but I have not cited it in my notes as this would have been disruptive, especially since I have been obliged to use author/date references to avoid conflict with the endnote and footnote numbering.

My thanks are also due to Tim Price who picked up a number of blunders in my Latin translations while we spent a pleasant evening imbibing spiritous liquors. I need hardly say that he cannot be held responsible for any errors which I may have introduced since then!

Finally, I must thank my wife, Elizabeth, whose love and understanding have helped me see this project through to its conclusion.

FURTHER READING

As this whole book can be regarded as a reading list, I shall only mention four publications which are of particular relevance to Dibdin's *Bibliomania*. There are two modern editions of Ferriar's poem, both slim A5 pamphlets. The Portico Library's edition [Ferriar 1996] contains the text of the 1809 edition and an appendix containing the 1812 additions. Both the introduction by David Thame and the notes by John Walker are excellent. This edition is particularly appropriate as Ferriar was founding Chairman of the Portico Library, a position he held at the time the poem appeared.

The Vanity Press edition [Ferriar 2001] contains the 1812 text of Ferriar's poem and Dibdin's poem 'Bibliography'. The Introducton by Marc Vaulbert de Chantilly is interesting and instructive.

Isaac D'Israeli's *Curiosities of literature* was a great influence on Dibdin. Fortunately, the British Library and Oak Knoll Press have recently published a handsome anthology of this engaging writer's works, *Isaac D'Israeli on books* [D'Israeli 2004].

Finally, for those who wish to see how over-inflated later editions of *Dibdin's Bibliomania* became, Thoemmes Continuum offer a reprint of the 1876 edition [Dibdin 2003], weighing in at 744 pages.

FURTHER LISTENING

It may seem odd to end this Introduction with music, but even the most avid bibliomaniac needs a break from reading, so I would like to suggest a few pieces which are, however remotely, connected with this book.

Pride of place must go to 'Tom Bowling' written about Thomas's father by his uncle, Charles Dibdin. It is an unashamedly sentimental ballad which was a favourite of such different types as the industrialist Andrew Carnegie [Carnegie 1920, p. 29] and the writer

Henry Thoreau [Lebeaux 1984, pp. 280, 283]. Robert Louis Stephenson quoted the song several times in his letters [Stephenson 1899, i, pp. 265, 366]. Robert Tear's moving rendition of it is available on a 2-CD compilation from EMI called *The very best of English song*. Three of Charles Dibdin's extremely enjoyable mini-operas performed by Opera Restor'd are available as volume 16 of Hyperion Records' *English Orpheus* series.

On the slender ground that Dibdin mentions Burton's *Anatomy of melancholy* (*Bibliomania*, p. 4) and that Milton drew on that work for his *L'allegro* and *Il penseroso*, I suggest that Handel's *L'allegro, il penseroso ed il moderato* will prove ideal listening for the cultured bibliomaniac. A very attractive recording performed by the Monteverdi Choir and English Baroque Soloists is available in a 2-CD set from Erato. Another recording is available from Hyperion Records, performed by the Choir of the King's Consort. Anyone wanting an excuse to listen to more Handel can turn to *Amadigi di Gaula, Flavio, Giulio Cesare, Ottone, Radamisto* and *Teseo*, secure in the knowledge that they have an equally tenuous connection to Dibdin's *Bibliomania*.

American readers will find, if they read the book, that even the 'Star spangled banner' is not immune from bibliomaniacal associations.

Richmond, 4 August 2004   *P. M. D.*

Advertisement

IN *laying before the public the following brief and superficial account of a disease, which, till it arrested the attention of Dr. Ferriar,*[7] *had entirely escaped the sagacity of all ancient and modern Physicians, it has been my object to touch chiefly on its leading characteristics; and to present the reader (in the language of my old friend Francis Quarles)*[8] *with an 'honest pennyworth' of information which may, in the end, either suppress or soften the ravages of so destructive a malady. I might easily have swelled the size of this Treatise by the introduction of much additional, and not incurious, matter; but I thought it most prudent to wait the issue of the present 'recipe,' at once simple in its composition and gentle in its effects.*

Some apology is due to the amiable and accomplished Character to whom my Epistle is addressed, as well as to the public, for the apparently confused and indigested manner in which the Notes are attached to the first part of this Treatise; but, unless I had thrown them to the end (a plan which modern custom does not seem to warrant), it will be obvious that a different arrangement could not have been adopted; and equally so, that the perusal, first, of the Text, and afterwards of the Notes, will be the better mode of passing judgment upon both.

Kensington, June 5, 1809.   *T. F. D.*

The Bibliomania

My dear sir,

When the poetical Epistle of Dr. Ferriar,[7] under the popular title of 'The Bibliomania,' was announced for publication, I honestly confess that, in common with many of my book-loving acquaintance, a strong sensation of fear and of hope possessed me: of fear, that I might have been accused, however indirectly, of having contributed towards the increase of this Mania; and of hope, that the true object of book-collecting, and literary pursuits, might have been fully and fairly developed. The perusal of this elegant epistle dissipated alike my fears and my hopes; for, instead of caustic verses, and satirical notes, (1) I found a smooth,

(1) There are, nevertheless, some satirical allusions which one could have wished had been suppressed. For instance;

He turns where Pybus rears his atlas-head,
Or Madoc's mass conceals its veins of lead;

What has Mr. Pybus's gorgeous book in praise of the late Russian Emperor Paul I[9] (which some have called the chef-dœuvre of Bensley's[10] press) to do with Mr. Southey's fine Poem of Madoc?[11] – in which, if there are 'veins of lead,' there are not a few 'of silver and gold.' Of the extraordinary talents of Mr. Southey, the indefatigable student in ancient

I

melodious, and persuasive panegyric; unmixed, however, with any rules for the choice of books, or the regulation of study.

lore, and especially in all that regards Spanish Literature and Old English Romances, this is not the place to make mention. His *'Remains of
Henry Kirk White,'*[12] the sweetest specimen of modern biography, has
sunk into every heart, and received an eulogy from every tongue. Yet is
his own life

> The more endearing song.

Dr. Ferriar's next satirical verses are levelled at Mr. THOMAS HOPE.[13]

> The lettered fop now takes a larger scope,
> With classic furniture, design'd by HOPE.
> (HOPE, whom upholsterers eye with mute despair,
> The doughty pedant of an elbow chair.)

It has appeared to me, that Mr. Hope's magnificent volume on *'Household Furniture,'* has been generally misunderstood, and, in a few instances, criticised upon false principles. – The first question is, does the *subject*
admit of illustration? and if so, has Mr. Hope illustrated it properly? I
believe there is no canon of criticism which forbids the treating of such
a subject; and while we are amused with archæological discussions on
Roman tiles and tesselated pavements, there seems to be no absurdity in
making the decorations of our sitting rooms, including something more
than the floor we walk upon, a subject at least of temperate and classical disquisition. Suppose we had found such a treatise in the volumes
of Gronovius[14] and Montfaucon?[15] (and are there not a few, apparently,
as unimportant and confined in these rich volumes of the Treasures of
Antiquity?) or suppose something similar to Mr. Hope's work had been
found among the ruins of Herculaneum? Or lastly, let us suppose the author had printed it only as a *private* book, to be circulated as a present? In
each of these instances, should we have heard the harsh censures which
have been thrown out against it? On the contrary, is it not very probable

To say that I was not gratified by the perusal of it,
would be a confession contrary to the truth; but to

that a wish might have been expressed that 'so valuable a work ought to
be made public.'

Upon what principle, *a priori*, are we to ridicule and condemn it? I
know of none. We admit Vitruvius, Inigo Jones, Gibbs, and Chambers,[16]
into our libraries; and why not Mr. Hope's book? Is decoration to be
confined only to the exterior? and, if so, are works, which treat of these
only, to be read and applauded? Is the delicate bas-relief, and beautifully carved column, to be thrust from the cabinet and drawing room,
to perish on the outside of a smoke-dried portico? Or, is not *that* the
most deserving of commendation, which produces the most numerous
and pleasing association of ideas? I recollect, when in company with the
excellent Dr. Jenner,[17]

——— [clarum et venerabile nomen
Gentibus, et multum nostræ quod proderat urbi]

and a half dozen more friends, we visited the splendid apartments in
Duchess-Street, Portland Place, we were not only struck with the appropriate arrangement of every thing, but, on our leaving them, and coming out into the dull foggy atmosphere of London, we acknowledged
that the effect produced upon our minds was something like that which
might have arisen had we been regaling ourselves on the silken couches,
and within the illuminated chambers, of some of the enchanted palaces
described in the Arabian Nights Entertainments.[18] I suspect that those
who have criticised Mr. Hope's work with asperity, have never seen his
house.

These sentiments are not the result of partiality or prejudice, for I
am wholly unacquainted with Mr. Hope. They are delivered with zeal,
but with deference. It is quite consolatory to find a gentleman of large
fortune, of respectable ancestry, and of classical attainments, devoting a
great portion of that leisure time which hangs like a leaden weight upon
the generality of fashionable people, to the service of the Fine Arts, and
in the patronage of merit and ingenuity. How much the world will again

say how ardently I anticipated an amplification of the subject, how eagerly I looked forward to a number of curious, apposite, and amusing anecdotes, and found them not therein, is an avowal of which I need not fear the rashness, when the known talents of the detector of Sterne's plagiarisms (2) are considered. I will not, however, disguise to you that I read it with uniform delight, and that I rose from the perusal with a keener appetite for

> The small, rare volume, black with tarnished gold.
> Dr. Ferriar's Ep. v. 138.

Whoever undertakes to write down the follies which grow out of an excessive attachment to any particular pursuit, be that pursuit horses, (3) hawks, dogs, guns,

---

be indebted to Mr. Hope's taste and liberality, may be anticipated from the 'Costume of the Ancients,' a work which has recently been published under his particular superintendence.

(2) In the fourth volume of the Transactions of the Manchester Literary Society, part iv. p. 45–87. will be found a most ingenious and amusing Essay, entitled 'Comments on Sterne,' which excited a good deal of interest at the time of its publication. This discovery may be considered, in some measure, as the result of the BIBLIOMANIA. In my edition of Sir Thomas More's Utopia, a suggestion is thrown out that even Burton may have been an imitator of Boiastuau: see vol. II. 143.[19]

(3) It may be taken for granted that the first book in this country which excited a passion for the *Sports of the Field*, was Dame Juliana Berners, or Barnes's, work, on *Hunting and Hawking*,[20] printed at St. Alban's, in the

snuff boxes, (4) old china, coins, or rusty armor, may
be thought to have little consulted the best means of

year 1486; of which Lord Spencer's[21] copy is, I believe, the only perfect
one known. It was fornerly the Poet Mason's,[22] and is mentioned in the
quarto edition of Hoccleve's Poems, p. 19, 1786. See too Bibl. Mason. pt.
iv. No. 153. Whether the forementioned worthy lady was really the author
of the work, has been questioned. Her book was reprinted by Wynkyn
De Worde[23] in 1497, with an additional Treatise on *Fishing*. The following specimen, from this latter edition, ascertains the general usage of the
French language with our Huntsmen in the 15th century.[24]

Beasts of Venery.

Where so ever ye fare by frith or by fell,
My dear child take heed how Trystam do you tell.
How many manner beasts of Venery there were:
Listen to your dame and she shall you *lere.*
Four manner beasts of Venery there are.
The first of them is the *Hart;* the second is the *Hare;*
The *Horse* is one of them; the *Wolf;* and not one *mo.*

Beasts of the Chace.

And where that ye come in plain or in place
I shall tell you which be beasts of enchace.
One of them is the *Buck;* another is the *Doe;*
The Fox and the *Marteron,* and the wild *Roe:*
And ye shall see my dear child other beastes all:
Where so ye them find *Rascal* ye shall them call.

Of the hunting of the Hare.

How to speke of the haare how all shall be wrought:
When she shall with houndes be founden and sought.
The fyrst worde to the houdis that the hunter shall out pit
Is at the kenell doore whan he openeth it.
That all maye hym here: he shall say *'Arere!'*
For his houndes would come to hastily

ensuring success for his labors, when he adopts the
dull vehicle of *Prose* for the communication of his

> That is the firste worde my sone of Venery.
> And when he hath couplyd his houndes echoon
> And is forth wyth theym to the felde goon,
> And whan he hath of caste his couples at wyll
> Thenne he shall speke and saye his houndes tyll
> *'Hors de couple avant sa avant!'* twyse soo
> And then *'So ho so ho!'* thryes, and no moo.

And then say *'Sacy avaunt so how,'* I thou praye, &c. The following are
a few more specimens. – *'Ha cy touz cy est yll —Venez ares sa how sa – La
douce la eit a venuz – Ho ho ore, swet a luy, douce a luy – So how, so how,
venez acoupler!!!'*

Whoever wishes to see these subjects brought down to later times, and
handled with considerable dexterity, may consult the last numbers of the
Censura Literaria[25] with the signature J. H. affixed to them. Those who
are anxious to procure the rare books mentioned in these bibliographical
treatises, may be pretty safely taxed with being infected by the BIBLIO-
MANIA. What apology my friend Mr. Haslewood,[26] the author of them,
has to offer in extenuation of the mischief committed, it is his business,
and not mine, to consider; and what the public will say to his curious
forthcoming reprint of the ancient edition of Wynkyn De Worde on
Hunting, Hawking, and Fishing, 1497, (with wood cuts) I will not pretend
to divine!

In regard to Hawking, I believe the enterprising Colonel Thornton[27]
is the only gentleman of the present day who keeps up this custom of
'good old times.'

The Sultans of the East seem not to have been insensible to the charms
of Falconry, if we are to judge from the evidence of Tippoo Saib[28] having a work of this kind in his library; which is thus described from the
Catalogue of it just published in a fine quarto volume, of which only 250
copies are printed.

'Shāhbār Nāmeh, 4to. a Treatise on Falconry; containing Instructions
for selecting the best species of Hawks, and the method of teaching

ideas; not considering that from *Poetry* ten thousand bright scintillations are struck off, which please and

them; describing their different qualities; also the disorders they are subject to, and method of cure. Author unknown.' – Oriental Library of Tippoo Saib, 1809, p. 96.

(4) Of *snuff boxes* every one knows what a collection the great Frederick, King of Prussia,[29] had – many of them studded with precious stones, and decorated with enamelled portraits. Dr. C. of G————,[30] has been represented to be the most successful rival of Frederick, in this 'line of collection' as it is called; some of his boxes are of uncommon curiosity. It may gratify a Bibliographer to find that there are other MANIAS beside that of the book; and that even physicians are not exempt from these diseases.

Of *Old China, Coins,* and *Rusty Armour,* the names of hundreds present themselves in these departments; but to the more commonly-known ones of Rawle and Grose,[31] let me add that of the late Mr. John White,[32] of Newgate-Street; a catalogue of whose curiosities, [including some very uncommon books] was published in the year 1788, in three parts, 8vo. Dr. Burney[33] tells us that Mr. White 'was in possession of a valuable collection of ancient rarities, as well as natural productions, of the most curious and extraordinary kind; no one of which however was more remarkable, than the obliging manner in which he allowed them to be viewed and examined by his friends.' – *History of Music,* vol. II. 539, note.

(5) The reader will find an animated eulogy on this great nobleman in Walpole's[34] *Anecdotes of Painters,* vol iv. 227: part of which was transcribed by Joseph Warton[35] for his Variorum edition of Pope's Works, and from thence copied into the recent edition of the same by the Rev. W. L. Bowles.[36] But PEMBROKE[37] deserved a more particular notice. Exclusively of his fine statues, and architectural decorations, the Earl contrived to procure a number of curious and rare books; and the testimonies of Maittaire[38] [who speaks indeed of him with a sort of rapture!] and Palmer,[39] shew that the productions of Jenson[40] and Caxton[41] were no strangers to his library. *Annales Typographici,* vol. I. 13. edit. 1719. *History of Printing,*

convince while they attract and astonish. Thus when Pope talks[42] of allotting for

> Pembroke (5) Statues, dirty Gods and Coins;
> Rare monkish manuscripts for Hearne[43] (6) alone;
> And books to Mead[44] (7) and butterflies to Sloane,[45] (8)

when he says that

> These Aldus[46] (9) printed, those Du Süeil[47] (10) has bound

moreover that

> For Locke or Milton (11) 'tis in vain to look;
> These shelves admit not any modern book;

p. v. 'There is nothing that so surely proves the pre-eminence of virtue more than the universal admiration of mankind, and the respect paid it even by persons in opposite interests; and more than this, it is a sparkling gem which even time does not destroy: it is hung up in the Temple of Fame, and respected for ever.' *Continuation of Granger,*[48] vol. I. 37. &c. 'He raised,' continues Mr. Noble,[49] 'a collection of Antiques that were unrivalled by any subject. His learning made him a fit companion for the literati. Wilton will ever be a monument of his extensive knowledge; and the princely presents it contains, of the high estimation in which he was held by foreign potentates, as well as by the many monarchs he saw and served at home. He lived rather as a primitive christian; in his behaviour, meek: in his dress, plain: rather retired, conversing but little.' Burnet, in the *History of his own Times,*[50] has spoken of the Earl with spirit and propriety.

(6) In the recent Variorum Edition of Pope's Works, all that is annexed to Hearne's name, as above introduced by the Poet, is, 'well known as an Antiquarian.'

he not only seems to illustrate the propriety of the foregoing remark, by shewing the immense superiority of verse to prose, in ridiculing reigning absurdities, but he seems to have had a pretty strong foresight of the BIBLIOMANIA which rages at the present day. However, as the ancients tell us that a Poet cannot be a *manufactured* creature, and as I have not the smallest

ALAS, POOR HEARNE!

thy merits, which are now fully appreciated, deserve an ampler notice! In spite of Gibbon's unmerciful critique [*Posthumous Works*, vol. II. 711.] [51] the productions of this modest, erudite, and indefatigable antiquary are rising in price proportionably to their worth. If he had only edited the *Collectanea* and *Itinerary* of his favourite *Leland*,[52] he would have stood on high ground in the department of literature and antiquities; but his other, and numerous works place him on a much loftier eminence. Of these, the present is not the place to make mention: suffice it to say, that for copies of his works, on LARGE PAPER, which the author used to advertise as selling for 7s. or 10s. or about which placards, to the same effect, used to be stuck on the walls of the colleges, – these very copies are now sometimes sold for more than the like number of guineas! It is amusing to observe, that the lapse of a few years only has caused such a rise in the article of HEARNE; and that the Peter Langtoft[53] on large paper, which at Rowe Mores's[54] sale [Bibl. Mores. No. 2191.] was purchased for £1. 2s. produced at a late sale, [A.D. 1808], £37! A complete list of Hearne's Pieces will be found at the end of his Life, printed with Leland's, &c. at the Clarendon Press, in 1772, 8vo. Of these the '*Acta Apostolorum*, Gr. Lat.;' and '*Aluredi Beverlacensis Annales*,'[55] are, I believe, the scarcest. It is wonderful to think how this amiable and excellent man persevered 'through evil report and good report,' in illustrating the antiquities of his country. To the very last he appears to have been molested; and among his persecutors, the learned editor of Josephus and Dionysius

pretensions, to the 'rhyming art,' [although in former
(12) times I did venture to dabble with it] I must of

Halicarnasseus, Dr. Hudson,[56] must be ranked, to the disgrace of
himself and the party which he espoused. 'Hearne was buried in
the church yard of St. Peter's (at Oxford) in the East, where is
erected over his remains, a tomb, with an Inscription written by
himself:'

Amicitiæ Ergo.
Here lyeth the Body of
THOMAS HEARNE. M. A.
Who studied and preserved
Antiquities.
He dyed June 10, 1735.
Aged 57 years.
Deut. xxxii: 7.
Remember the days of old
consider the years
of many generations
ask thy Father
and he will shew thee
thy elders
and they will tell thee
Job. viii. 8. 9. 10.
Enquire I pray thee.

Life of Hearne, p. 34.

(7) Of Dr. MEAD and his Library a particular account is given in the
following pages.[44]

(8) For this distinguished character consult Nichols's *Anecdotes of Bowyer,*
550, note*; which, however, relates entirely to his ordinary habits and
modes of life. His manifcent collection of Natural Curiosities and MSS.
is now in the British Museum.

necessity have recourse to *Prose;* and, at the same time, to your candor and forbearance in perusing the pages which ensue.

(9) The annals of the Aldine Press have had ample justice done to them in the beautiful and accurate work published by Renouard, under the title of *'Annales de L'Imprimerie des Alde,'* in two vols. 8vo. 1804.[57] One is rather surprised at not finding any reference to this masterly piece of bibliography in the last edition of Mr. Roscoe's Leo X. where there is a pleasing account of the establishment of the Aldine Press.[58]

(10) I do not recollect having seen any book bound by this binder. Of Padaloup,[59] De Rome,[60] and Baumgarten,[61] where is the fine collection that does not boast of a few specimens? We will speak 'anon' of the Roger Paynes,[62] Kalthoebers,[63] Herrings,[64] Staggemiers,[65] and Mackinlays[66] of the day!

(11) This is not the reproach of the age we live in; for reprints of Bacon, Locke, and Milton have been published with complete success. It would be ridiculous indeed for a man of sense, and especially a University man, to give 5 or £6 for *'Gosson's School of Abuse, against Pipers and Players,'*[67] or £3 3s. for a clean copy of *'Recreation for Ingenious Head Pieces,* or a *Pleasant Grove for their Wits to walk in,'*[68] and grudge the like sum for a dozen handsome octavo volumes of the finest writers of his country.

(12) About twelve years ago I was rash enough to publish a small volume of Poems, with my name affixed. They were the productions of my juvenile years; and I need hardly say, at this period, how ashamed I am of their authorship. The Monthly and Analytical Reviews did me the kindness of just tolerating them, and of warning me not to commit any future trespass upon the premises of Parnassus. I struck off 500 copies, and was glad to get rid of half of them as waste paper; the remaining half has been partly destroyed by my own hands, and has partly mouldered away in oblivion amidst the dust of Booksellers' shelves. My only consolation is, that the volume is *exceedingly rare!*[69]

If ever there was a country upon the face of the globe – from the days of Nimrod the beast- to Bagford[70] (13) the book-hunter – distinguished for the variety, the justness, and magnanimity of its views; if ever there was a nation which really and unceasingly 'felt for another's woe:' [I call to witness our Infirmaries,

(13) 'JOHN BAGFORD, by profession a bookseller, frequently travelled into Holland and other parts, in search of scarce books and valuable prints, and brought a vast number into this kingdom, the greatest part of which were purchased by the Earl of Oxford.[71]He had been in his younger days a shoemaker; and, for the many curiosities wherewith he enriched the famous library of Dr. John Moore, Bishop of Ely,[72] his Lordship got him admitted into the Charter House. He died in 1706, aged 65: after his death, Lord Oxford purchased all his collections and papers for his library: these are now in the Harleian collection in the British Museum. In 1707 were published, in the Philosophical Transactions, his Proposals for a General History of Printing.' – Bowyer and Nichols's *Origin of Printing*, p 164. 189, note.

It has been my fortune (whether good or bad remains to be proved) not only to transcribe the slender memorial of Printing in the Philosophical Transactions, drawn up by Wanley[73] for Bagford, but to wade through *forty-two* folio volumes, in which Bagford's materials for a History of Printing are incorporated, in the British Museum: and from these, I think I have furnished myself with a pretty fair idea of the said Bagford. He was the most hungry and rapacious of all book and print collectors; and, in his ravages, spared neither the most delicate nor costly pecimens. His eyes and his mouth seem to have been always open to express his astonishment at, sometimes, the most common and contemptible productions; and his paper in the Philosophical Transactions, betrays such simplicity and ignorance, that one is astonished how my Lord Oxford and the learned Bishop of Ely could have employed so credulous a bibliographical forager.

Hospitals, Asylums, and other public and private Institutions of a charitable nature, which, like so many
belts of adamant, unite and strengthen us in the great
cause of HUMANITY] if ever there was a country and a
set of human beings, pre-eminently distinguished for
all the social virtues which soften and animate the soul
of man, surely OLD ENGLAND and ENGLISHMEN are
THEY! The common cant, it may be urged, of all writers in favor of the country where they chance to live!
And what, you will say, has this to do with Book Collectors and Books? – Much, every way: a nation thus
glorious, is, at this present eventful moment, afflicted
not only with the Dog (14) but the BOOK disease —

A modern collector and lover of *perfect* copies, will witness, with
shuddering, among Bagford's immense collection of Title Pages, in
the Museum, the frontispieces of the Complutensian Polyglot[74] and
Chauncy's History of Hertfordshire,[75] torn out to illustrate an History of Printing. His enthusiasm, however, carried him through a
great deal of laborious toil; and he supplied in some measure, by this
qualification, the want of other attainments. His whole mind was
devoted to book-hunting; and his integrity and diligence probably
made his employers overlook his many failings. His hand writing is
scarcely legible, and his orthography is still more wretched; but if he
was ignorant, he was humble, zealous, and grateful; and he has certainly done something towards the accomplishment of that desirable
object, an accurate General History of Printing. In my edition of
Ames's Typographical Antiquities,[76] I shall give an analysis of Bagford's
papers, with a specimen or two of his composition.

(14) For an eloquent account of this disorder consult the letters of Dr.
Mosely[77] inserted in the Morning Herald of last year. I have always been

Fire in each eye, and paper in each hand

They rave, recite, —————

Let us enquire, therefore, into the origin and tendency of the BIBLIOMANIA.

In this enquiry I purpose considering the subject under three points of view: I. THE HISTORY OF THE DISEASE, or an account of the eminent men who have fallen victims to it; II. THE NATURE, OR SYMPTOMS OF THE DISEASE; and III. THE PROBABLE MEANS OF ITS CURE. We are to consider, then,

I. THE HISTORY OF THE DISEASE. In treating of the history of this disease, it will be found to have been attended with this remarkable circumstance; namely, that it has almost uniformly confined its attacks to the *male* sex, and among these, to people in the higher and middling classes of society, while the artificer, labourer, and peasant have escaped wholly uninjured. It has raged chiefly in palaces, castles, halls, and gay mansions; and those things, which in general are supposed not to be inimical to health, such as cleanliness,

surprised, and a little vexed, that these animated pieces of composition should be relished and praised by every one – *but the Faculty!*

(15) The writings of the Roman philologers seem to bear evidence of this fact. Seneca, when an old man, says, that 'if you are fond of books, you will escape the ennui of life; you will neither sigh for evening, disgusted with the occupations of the day – nor will you live dissatisfied with yourself,

spaciousness, and splendor, are only so many induce-
ments towards the introduction and propagation of
the Bibliomania! What renders its character particularly formidable is, that it rages in all seasons of the
year, and at all periods of human existence. The emotions of friendship or of love are weakened or subdued
as old age advances; but the influence of this passion,
or rather disease, admits of no mitigation: 'it grows
with our growth, and strengthens with our strength;'
and is oft-times

————— The ruling passion strong in death. (15)

We will now, my dear Sir, begin 'making out the catalogue' of victims to the Bibliomania! The first eminent character who appears to have been infected with
this disease was Richard De Bury, one of the tutors
of Edward III, and afterwards Bishop of Durham; a
man, who has been uniformly praised for the variety

or unprofitable to others.' *De Tranquilitate*, ch. 3. Cicero has positively
told us that 'study is the food of youth, and the amusement of old age.'
Orat. Pro Archiciâ. The younger Pliny was a downright Bibliomaniac. 'I
am quite transported and comforted,' says he, 'in the midst of my books:
they give a zest to the happiest, and assuage the anguish of the bitterest,
moments of existence! Therefore, whether distracted by the cares or the
losses of my family, or my friends, I fly to my library as the only refuge in
distress: here I learn to bear adversity with fortitude.' *Epist.* lib. viii. cap.
19. But consult Cicero *De Senectute*. All these treatises afford abundant
proof of the hopelessness of cure in cases of the Bibliomania.

of his erudition, and the intenseness of his ardor in book-collecting. (16) I do not discover any other notorious example of the fatality of the BIBLIOMANIA until the time of Henry VII; when the monarch himself may be considered as having added to the number.

(16) It may be expected that I should notice a few book-lovers, and probably BIBLIOMANIACS, previously to the time of Richard De Bury;[78] but so little is known with accuracy of Johannes Scotus Erigena,[79] and his patron Charles the Bald, King of France, or of the book tête-a-têtes they used to have together – so little, also, of Nennius,[80] Bede, and Alfred, [although the monasteries at this period, from the evidence of Sir William Dugdale,[81] in the first volume of the Monasticon were 'opulently endowed.' – inter alia, I should hope, with magnificent MSS. on vellum, bound in velvet, and embossed with gold and silver] or the illustrious writers in the Norman period, and the fine books which were in the abbey of Croyland – so little is known of book-collectors previously to the 14th century, that I thought it the most prudent and safe way to begin with the above excellent prelate.

RICHARD DE BURY was the friend and correspondent of Petrarch; and is said by Mons. de Sade,[82] in his Memoires pour la vie de Petrarque, 'to have done in England what Petrarch did all his life in France, Italy, and Germany, towards the discovery of MSS. of the best ancient writers, and making copies of them under his own superintendence.' His passion for book-collecting was unbounded; ['vir ardentis ingenii,' says Petrarch of him] and in order to excite the same ardor in his countrymen, or rather to propagate the disease of the BIBLIOMANIA with all his might, he composed a bibliographical work under the title of *Philobiblion;* concerning the first edition of which, printed at Spires in 1483,[83] Clement[84] (tom. v. 142) has a long gossiping account; and Morhof[85] tells us that it is 'rarissima, et in paucorum manibus versatur.' It was reprinted at Paris in 1500, 4to. by the elder Ascensius,[86] and frequently in the subsequent century; but the best editions of it are those by Goldastus[87] in 1674, 8vo. and Hummius[88] in 1703. Morhof observes that 'however De Bury's work

Although our venerable typographer, Caxton, lauds and magnifies, with equal sincerity, the whole line of British Kings, from Edward IV to Henry VII [under whose patronage he would seem, in some measure, to have carried on his printing business] yet, of all these monarchs, the latter alone was so unfortunate as to fall a victim to this disease. His library must have been a magnificent one, if we may judge from the splendid specimens of it which now remain. (17) It would appear too, that, about this time, the BIBLIOMANIA was

savors of the rudeness of the age, it is rather elegantly written, and many things are well said in it relating to Bibliothecism.' *Polyhist. Literar.* vol. i. 187, edit. 1747.

For further particulars concerning De Bury, read Bale,[89] Wharton,[90] Cave,[91] and Godwin's Episcopal Biography.[92] He left behind him a fine library of MSS. which he bequeathed to Durham, now Trinity, College, Oxford.[93]

It may be worth the antiquary's notice, that, in consequence (I suppose) of this amiable prelate's exertions, 'in every convent was a noble library and a great: and every friar, that had state in school, such as they be now, hath AN HUGE LIBRARY.' See the curious Sermon of the Archbishop of Armagh, Nov. 8, 1387, in Trevisa's works among the *Harleian MSS.* No. 1900. Whether these Friars, thus affected with the frensy of book-collecting, ever visited the 'old chapelle at the Est End of the church of S. Saink, [Berkshire], whither of late time resorted in pilgrimage many folkes for the disease of *madness*,' [see Leland's *Itinerary*, vol. ii. 29. edit. 1770] I have not been able, after the most diligent investigation, to ascertain.

(17) The British Museum contains a great number of books which bear the royal stamp of Henry VII's arms. Some of these printed by Verard,[94]

increased by the introduction of foreign printed books; and it is not very improbable that a portion of Henry's immense wealth was devoted towards the purchase of VELLUM copies, which were now beginning to be published by the great typographical triumvirate, Verard,[94] Eustace,[95] and Pigouchet.[96]

During the reign of Henry VIII, I should suppose that the Earl of Surrey (18)[97] and Sir Thomas Wyatt[98] were a little attached to book-collecting; and that Dean Colet (19)[99] and his friends Sir Thomas More[100] and Erasmus[101] were downright Bibliomaniacs. There can be little doubt but that neither the great LELAND

UPON VELLUM, are magnificent memorials of a library, the dispersion of which is for ever to be regretted. As Henry VIII knew nothing of, and cared less for, fine books,[102] it is not very improbable that some, of the choicest volumes belonging to the late king were presented to Cardinal Wolsey.

(18) The EARL OF SURREY and SIR THOMAS WYATT were among the first who taught their countrymen to be charmed with the elegance and copiousness of their own language. How effectually they accomplished this laudable object, will be seen from the forthcoming beautiful and complete edition of their works by the Rev. Dr. Nott.[103]

(19) COLET, MORE and ERASMUS [considering the latter when he was in England] were *here* undoubtedly the great literary triumvirate of the early part of the 16th century. The lives of More and Erasmus are generally read and known; but of DEAN COLET it may not be so generally known that his ardor for books and for classical literature was keen and insatiable; that, in the foundation of ST. PAUL'S SCHOOL, he has left behind a name, which entitles him to rank in the foremost of those who

(20) nor his Biographer Bale,[89] (21) were able to escape the contagion; and that, in the ensuing period,

have fallen victims to the BIBLIOMANIA. How anxiously does he seem to
have watched the progress, and pushed the sale, of his friend Erasmus's
first edition of the Greek Testament! 'Quod scribis de Novo Testamento
intelligo. Et libri *novæ editionis tuæ hic avide emuntur e passim leguntur!*'
The entire epistle (which may be seen in Dr. Knight's dry Life of Colet,
p. 315) is devoted to an account of Erasmus's publications. 'I am really
astonished, my dear Erasmus [does he exclaim], at the fruitfulness of
your talents; that, without any fixed residence, and with a precarious
and limited income, you contrive to publish so many and such excellent
works.' Adverting to the distracted state of Germany at this period, and
to the wish of his friend to live secluded and unmolested, he observes
– 'As to the tranquil retirement which you sigh for, be assured that you
have my sincere wishes for its rendering you as happy and composed as
you can wish it. Your age and erudition entitle you to such a retreat. I
fondly hope indeed, that you will choose this country for it, and come
and live amongst us, whose disposition you know, and whose friendship
you have proved.'

There is hardly a more curious picture of the custom of the times relating the education of boys, than the Dean's own Statutes for the regulation
of St. Paul's School, which he had founded. These shew, too, the *popular
books* then read by the learned. 'The children shall come unto the School
in the morning at seven of the clock, both winter and summer, and tarry
there until eleven; and return again at one of the clock, and depart at five,
&c. In the school, no time in the year, they shall use tallow candle in no
wise, but *only wax candle,* at the costs of their friends. Also I will they
bring no meat nor drink, nor bottle, nor use in the school no breakfasts,
nor drinkings, in the time of learning in no wise, &c. I will they use no
cock fightings, nor riding about of victory, nor disputing at Saint Bartholomew, which is but foolish babbling and loss of time.' The master is
then restricted, under the penalty of 40 shillings, from granting the boys
a holiday, or 'remedy' [playday,] as it is here called 'except the King, an
Archbishop, or a Bishop, present in his own person in the school, desire

Roger Ascham[104] became notorious for the Book-disease. He purchased most probably, during his travels

it.' The studies for the lads were, 'Erasmus's Copia & Institutum Christiani Hominis, (composed at the Dean's request) Lactantius, Prudentius, Juvencus, Proba and Sedulius, and Baptista Mantuanus,' and such other as shall be thought convenient and most to purpose unto the true latin speech: all barbary, all corruption, all Latin adulterate, which ignorant blind fools brought into this world, and with the same hath distained and poisoned the old Latin speech, and the *veray* Roman tongue, which in the time of Tully and Sallust and Virgil and Terence was used – I say that filthiness, and all such abusion, which the later blind world brought in, which more rather may be called *Bloterature* than *Literature,* I utterly banish and exclude out of this school.' Knight's *Life of Colet,* 362, 4.

What was to be expected, but that boys, thus educated, would hereafter fall victims to the BIBLIOMANIA?!

(20) The history of this great man, and of his literary labors, is most interesting. He was a pupil of William Lilly, the first headmaster of St. Paul's School; and by the kindness and liberality of a Mr. Myles, he afterwards received the advantage of a College education, and was supplied with money in order to travel abroad, and make such collections as he should deem necessary for the great work which even then seemed to dawn upon his young and ardent mind. Leland endeavoured to requite the kindness of his benefactor by an elegant copy of Latin verses, in which he warmly expatiates on the generosity of his patron, and acknowledges that his acquaintance with the *Almæ Matres* [for he was of both Universities] was entirely the result of such beneficence. While he resided on the continent, he was admitted into the society of the most eminent Greek and Latin Scholars, and could probably number among his correspondents the illustrious names of Budæus,[105] Erasmus, the Stephani,[106] Faber[107] and Turnebus.[108] Here, too, he cultivated his natural taste for poetry; and, from inspecting the fine BOOKS which the Italian and French presses had produced, as well as fired by the love of Grecian learning, which had fled, on the sacking of Constantinople, to take shelter in the academic bow-

abroad (22), many a fine copy of the Greek and Latin
Classics from which he read to his illustrious pupils,

ers of the Medici, he seems to have matured his plans for carrying into
effect the great work which had now taken full possession of his mind.
He returned to England, resolved to institute an inquiry into the state
of the Libraries, Antiquities, Records and Writings then in existence.
Having entered into holy orders, and obtained preferment at the express
interposition of the King, (Henry VIII) he was appointed his Antiquary
and Library Keeper, and a royal commison was issued in which Leland
was directed to search after 'England's Antiquities, and peruse the
libraries of all Cathedrals, Abbies, Priories, Colleges, &c. as also all the
places wherein Records, Writings, and Secrets of Antiquity were reposit-
ed.' 'Before Leland's time,' says Hearne, in the Preface to the Itinerary, 'all
the literary monuments of Antiquity were totally disregarded; and Stu-
dents of Germany apprised of this culpable indifference, were suffered
to enter our libraries unmolested, and to cut out of the books deposited
there whatever passages they thought proper – which they afterwards
published as relics of the ancient literature of their own country.'

Leland was occupied, without intermission, in this immense under-
taking, for the space of six years; and, on its completion, he hastened
to the metropolis to lay at the feet of his Sovereign the result of his
researches. This was presented to Henry under the title of A New Year's
Gift; and was first published by Bale in 1549, 8vo. 'Being inflamed,' says
the author, 'with a love to see thoroughly all those parts of your opulent
and ample realm, in so much that all my other occupations intermitted, I
have so travelled in your dominions, both by the sea coasts and the middle parts, sparing neither labor nor costs, by the space of six years past,
that there is neither cape nor bay, haven, creek or pier, river or confluence
of rivers, breeches, wastes, lakes, moors, fenny waters, mountains, vallies,
heaths, forests, chases, woods, cities, burghes, castles, principal manor
places, monasteries and colleges, but I have seen them; and noted, in so
doing, a whole world of things very memorable.' Leland moreover tells
his Majesty – that 'By his laborious journey and costly enterprise, he had
conserved many good authors, the which otherwise had been like to have

Lady Jane Grey, and Queen Elizabeth: but whether he
made use of an *Editio Princeps*, or a *Large paper copy*, I

perished; of the which, part remained in the royal palaces, part also in
his own custody, &c.'

As Leland was engaged six years in this literary tour, so he was occupied for a no less period of time in digesting and arranging the pro-
digious number of MSS. he had collected. But he sunk beneath the im-
mensity of the task! The want of amanuenses, and of other attentions and
comforts, seems to have deeply affected him: in this melancholy state,
he wrote to Archbishop Cranmer a latin epistle, in verse, of which the
following is the commencement – very forcibly describing his situation
and anguish of mind.

> Est congesta mihi domi supellex
> Ingens, aurea, nobilis, venusta,
> Qua totus studeo Britanniarum
> Vero reddere gloriam nitori.
> Sed fortuna meis noverca cœptis
> Jam felicibus invidet maligna.
> Quare, ne pereant brevi vel hora
> Multarum mihi noctium labores
> Omnes ———
> CRANMERE, eximium decus piorum!
> Implorare tuam benignitatem
> Cogor:[109]

The result was, that Leland lost his senses; and after lingering two years
in a state of total derangement, he died on the 18th of April, 1552. 'Proh
tristes rerum humanarum vices! prôh viri optimi deplorandam infelicis-
simamque sortem,' exclaims Dr. Smith, in his Preface to Camden's Life,
1691, 4to.[110]

The precious and voluminous MSS. of Leland were doomed to suffer a
fate scarcely less pitiable than that of their owner. After being pilfered by
some, and garbled by others, they served to replenish the pages of Stow,[111]
Lambard,[112] Camden,[110] Burton,[19] Dugdale,[81] and many other antiquar-

have hitherto not been lucky enough to discover. This
learned character died in the vigour of life, and in the

ies and historians. Polydore Virgil,[113] who had stolen from them pretty
freely, had the insolence to abuse Leland's memory – calling him 'a vain
glorious man'; but what shall we say to this flippant egotist? who, according to Caius's[114] testimony [*De Antiq. Cantab. head. lib.* i.] 'to prevent a
discovery of the many errors of his own history of England, collected and
burnt a greater number of ancient histories and manuscripts than would
have loaded a waggon.' The imperfect remains of Leland's MSS. are now
deposited in Bodleian Library, and in the British Museum.

Upon the whole, it must be acknowledged that Leland is a melancholy,
as well as illustrious, example of the influence of the Bibliomania!

(21) In spite of Bale's[89] coarseness, positiveness, and severity, he has done
much towards the cause of learning; and, perhaps, towards the propagation of the disease under discussion. His regard for Leland does him
great honor; and although his plays are miserably dull, notwithstanding
the high prices which the original editions of them bear, [vide ex gr. Cat.
Steevens, No. 1221; which was sold for £12 12s. see also the reprints in the
Harleian Miscellany] the lover of literary antiquities must not forget that
his '*Scriptores Britanniæ*' are yet quoted with satisfaction by some of the
most respectable writers of the day. That he wanted delicacy of feeling,
and impartiality of investigation, must he admitted; but a certain rough
honesty and prompt benevolence which he had about him, compensated
for a multitude of offences. The abhorrence with which he speaks of the
dilapidation of some of our old libraries, must endear his memory to
every honest bibliographer: 'Never' (says he) 'had we been offended for
the loss of our LIBRARIES, being so many in number, and in so desolate
places for the more part, if the chief monuments and most notable works
of our excellent writers had been reserved. If there had been in every
shire of England, but one SOLEMPNE LIBRARY, to the preservation of
those noble works, and preferment of good learning in our posterity, it
had been yet somewhat. But to destroy all without consideration, is, and
will be, unto England for ever, a most horrible infamy among the grave

bloom of reputation; and, as I suspect, in consequence
of the BIBLIOMANIA – for he was always collecting

seniors of other nations. A great number of them which purchased those
superstitious mansions, reserved of those library-books, some to serve
the *jakes,* some to scour their candlesticks, and some to rub their boots:
some they sold to the grocers and soap sellers; some they sent over sea to
the book-binders, not in small number, but at times whole ships full, to
the wondering of the foreign nations, Yea, the Universities of this realm
are not all clear of this detestable fact. But cursed is that belly which
seketh to be fed with such ungodly gains, and shameth his natural country. I know a merchant man, which shall at this time be nameless, that
bought the contents of two noble libraries for forty shillings price; a shame it
is to be spoken! This stuff hath he occupied in the stead of grey paper,
by the space of more than ten years, and yet he hath store enough for as
many years to come!' Bale's Preface to Leland's '*Laboryouse Journey, &c.*'
Emprented at London by John Bale. Anno. M. D. xlix. 8vo.

After this, who shall doubt the story of the Alexandrian Library supplying the hot baths of Alexandria with fuel for six months!? See Gibbon
on the latter subject; vol. ix. 440.

(22) ASCHAM's[104] English letters, written when he was abroad, will be
found at the end of Bennet's edition of his works, in 4to. They are curious and amusing. What relates to the BIBLIOMANIA I here select from
similar specimens. 'Oct. 4. at afternoon I went about the town [of Brux-
elles.] I went to the frier Carmelites house, and heard their even song:
after, I desired to see the LIBRARY. A frier was sent to me, and led me
into it. There was not one good book but *Lyra.*[115] The friar was learned,
spoke latin readily, entered into Greek, having a very good wit, and a
greater desire to learning. He was gentle and honest &c.' p. 370–1. 'Oct.
20. to Spira: a good city. Here I first saw *Sturmius de periodis.*[116] I also
found here *Ajax, Electra,* and *Antigone* of *Sophocles,* excellently, by my
good judgment, translated into verse, and fair printed this summer by
Gryphius.[117] Your stationers do ill, that at least do not provide you the
register of all books, especially of old authors, &c.' p. 372. Again: 'Hi-
eronimus Wolfius,[118] that translated Demosthenes and Isocrates, is in

books, and always studying them. His 'Schoolmaster' is a work which can only perish with our language.

If we are to judge from the beautiful Missal lying open before Lady Jane Grey, in Mr. Copley's[119] elegant picture now exhibiting at the British Institution,[120] it would seem rational to infer that this amiable and learned female was slightly attacked by the disease. It is to be taken for granted that Queen Elizabeth was not exempt from it; and that her great Secretary, (23) Cecil,[121] sympathised with her!

this town. I am well acquainted with him, and have brought him twice to my Lord's to dinner. He looks very simple. He telleth me that one Borrheus,[122] that hath written well upon Aristot. priorum, &c. even now is printing goodly commentaries upon Aristotle's Rhetoric. But Sturmius[116] will obscure them all.' p. 381.

It is impossible to read these extracts without being convinced that Roger Ascham was a book-hunter, and infected with the BIBLIOMANIA!

(23) It is a question, which requires more time for the solution than I am able to spare, whether CECIL's name stands more frequently at the head of a Dedication, in a printed book, or of State Papers and other political documents in MS. He was a wonderful man; but a little infected – as I suspect – with the BOOK-DISEASE.

———— Famous Cicill, treasorer of the land,
Whose wisedome, counsell, skill of Princes state
The world admires ————————————
The house itselfe doth shewe the owners wit,
And may for bewtie, state, and every thing,
Compared be with most within the land.
          Tale of Two Swannes, 1590. 4to.[123]

In regard to Elizabeth, her *Prayer-Book*[124] (24) is quite evidence sufficient for me that she found the BIBLIOMANIA irresistible! During her reign, how vast and how frightful were the ravages of the Book-madness! If we are to credit Laneham's celebrated Letter,[125] it had extended far into the country, and infected some of the worthy inhabitants of Coventry; for one 'Captain Cox,'[126] (25) by profession a mason, and that right

I have never yet been able to ascertain whether the owner's attachment towards VELLUM, or LARGE PAPER, Copies was the more vehement!

(24) Perhaps this conclusion is too precipitate. But whoever looks at Elizabeth's portrait, on her bended knees, struck off on the reverse of the title page to her prayer book [first printed in 1565 or 1575] may suppose that the Queen thought the addition of her own portrait would be no mean decoration to the work. Every page is adorned with borders, engraved on wood, of the most spirited execution: representing, amongst other subjects, 'The Dance of Death.' My copy is the reprint of 1608 – in high preservation. I have no doubt that there was a *presentation* copy printed UPON VELLUM; but in what cabinet does this precious gem now slumber?

(25) Laneham gives a splendid list of Romances and Old Ballads possessed by this said CAPTAIN COX; and tells us, moreover, that 'he had them all at his fingers ends.' Among the ballads we find 'Broom broom on Hil; So Wo is me begon twlly lo. Over a Whinny Meg; Hey ding a ding; Bony lass upon Green; My bony on gave me a bek; By a bank as I lay; and two more he had fair wrapt up in parchment, and bound with a whip-cord.' Edit. 1784. p. 36.7.8. Ritson,[127] in his Historical Essay on *Scotish Song*, speaks of some of these, with a zest, as if he longed to untie the 'whip-cord' packet.

(26) SIR JOHN HARRINGTON, knt. Sir John, and his father John Harrington, were very considerable literary characters in the 16th century;

skilful' had 'as fair a library of sciences, and as many goodly monuments both in Prose and Poetry, and at afternoon could talk as much without book, as any Innholder betwixt Brentford and Bagshot, what degree soever he be!'

While the country was thus giving proofs of the prevalence of this disorder, the two Harringtons (especially the younger) (26)[128] and the illustrious Spenser (27) were unfortunately seized with it in the metropolis.

and whoever has been fortunate enough to read through Mr. Park's new edition of the *Nugæ Antiquæ*, 1804, 8vo.[129] will meet with numerous instances in which the son displays considerable bibliographical knowledge – especially in *Italian* literature; Harrington and Spenser seem to have been the Matthias[130] and Roscoe[58] of the day. I make no doubt but that the former was as thoroughly acquainted with the *vera edizione* of the Giuntæ edition of Boccaccio's Decamerone, 1527, 4to.[131] as either Haym,[132] Orlandi,[133] or Bandini.[134] Paterson,[135] with all his skill, was mistaken in this article when he catalogued Crofts's books. See Bibl. Crofts. No. 3976: his true edition was knocked down for 6s.!!![136]

(27) Spenser's general acquaintance with Italian literature has received the best illustration in Mr. Todd's Variorum edition of the Poet's works;[137] where the reader will find, in the notes, a constant succession of anecdotes of, and references to, the state of anterior and contemporaneous literature, foreign and domestic.

(28) 'The story is extant, and written in very choice *French.*' Consult Chauffepié's *Supplement to Bayle's Dictionary*, vol. iv. p. 621. note Q.[138] Vossius's library was magnificent and extensive. The University of Leyden offered not less than 36,000 florins for it. *Idem.* p. 631.

(29) Of MICHAEL MAITTAIRE I have given a brief sketch in my Introduction to the *Greek and Latin Classics*, vol. 1.148. Mr. Beloe, in the 3d vol.

In the seventeenth century, from the death of Elizabeth to the commencement of Anne's reign, it seems to have made considerable havoc; yet, such was our blindness to it, that we scrupled not to engage in overtures for the purchase of Isaac Vossius's[139] (28) fine library, enriched with many treasures from the Queen of Sweden's, which this versatile genius scrupled not to pillage without confession or apology. During this century our great reasoners and philosophers began to be in motion; and, like the fumes of tobacco, which drive the concealed and clotted insects from the interior to the extremity of the leaves, the infectious particles of the Bibliomania set a thousand busy brains a-thinking, and produced ten thousand capricious works, which, over-shadowed by the majestic remains of Bacon, Locke, and Boyle, perished for want of air, and warmth, and moisture.

The reign of Queen Anne was not exempt from the influence of this discase; for, during this period, Maittaire[38] (29) began to lay the foundation of his exten-

---

of his *Anecdotes of Literature,* p. ix. has described his merits with justice. The principal value of Maittaire's *Annales Typographici* consists in a great deal of curious matter detailed in the notes; but the absence of the 'lucidus ordo,' renders the perusal of these fatiguing and dissatisfactory. The author brought a full and well-informed mind to the task he undertook – but he wanted taste and precision in the arrangement of his materials. The eye wanders over a vast indigested mass; and information, when it is to be acquired with excessive toil, is, comparatively, seldom acquired.

sive library, and to publish some bibliographical works which may be thought to have rather increased, than diminished, its force. Meanwhile, Harley (30) Earl of Oxford[71] watched its progress with an anxious eye; and

Panzer[140] has adopted an infinitely better plan, on the model of Orlandi; and if his materials had been *printed* with the same beauty with which they appear to have been composed, and his annals had descended to as late a period as those of Maittaire, his work must have made us, eventually, forget that of his predecessor. The bibliographer is, no doubt, aware that of Maittaire's first volume there are two editions. Why the author did not reprint, in the second edition (1733), the fac-simile of the epigram and epistle of Lascar prefixed to the edition of the Anthology 1496, and the disquisition concerning the ancient editions of Quintilian, (both of which were in the first edition of 1719) is absolutely inexplicable. Maittaire was sharply attacked for this absurdity, in the 'Catalogus Auctorum,' of the *Annus Tertius Sæcularis Inv. Art. Topog.* ' Harlem, 1741, 8vo. p. 11. 'Rara certe Librum augendi methodus!' (exclaims the author) 'Satis patet auctorem hoc eo fecisse consilio, ut et primæ et secundæ Libri sive editioni pretium suum constaret, et una æque ac altera Lectoribus necessaria esset.'[141]

The catalogue of Maittaire's library, [1748, 2 parts, 8vo.] which affords ample proof of the BIBLIOMANIA of its collector, is exceedingly scarce. A good copy of it, even unpriced, is worth a guinea: it was originally sold for 4 shillings; and was drawn up by Maittaire himself.

(30) In a periodical publication called *'The Director,'* to which I contributed under the article of *'Bibliographiana'* (and of which the printer of this work, Mr. William Savage,[142] is now the sole publisher) there was rather a minute analysis of the famous library of HARLEY, EARL OF OXFORD: a library, which seems not only to have revived, but eclipsed, the splendor of the Roman one formed by Lucullus. The following is an abridgement of this analysis:

although he might have learnt experience from the fatal examples of R. Smith,[143] (31) and T. Baker,[144] (32)

			Volumes.
1. Divinity: *Greek, Latin, French and Italian* – about			2000
————*English*	–	–	2500
2. History an Antiquities	–	–	4000
3. Books of Prints, Sculpture, and Drawings –			
Twenty Thousand Drawings and Prints.			
Ten Thousand Portraits.			
4. Philosophy, Chemistry, Medicine, &c.	–		2500
5. Geography, Chronology, General History	–		600
6. Voyages and Travels	–	–	800
7. Law	–	–	800
8. Sculpture and Architecture	–	–	900
9. Greek and Latin Classics	–	–	2400
10. Books printed on VELLUM	–	–	220
11. English Poetry, Romances, &c.	–	–	1000
12. French and Spanish do.	–	–	700
13. Parliamentary Affairs	–	–	400
14. Trade and Commerce	–	–	300
15. Miscellaneous Subjects	–	–	4000
16. Pamphlets – *Four Hundred Thousand!*			

Mr. Gough[145] says, these books 'filled thirteen handsome chambers, and two long galleries.' Osborne the bookseller[146] purchased them for £13,000: a sum, little more than two thirds of the price of the binding, as paid by Lord Oxford. The bookseller was accused of injustice and parsimony; but the low prices which he afterwards affixed to the articles, and the tardiness of their sale, are sufficient refutations of this charge. Osborne opened his shop for the inspection of the books on Tuesday the 14th of February, 1744; for fear 'of the curiosity of the spectators, before the sale, producing disorder in the disposition of the books.' The dispersion of the HARLEIAN COLLECTION is a blot in the literary annals of our country; had there then been such a Speaker, and such a spirit in the

and the more recent ones of Thomas Rawlinson,[147]
(33) Bridges,[148] (34) and Collins,[149] (35) yet he seemed

House of Commons, as we now possess, the volumes of Harley would
have been reposing with the MARBLES OF TOWNLEY[150]!

(31) 'BIBLIOTHECA SMITHIANA: sive Catalogus Librorum in quavis facultate insigniorum, quos in usum suum et Bibliothecæ ornarnentum
multo ære sibi comparavit vir clarissimus doctissimusque D. RICHARDUS
SMITH, &c. Londini, 1682,' 4to. I recommend the collector of curious
and valuable catalogues to lay hold upon the present one (of which a
more particular description will be given in another work) whenever it
comes in his way. The address 'To the Reader,' in which we are told that
'this so much celebrated, so often desired, so long expected library is now
exposed to sale,' gives a very interesting account of the owner. Inter alia,
we are informed that Mr. Smith 'was as constantly known every day to
walk his rounds through the shops, as to sit down to his meals, &c.' and
that 'while others were forming arms, and new-modelling kingdoms, *his*
great ambition was to become master of a good book.'

The catalogue itself justifies every thing said in commendation of the
collector of the library. The arrangement is good; the books in almost all
departments of literature, foreign and domestic, valuable and curious; and
among the english ones I have found some of the rarest Caxtons to refer to
in my edition of Ames. What would Mr. Bindley,[151] or Mr. Malone,[152] or Mr.
Deuce,[153] give to have the *creaming* of such a collection of 'Bundles of Stitcht
Books and Pamphlets,' as extends from page 370 to 395 of this catalogue!
But alas! while the Bibliographer exults in, or hopes for, the possession of
such treasures, the physiologist discovers therein fresh causes of disease,
and the philanthropist mourns over the ravages of the BIBLIOMANIA!

(32) Consult Masters's[154] *'Memoirs of the Life and Writings of the late Rev.*
THOMAS BAKER,' Camb. 1784, 8vo. Let any person examine the catalogue
of *Forty-two* folio volumes of 'MS. collections by Mr. Baker' (as given at
the end of this piece of biography) and reconcile himself, if he can, to
the supposition that the said Mr. Baker did not fall a victim to the *Book-
disease!* For some cause, I do not now recollect what, Baker took his name

resolved to brave and to baffle it; but, like his predeces-
sors, he was suddenly crushed within the gripe of the

off the books of St. John's College, Cambridge, to which he belonged;
but such was his attachment to the place, and more especially the library, that he spent a great portion of the ensuing twenty years of his life
within the precincts of the same; frequently comforted and refreshed, no
doubt, by the sight of the magnificent LARGE PAPER copies of Walton[155]
and Castell,[156] and of Cranmer's Bible UPON VELLUM!

(33) This THOMAS RAWLINSON, who is introduced in the Tatler, under
the name *Tom Folio,* was a very extraordinary character, and most des-
perately addicted to book-hunting. Because his own house was not large
enough, he hired *London House,* in Aldersgate Street, for the reception
of his library; and here he used to regale himself with the sight and the
scent of innumerable black letter volumes, arranged in 'sable garb,' and
stowed perhaps 'three deep,' from the bottom to the top of his house.
He died in 1725; and Catalogues of his books for sale continued, for nine
succeeding years, to meet the public eye. The following is a list of all
the parts which I have ever met with; taken from copies in Mr. Heber's
possession.

Part 1. *A catalogue of choice and valuable Books in most Faculties and Lan-
    guages;* being the sixth part of the collection made by THOMAS RAW-
    LINSON, Esq. &c. to be sold on Thursday, the 2d day of March, 1726;
    beginning every evening at 5 of the clock, by Charles Davis, Book-
    seller, 'Qui non credit, cras credat.' Ex Autog. T. R.

2. *Bibliotheca Rawlinsoniana;* sive Delectus Librorum in omni ferè Lin-
    gua et Facultate præstantium – to be sold on Wednesday 26th April,
    [1726] by Charles Davis, Bookseller. 2600 Numbers.

3. *The Same:* January 172⅞. By Thomas Ballard, Bookseller. 3520 Num-
    bers.

4. *The Same:* March, 172⅞. By the Same. 3840 Numbers.

5. *The Same:* October, 1727. By the same, 3200 Numbers.

6. *The Same:* November, 1727. By the same, 3520 Numbers.

7. *The Same:* April, 1729. By the same, 4161 Numbers.

demon, and fell one of the most splendid of his victims. Even the unrivalled medical skill of Mead⁴⁴ (36)

8. *The Same:* November, 1729. By the same, 2700 Numbers.
9. *The Same:* [Of Rawlinson's MANUSCRIPTS] By the same. March 1733/4.
    800 Numbers.
10. *Picturæ Rawlinsonianæ.* April, 1734, 117 Articles.
    At the end, it would seem that a catalogue of his prints, and MSS.
missing in the last sale, were to be published the ensuing winter.
    N. B. The black letter books are catalogued in the gothic letter.

(34) 'BIBLIOTHECÆ BRIDGESIANÆ CATALOGUS: or a catalogue of the entire library of John Bridges, late of *Lincoln's Inn,* Esq. &c.¹⁴⁸ which will
begin to be sold by Auction, on Monday the seventh day of February,
172⁵/₆, at his Chambers in *Lincoln's Inn,* No. 6.'
    From a priced copy of this sale catalogue, in my possession, once be-
longing to Nourse the bookseller¹⁵⁷ in the Strand, I find that the following was the produce of the Sale:

The Amount of the books	£3730	0	0
Prints and books of Prints	394	17	6
Total Amount of the Sale	£4124	17	6

Two different catalogues of this valuable collection of books were
printed. The one was analysed, or a *catalogue raisonné;* to which was prefixed a print of a Grecian portico, &c. with ornaments and statues: the
other (expressly for the sale) was an indigested and extremely confused
one – to which was prefixed a print, designed and engraved by A. Motte,
of an oak felled, with a number of men cutting down and carrying away
its branches; illustrative of the following Greek motto inscribed on a
scroll above – Δρύος πεσούσης πᾶς ἀνὴρ ξυλενεται:¹⁵⁸ 'An affecting me-
mento' (says Mr. Nichols,¹⁵⁹ very justly, in his *Anecdotes of Bowyer,* p. 557)
'to the collectors of great libraries, who cannot, or do not, leave them to
some public accessible repository.'

could save neither his friend nor himself. The Doctor survived his Lordship about twelve years; dying of

(35) In the year 1730–1, there was sold by auction, at St. Paul's Coffee House, in St. Paul's Church Yard (beginning every evening at five o'clock), the library of the, celebrated Free Thinker,

ANTONY COLLINS, ESQ.

'Containing a collection of several thousand volumes in Greek, Latin, English, French, and Spanish; in divinity, history, antiquity, philosophy, husbandry and all polite literature: and especially many curious travels and voyages; and many rare and valuable pamphlets.' This collection, which is divided into two parts, (the first containing 3451 articles, the second 3442) is well worthy of being consulted by the theologian, who is writing upon any controverted point of divinity: there are articles in it of the rarest occurrence. The singular character of its owner and of his works is well known: he was at once the friend and the opponent of Locke[160] and Clarke,[161] who were both anxious for the conversion of a character of such strong, but misguided talents. The former, on his death-bed, wrote Collins a letter to be delivered to him, after his decease, which was full of affection and good advice.

(36) It is almost impossible to dwell on the memory of this GREAT MAN, without emotions of delight – whether we consider him as an eminent physician, a friend to literature, or a collector of books, pictures, and coins. Benevolence, magnanimity, and erudition were the striking features of his character: his house was the general receptacle of men of genius and talent, and of every thing beautiful, precious, or rare. His curiosities, whether books, or coins, or pictures, were freely laid open to the public; and the enterprising student, and experienced antiquary, alike found amusement and a courteous reception. He was known to all foreigners of intellectual distinction, and corresponded both with the artisan and the potentate. The great patron of literature, and the leader of his profession (which he practised with a success unknown before), it was hardly possible for unbefriended merit, if properly introduced to him,

the complaint called the BIBLIOMANIA! He left behind
an illustrious character; sufficient to flatter and soothe

to depart unrewarded. The clergy, and, in general, all men of learning,
received his advice *gratuitously:* and his doors were open every morning
to the most *indigent,* whom he frequently assisted with money. Although
his income, from his professional practice, was very considerable, he died
by no means a rich man – so large were the sums which he devoted to
the encouragement of literature and the fine arts!

The sale of Dr. Mead's *books* commenced on the 18th of November,
1754, and again on the 7th of April, 1755: lasting together 57 days. The sale
of the *prints* and *drawings* continued 14 nights. The *gems, bronzes, busts,*
and *antiquities,* 8 days.

His Books produced			£5496 15 0
Pictures -	-	-	3417 11 0
Prints and drawings	-	-	1908 14 0
Coins and medals	-	-	1977 17 0
Antiquities	-	-	3246 15 0
	Amount of all the sales		£16047 12 0

It would be difficult to mention, within a moderate compass, all the
rare and curious articles which his library contained – but the following
are too conspicuous to be passed over. The *Spira Virgil* of 1470, *Pfintzing's Tewrdrancks,* 1527,[162] *Brandt's Stultifera Navis,* 1498, and the *Aldine
Petrarch* of 1501, ALL UPON VELLUM. The large paper *Olivet's Cicero* was
purchased by Dr. Askew for £14. 14s. and was sold again at his sale for £36
15s. The King of France bought the editio princeps of *Pliny Senr.* for £11
11s; and Mr. Willock, a bookseller, bought the magnicentiy illuminated
Pliny by Jensen of 1472, for £18 18s: of which Maittaire has said so many
fine things. The *French* books, and all the works upon the *Fine Arts,* were
of the first rarity and value, and bound in a sumptuous manner. Winstanley's[163] *Prospects of Audley End* brought £50. An amusing account of
some of the pictures will be found in Mr. Beloe's *Anecdotes* of *Literature
and Scarce Books,* vol. I. 166. 71. But consult also *Nichols's Anecdotes of Bow-*

those who may tread in his footsteps, and fall victims to a similar disorder.

The years 1755–6, were singularly remarkable for the mortality excited by the BIBLIOMANIA; and the well known names of Folkes[164] (37) and Rawlinson,[165] (38)

---

yer, p. 225. &c. Of the catalogue of Dr. Mead's books there were only six copies printed on LARGE PAPER. See Bibl. Lort. n°. 1149.

(37) 'A Catalogue of the entire and valuable library of MARTIN FOLKES, ESQ. President of the Royal Society, and Member of the Royal Academy of Sciences at Paris, lately deceased; which will be sold by auction by Samuel Baker,[166] at his house, in York Street, Covent Garden. To begin on Monday, February 2, 1756, and to continue for forty days successively (Sundays excepted). Catalogues to be had at most of the considerable places in Europe, and all the booksellers of Great Britain and Ireland, Price Sixpence.'

This collection was an exceedingly fine one; enriched with many books of the choicest description, which Mr. Folkes had acquired in his travels in Italy and Germany. The works on natural history, coins, medals, and inscriptions, and on the fine arts in general, formed the most valuable department – those on the Greek, Latin, and English classics, were comparatively of inferior importance. It is a great pity the catalogue was not better digested; or the books classed according to the nature of their contents.

The following prices, for some of the more rare and interesting articles, will amuse a bibliographer of the present day. The chronicles of Fabian,[167] Hall,[168] and Grafton,[169] did not altogether bring quite £2; though the copies are described as perfect and fair. There seems to have been a fine set of Sir Wm. Dugdale's Works (Nos. 3074-81) in 13 vols, which, collectively, produced about 30 guineas.

In *Spanish literature,* the history of South America, by Don Juan and Ant. di Ulloa, Madr. fol. in 5 vols,[170] was sold for £5; a fine large paper copy of the description of the Monastery of St. Lorenzo, and the Esco-

might have supplied a modern Holbein with a hint for the introduction of a new subject in the *'Dance of Death.'* The close of George the Second's reign

rial, Madr. 1657, brought £1 2*s*: de Lastanosa's Spanish Medals, Huesca, fol, 1645, £2 2*s*.[171]

In *English*, the first edition of Shakspeare, 1623, which is now, what a French bibliographer would say, 'presque introuvable,' produced the sum of £3 3*s*; and Fuller's Worthies, 18*s*![172]

Fine Arts, Antiquities, and *Voyages*. Sandrart's works, in 9 folio volumes (of which a fine perfect copy is now rarely to be met with, and of very great value) were sold for £13 13*s*. only: Desgodetz[173] Roman edifices, Paris, 1682, £4 10*s*: Galleria Giustiniano, 2 vols. fol. £13 13s. Le Brun's Voyages in Muscovy, &c. in large paper, £4. 4*s*. De Rossi's Raccolta de Statue, &c. Rom. 1704, £6 10*s*. Medailles du Regne de Louis le Grand. de l'Imp. Roy. 1. p. fol. 1702, £5 15*s*. 6*d*.

The works on *Natural History* brought still higher prices; but the whole, from the present depreciation of specie, and increased rarity of the articles, would now bring thrice the sums then given.

Of the *Greek and Latin Classics*, the Pliny of 1469 and 1472 were sold to Dr. Askew for £11 11*s*. and £7. 17*s*. 6*d*. At the Doctor's sale they brought £43 and £23: although the first was lately sold (A.D. 1805) among some duplicates of books belonging to the British Museum, at a much lower price: the copy was, in fact, neither large nor beautiful. Those in the Hunter[174] and Cracherode[175] collections are greatly superior, and would each bring more than double the price.

From a priced copy of the sale catalogue, in my possession, I find that the amount of the sale, consisting of 5126 articles, was £3091 5*s*.

The *Prints and Drawings* of Mr. Folkes occupied a sale of 8 days; and his *pictures, gems, coins*, and *mathematical instruments*, of five days.

Mr. Martin Folkes may justly be ranked among the most useful, as well as splendid literary characters, of which this country can boast. He appears to have imbibed, at a very early age, an extreme passion for science and literature; and to have distinguished himself so much at the University of Cambridge, under the able tuition of Dr. Laughton,[176]

witnessed another instance of the fatality of this disease. Henley[177] (39) 'bawl'd till he was hoarse' against

that, in his 23d year, he was admitted a Fellow of the Royal Society.
About two years afterwards he was chosen one of the council, and rose,
in gradual succession, to the chair of the presidentship, which he filled
with a credit and celebrity that has since never been surpassed. On
this occasion he was told by Dr. Jurin,[178] the Secretary, who dedicated
to him the 34th vol. of the Transactions, that 'the greatest man that
ever lived, (Sir Isaac Newton) singled him out to fill the chair, and to
preside in the society, when he himself was so frequently prevented by
indisposition: and that it was sufficient to say of him that he was *Sir
Isaac's friend.*'

Within a few years after this, he was elected President of the Society
of Antiquaries. Two situations, the filling of which may be considered
as the *ne plus ultra* of literary distinction. Mr. Folkes travelled abroad,
with his family, about two years and a half, visiting the cities of Rome,
Florence, and Venice – where he was noticed by almost every person of
rank and reputation, and from whence he brought away many a valuable
article to enrich his own collection. He was born in the year 1690, and
died of a second stroke of the palsy, under which he languished for three
years, in 1754. Dr. Birch[179] has drawn a very just and interesting character
of this eminent man, which may be found in Nichols's *Anecdotes of Bowyer,* 562. 7. Mr. Edwards,[180] the late ornithologist, has described him, in a
simple, but appropriate manner. 'He seemed,' says he, 'to have attained
to universal knowledge; for, in the many opportunities I have had of being in his company, almost every part of science has happened to be the
subject of discourse, all of which he handled as an adept. He was a man
of great politeness in his manners, free from all pedantry and pride, and,
in every respect, the real unaffected fine gentleman.'

(38) 'BIBLIOTHECA RAWLINSONIANA, sive Catalogus Librorum Richardi
Rawlinson, LL.D. Qui prostabunt Venales sub hasta, Apud Samuelem
Baker. In Vico dicto *York Street, Covent Garden, Londini, Die Lunæ* 29
Martii, MDCCLVI.'

the cruelty of its attack; while his library has informed posterity how severely and how mortally he suffered from it.

This valuable library must have contained about 20,000 volumes; for the number of articles amounted to 9405. On examining a priced catalogue of it, which now lies before me, I have not found any higher sum offered for a work than £4 1s. for a collection of fine prints, by Aldegrave.[181] (No. 9405) The Greek and Latin classics, of which there were few *Editiones Principes*, or on *large paper*, brought the usual sums given at that period. The old English black lettered books, which were pretty thickly scattered throughout the collection, were sold for exceedingly low prices – if the copies were perfect. Witness the following:

	£.	s.	d
The Newe Testament in English, 1530 —	0	2	9
The Ymage of both Churches, after the Revelation of St. John, by Bale, 1550 — —	0	1	6
The boke called the Pype or Tonne of Perfection, by Richard Whytforde, 1532 — —	0	1	9
The Visions of Pierce Plowman, 1561 —	0	2	0
The Creede ot Pierce Plowman, 1553 —	0	1	6
The Bookes of Moses, in English, 1530 —	0	3	9
Bale's Actes of Englishe Votaries, 1550 —	0	1	3
The Boke of Chivalrie, by Caxton — —	0	11	0
The Boke of St. Albans, by W. de Worde —	1	1	0

These are only very few of the rare articles in English literature; of the whole of which (perhaps upwards of 200 in number) I believe, the 'Boke of St. Albans,' brought the highest sum. Hence it will be seen, that this was not the age of curious research into the productions of our ancestors. Shakspeare had not then appeared in a proper *Variorum edition*. Theobald,[182] and Pope, and Warburton,[183] had not investigated the blackletter lore of ancient English writers, for the illustration of their favourite author. This was reserved for Farmer,[184] for Steevens,[185] for Malone,[152] for Chalmers,[186] Reed[187] and Douce:[153] and it is expressly to these latter

We are now, my dear Sir, descending rapidly to our own times; and, in a manner sufficiently rough,

gentlemen (for Johnson[188] and Hanmer[189] were very sparing, or very shy, of the black letter), that we are indebted for the present spirit of research into the works of our ancestors.

The sale of the books lasted 50 days. There was a second sale of pamphlets, books of prints, &c. in the following year, which lasted 10 days; and this was immediately succeeded by a sale of the Doctor's single prints and drawings, which continued 8 days.

(39) This gentleman's library, not so remarkable for the black letter, as for whimsical publications, was sold by auction, by Samuel Paterson,[135] [the earliest sale in which I find this well known book-auctioneer engaged] in June, 1759, and the three ensuing evenings. The title of the Sale Catalogue is as follows:

'A Catalogue of the original MSS. and manuscript collections of the late Reverend Mr. JOHN HENLEY,[177] A. M. Independent Minister of the Oratory, &c. in which are included sundry collections of the late Mons. des Maizeaux,[190] the learned editor of Bayle,[191] &c. Mr. Lowndes,[192] author of the Report for the Amendment of Silver Coins, &c. Dr. Patrick Blair,[193] Physician at Boston, and F. R. S. &c. together with original letters and papers of State, addressed to Henry d'Avenant, Esq. her Britannic Majesty's Envoy at Francfort, from 1703 to 1708 inclusive.'

Few libraries have contained more curious and remarkable publications than did this. The following articles, given as notable specimens, remind us somewhat of Addison's Memoranda for the Spectator,[194] which the waiter at the coffee house picked up and read aloud for the amusement of the company.

No. 166. God's Manifestation by a Star to the Dutch. A mortifying Fast Diet at Court. On the Birth Day of the first and oldest young Gentleman. All corrupt: none good; no, not one.

No. 168. General Thumbissimo. The Spring reversed, or the Flanderkin's Opera and Dutch Pickle Herrings. The Creolean Fillip, or

have traced the *History of the Bibliomania* to the commencement of the present illustrious reign: when we discover, among its victims, a General, who had probably faced many a cannon, and stormed many a rampart, uninjured. The name of Dormer[195] (40) will remind you of the small but choice library which affords

> Royal Mishap. A Martial Telescope, &c. England's Passion Sunday, and April Changelings.

No. 170. Speech upon Speech. A Telescope for Tournay. No Battle, but worse, and the True Meaning of it. An Army Beaten and interred.

No. 174. Signs when the P. will come. Was Captain Sw-n a Prisoner on Parole, to be catechised? David's Opinion of like Times. The Seeds of the plot may rise, though the leaves fall. A Perspective, from the Blair of Athol, The Pretender's Popery. Murder! Fire! Where! Where!

No. 178. Taking Carlisle, catching an eel by the tail. Address of a Bishop, Dean and Clergy. Swearing to the P———r, &c. Anathema denounced against those Parents, Masters, and Magistrates, that do not punish the Sin at Stokesley. A Speech, &c. A Parallel between the Rebels to K. Charles I. and those to his Successor. *Jane Cameron* looked killing at *Falkirk*.

No. 179. Let Stocks be knighted, write, Sir Bank, &c. the Ram-head Month. A Proof that the Writers against Popery fear it will be established in this Kingdom. A Scheme wisely blabbed to root and branch the Highlanders. Let St. Patrick have fair Play, &c.

Of ORATOR HENLEY I have not been able to collect any biographical details more interesting than those which are to be found in Warburton's notes to Pope's Dunciad.

such a melancholy proof of its owner's fate; while the more splendid examples of Smith[196] (41) and West[197] (42) serve to shew the increased ravages of a disease,

(40) 'A Catalogue of the genuine and elegant Library of the late Sir C. C. DORMER, collected by Lieutenant General James Dormer; which will be sold, &c. by Samuel Baker, at his house in York Street, Covent Garden; to begin on Monday, February the 20th, 1764, and to continue the nine-teen following evenings.' At the end of the catalogue we are told that the books were 'in general of the best editions, and in the finest condition, many of them in large paper, bound in morocco, gilt leaves, &c.'

This was a very choice collection of books, consisting almost entirely of Greek, Latin, Italian, Spanish and French. The number of articles did not exceed 3082, and of volumes, probably not 7000. The catalogue is neatly printed, and copies of it on *large paper* are exceedingly scarce. Among the most curious and valuable articles were those numbered 599, 604, 2249, 2590; from n°. 2680 to the end, was a choice collection of Ital-ian and Spanish books.

(41) In the year 1755 wus published at Venice, printed by J. B. Pasquali,[198] a catalogue of the books of JOSEPH SMITH, Esq. Consul at Venice:

The catalogue was published under the following Latin title: 'Bibli-otheca Smithiana, seu Catalogus Librorum D. Josephi Smithii, Angli, per Cognomina Authorum dispositus, Venetiis, typis Jo. Baptistæ Pas-quali M, DCCLV.' in quarto; with the arms of Consul Smith. The title page is succeeded by a Latin preface of Pasquali, and an alphabetical list of 43 pages of the authors mentioned in the catalogue: then follow the books, arranged alphabetically, without any regard to size, language, or subject. These occupy 519 pages, marked with the Roman numerals; after which are 66 pages, numbered in the same manner, of 'addenda et corrigenda.' The most valuable part of the volume, is 'The Prefaces and Epistles prefixed to those works in the Library, which were printed in the 15th century:' these occupy 348 pages. A Catalogue, (in three pages) of the Names of the illustrious Men mentioned in these prefaces, &c. closes the book.

which seemed to threaten the lives of all, into whose
ears (like those of 'Visto,')[199] some demon had 'whis-

It would be superfluous to mention to bibliographers the rare articles
contained in this collection, which are so generally known and so justly
appreciated. They consist chiefly of early editions of *Italian, Greek,* and
Latin classics; and of many copies of both printed UPON VELLUM. The
library, so rich in these articles, was, however, defective in English Literature and Antiquities. There was scarcely any thing of Shakspeare or
Dugdale.

On the death of Mr. Smith, in 1772, his collection was sold in 1773,[200]
by Baker and Leigh; and the books were announced to the public, as being 'in the finest preservation, and consisting of the very best and scarcest
editions of the Latin, Italian, and French authors, from the invention of
printing; with manuscripts and missals, upon vellum, finely illuminated.'
A glance upon the prices for which most of these fine books were sold,
made Mr. Cuthell[201] exclaim, in my hearing, that *'they were given away.'*
On these occasions, one cannot help now and then wishing with father
Evander,

'O mihi præteritos referat si Juppiter annos!'[202]

On comparing Pasquali's with the sale, catalogue, it will be obvious
that a great number of rare and valuable articles was disposed of before
the books came to public auction. Indeed it is known that his present
MAJESTY enriched his magnificent collection with many of the Consul's
first editions, and *vellum copies,* during the life of the latter. The sale continued thirteen days only; and on the last day were sold all the English
books in the *black letter.* Some of these are rather curious.

Of CONSUL SMITH I am unable to present the lover of VIRTU with any
particulars more acceptable than the following. Pasquali (whose Latin
preface is curious enough – abounding with as many interrogatories as
Hamlet's soliloquies) has told us that 'as the Consul himself was distinguished for his politeness, talents, and prudence, so was his house for
splendid and elegant decorations. You might there view,' says he, 'the
most beautifully painted pictures, and exquisite ornaments, whether

pered' the sound of 'TASTE.' These three striking instances of the fatality, of the Bibliomania occurred –
the first in the year 1764; and. the latter in 1773. The
following year witnessed the sale of the Fletewode[203]
(43) library; so that nothing but despair and havoc ap-

gems, vases, or engravings. In short, the whole furniture was so brilliant
and classical, that you admired at once the magnificence and judgment
of the owner.' He tells us a little further, that he had frequently solic-
ited the Consul to print a catalogue of his books; which proposition his
modesty at first induced him to reject; but, afterwards, his liberality, to
comply with. He then observes that, 'in the compilation of the catalogue,
he has studied brevity as much as it was consistent with perspicuity; and
that he was once desirous of stating the *value* and *price* of the books, but
was dissuaded from it by the advice of the more experienced, and by the
singular modesty of the Collector.'

It must be confessed that Pasquali has executed his task well; and that
the catalogue ranks among the most valuable, as well as rare, books of
the kind.

(42) 'BIBLIOTHECA WESTIANA; A Catalogue of the curious and truly
valuable library of the late James West, Esq. President of the Royal Society, deceased, &c. Including the works of CAXTON, LETTOU,[204] MACH-
LINIA,[205] the anonymous St. ALBANS SCHOOLMASTER,[206] WYNKYN DE
WORDE, PYNSON,[207] and the rest of the old English typographers. Digested by Samuel Paterson,'[135] 1773, 8vo.

ANALYSIS OF THE CATALOGUE.

1. *Volumes of Miscellaneous Tracts.*

These volumes extend from No. 148 to 200, from 915 to 992, from 1201 to
1330, and from No. 1401 to 1480.

2. *Divinity.*

In the whole, 560 articles; probably about 1200 volumes; some of them
exceedingly scarce and valuable.

peared to move in the train of this pestiferous malady. In the year 1775 died the famous Dr. Anthony
Askew,[208] another illustrious victim to the Bibliomania. Those who recollect the zeal and scholarship of
this great book-collector, and the precious gems with

3. *Education, Languages, Criticism, Classics, Dictionaries, Catalogues of Libraries, &c.*

There were about 700 volumes in these departments. The catalogues of
English books, from that of Maunsell, in 1595,[209] to the latest before Mr.
West's time, were very complete. The treatises on education, and translations of the ancient classics, comprehended a curious and uncommon
collection. The Greek and Latin classics were rather select than rare.

4. *English Poetry, Romances, and Miscellanies.*

This interesting part of the collection comprehended about 355 articles,
or probably about 750 volumes; and if the singularly rare and curious
books which may be found *under these heads alone,* were now concentrated in one library, the owner of them might safely demand 4000 guineas
for such a treasure.

5. *Philosophy, Mathematics, Inventions, Agriculture and Horticulture, Medicine, Cookery, Surgery, &c.*

Two hundred and forty articles, or about 560 volumes.

6. *Chemistry, Natural History, Astrology, Sorcery, Gigantology.*

Probably not more than 100 volumes.

7. *History and Antiquities.*

This comprehended a great number of curious and valuable productions,
relating both to foreign and domestic transactions.

8. *Heraldry and Genealogy.*

A great number of curious and scarce articles may be found under these
heads.

which his library (44) was stored from the cabinets of De Boze[210] and Gaignat,[211] as well as of Mead and Folkes, cannot but sigh with grief of heart on the thought

9. *Ancient Legends and Chronicles.*

To the English antiquary, few departments of literature are more interesting than these. Mr. West seems to have paid particular attention to them, and to have enriched his library with many articles of this description, of the rarest occurrence. The lovers of Caxton, Fabian,[167] Hardyng,[212] Hall,[168] Grafton,[169] and Holinshed,[213] may be highly gratified by inspecting the various editions of these old chroniclers. I entreat the diligent bibliographer to examine the first 8 articles of page 209 of the catalogue. Alas, when will all these again come under the hammer at one sale?!

10. *Topography.*

Even to a veteran, like the late Mr. GOUGH, such a collection as may be found from p. 217 to p. 239 of this catalogue, would be considered a first-rate acquisition. I am aware that the gothic wainscot, and stained glass windows, of *Enfield Study* enshrined a still more exquisite topographical collection! But we are improved since the days of Mr. West; and every body knows to *whom* these improvements are, in a great measure, to be attributed. When I call to mind the author of *'British Topography'* and *'Sepulchral Monuments,'*[214] I am not insensible to the taste, diligence, and erudition of the 'par nobile fratrum,' who have gratified us with the *'Environs of London,' 'Roman Remains,'* and the first two *volumes of 'Magna Britannia!'*[215]

The preceding is to be considered as a very general, and therefore superficial, analysis of the catalogue of Mr. West's library: copies of it, with the sums for which the books were sold, are now found with difficulty, and bring a considerable price. I never saw or heard of one on LARGE PAPER!

(43) 'A Catalogue of rare books and tracts in various languages and faculties; including *the Antient Conventual Library* of Missenden-Abbey, in Buckinghamshire; together with some choice remains of that of the

of such a victim! How ardently, and how kindly [as I remember to have heard his friend Dr. Burges[216] say], would Askew[208] unfold his glittering stores – open the magnificent folio, or the shining duodecimo, UPON

late eminent Serjeant at Law, WILLIAM FLETEWODE, Esq. Recorder of London, in the Reign of Queen Elizabeth; among which are several specimens of the earliest Typography, foreign and English, including CAXTON, WYNKYN DE WORDE, PYNSON,[207] and others; a fine collection of English Poetry, some scarce old law books, a great number of old English plays, several choice MSS. upon vellum, and other subjects of literary curiosity. Also several of the best editions of the classics, and modern English and French books. To begin *December* 5, 1774, and the 17 following evenings, precisely at half an hour after five.'

I am in possession of a *priced Catalogue* of this collection, which once belonged to Herbert,[217] and which contains all the purchasers' names, as well as the sums given. The purchasers were principally Herbert, Garrick,[218] Dodd,[219] Elmsley,[220] T. Payne,[221] Richardson,[222] Chapman,[223] Wagstaff,[224] Bindley,[151] and Gough.[145] The following is a specimen of some curious and interesting articles contained in this celebrated library, and of the prices for which they once sold!

£. s. d.

No. 172	Bale's *brefe Chronycle relating to Syr Johan Oldecastell*, 1544.[225] The Life off the 70th Archbishopp off Canterbury presentlye sittinge, 1574, &c. Life of Hen. Hills, Printer to O. Cromwell,[226] *with the Relation of what passed between him and the Taylor's Wife in Black Friars*, 1688, &c.	0 7 9
	Purchased by Mores[54]	
Nos. 361 to 367.	Upwards of thirty *scarce Theological Tracts*, in Latin and English	1 5 0

VELLUM, embossed and fast held together with golden knobs and silver clasps! How carefully would he unroll the curious MS. – decipher the half effaced char-

		£. s. d.
Nos. 746 to 784.	A fine collection of early English Translations, in black letter, with some good foreign editions of the classics. Not exceeding, in the whole	10 10 0
Nos. 837, 838.	Two copies of the *first edition* of Bacon's Essays, 1597!	0 0 6
	The reader will just glance at No. 970, in the catalogue, en passant, to	

Nos. 1082 (£1 2s.) and 1091 (12s.); but more particularly to

No. 1173.	*Caxton's Boke of Tulle of Olde Age*, &c. 1481. Purchased by the late Mr. T. Payne[221]	8 8 0
No. 1174.	CAXTON'S *Boke which is sayd or called Cathon*, &c. 1483.	5 0 0
	Purchased by Alchorn,[227]	
No. 1256.	CAXTON'S *Doctrinal of Sapyence*, 1489	
	Purchased by Alchorn.	6 6 0
No. 1257.	CAXTON'S *Cordyal*, 1479	6 12 6
No. 1258.	WYNKYN DE WORDE'S *Orcharde of Syon*, &c. 1519	1 13 0

I will, however, only add that there were upwards of 150 articles of *Old Plays*, mostly in quarto. See pages 71–2. Of *Antiquities, Chronicles*, and *Topography*, it would be difficult to pitch upon the rarest volumes. The collection, including very few MSS, contained 3641 articles, or probably nearly 7000 volumes. The Catalogue is uncommon.

(44) I am now arrived, pursuing my chronological arrangement, at a very important period in the annals of book-sales. The name and collection

acters – and then, casting an eye of ecstacy over the shelves upon which similar treasures were lodged, exult in the glittering prospect before him! But death – who, as Horace tells us, raps equally at the palaces of kings and cottages of peasants, made no scruple to exercise the knocker of the Doctor's door, and sent, as his avant-courier, THIS DEPLORABLE MANIA! It ap-

of Dr. ASKEW are so well known in the bibliographical world, that the reader need not be detained with laboured commendations on either: in the present place, however, it would be a cruel disappointment not to say a word or two by way of *preface* or *prologue*.

Dr. ANTHONY ASKEW had eminently distinguished himself by a refined taste, a sound knowledge, and an indefatigable research relating to every thing connected with Grecian and Roman literature. It was to be expected, even during his life, as he was possessed of sufficient means to gratify himself with what was rare, curious, and beautiful in literature and the fine arts, that the public would, one day, be benefited by such pursuits: especially as he had expressed a wish that his treasures might be unreservedly submitted to sale, after his decease. In this wish the Doctor was not singular. Many eminent collectors had indulged it before him: and to my knowledge, many modern ones still indulge it. Accordingly on the death of Dr. Askew, in 1774, appeared, in the ensuing year, a catalogue of his books for sale, by Messrs. Baker and Leigh, under the following title:

'BIBLIOTHECA ASKEVIANA, sive Catalogus Librorum Rarissimorum ANTONII ASKEW, M. D. quorum Auctio fiet apud S. Baker et G. Leigh,[228] in Vico dicto *York Street, Covent Garden,* Londini. *Die Lunæ,* 13 *Februarii,* MDCCLXXV, et in undeviginti sequentes dies.' A few copies were struck off on large paper.

We are told by the compiler of the catalogue, that it was thought unnecessary to say much with respect to this Library of the late Dr. Anthony Askew, 'as the Collector and Collection were so well known in

peared; and even Askew, with all his skill in medicine and books, fell lifeless before it – bewailed, as he was beloved and respected!

After this melancholy event, one would have thought that future *Virtuosi* would have barricadoed their doors, and fumigated their chambers, to keep out such a pest! – but how few are they who profit by experience, even when dearly obtained! The subsequent

almost all parts of Europe.' Afterwards it is observed that 'The books in general are in very fine condition, many of them bound in morocco, and russia leather, with gilt leaves. To give a particular account,' continues the Compiler, 'of the *many scarce editions* of books in this Catalogue would be almost endless, therefore the *first editions* of the classics, and some *extremely rare books* are chiefly noticed. The Catalogue, without any doubt, contains the best, rarest, and most valuable collection of GREEK and LATIN BOOKS that were ever sold in England.' This account is not overcharged. The collection, in regard to Greek and Roman literature, was *unique* in its day.

The late worthy and learned Mr. M. CRACHERODE,[175] whose library now forms one of the most splendid acquisitions of the British Museum, and whose *bequest* of it will immortalize his memory, was also among the 'Emptores literarii' at this renowned sale. He had enriched his collection with many '*Exemplar Askevianum;*' and, in his latter days, used to elevate his hands and eyes, and exclaim against the prices now offered for EDITIONES PRINCIPES!

The fact is, Dr. Askew's sale has been considered a sort of *æra* in bibliography. Since that period, rare and curious books in Greek and Latin literature have been greedily sought after, and obtained at most extravagant prices. It is very well for a veteran in bibliography, as was Mr. Cracherode, or as are Mr. Wodhull[229] and Dr. Gosset,[230] whose collections were formed in the days of Gaignat, Askew, Duke de la Valliere,[231] and Lamoignon[232] – it is very well for such gentlemen to declaim against

history of the disease is a striking proof of the truth of this remark; for the madness of book-collecting rather increased – and the work of death still went on. In the year 1776 died John Ratcliffe[233] (45), another, and a very singular, instance of the fatality of the BIBLIOMANIA. If he had contented himself with his former occupa-

modern prices! But what is to be done? Books grow scarcer every day, and the love of literature, and of possessing rare and interesting works, increases in an equal ratio. Hungry bibliographers meet, at sales, with well-furnished purses, and are resolved upon sumptuous fare. Thus the hammer *vibrates*, after a bidding of *Forty pounds*, where formerly it used regularly to *fall* at *Four!*

But we lose sight of Dr. Askew's *rare editions*, and *large paper copies*. The following, gentle Reader, is but an imperfect specimen!

		£.	s.	d.
No. 168.	Chaucer's Works, by PYNSON, no date	7	17	6
No. 172.	Cicero of Old Age, by Caxton, 1481	13	13	0
No. 518.	Gilles (Nicole) Annales, &c. de France.[234] Paris. fol. 1520. 2 tom. SUR VELIN	31	10	6
No. 647.	Æginetæ (Pauli) Præcepta Salubria. Paris, quarto, 1510. ON VELLUM	11	0	0
No. 666.	Æsopi Fabulæ. EDIT. PRIN. *circ.* 1480	6	6	0
No. 684.	Boccacio, la Teseide, *Ferar.* 1475. PRIMA EDIZIONE	85	0	0
No. 1433.	Catullus, Tibullus, et Propertius, Aldi. 8vo. 1502. IN MEMBRANA	17	10	0

No. 1433. This copy was purchased by the late Mr. M. C. Cracherode, and is now, with his library, in the British Museum. It is a beautiful book, but cannot be compared with Lord Spencer's Aldine VELLUM Virgil, of the same size.

tion, and frequented the butter and cheese, instead of the book, market – if he could have *fancied himself* in a brown peruke, and Russian apron, instead of an embroidered waistcoat, velvet breeches, and flowing perriwig, he might, perhaps, have enjoyed greater longevity; but infatuated by the Caxtons and Wynkyn De Wordes of Fletewode and of West, he fell into the snare; and the more he struggled to disentangle himself, the more certainly did he become a prey to the disease.

		£.	s.	d.
No. 1576.	Durandi Rationale, &c. 1459. In Membrana The beginning of the 1st chapter was wanting. Lord Spencer has a perfect copy of this rare book on spotless vellum!	61	0	0
No. 2656.	Platonis Opera, apud Aldum, 2 vol. fol. 1513. *Edit. Prin.* On vellum Purchased by the late Dr. W. Hunter; and is, at this moment, in his Museum at Glasgow. The reader who has not seen them can have no idea of the beauty of these vellum leaves. The ink is of the finest lustre, and the whole typographical arrangement may be considered a masterpiece of printing. Lord Oxford told Dr. Mead that he gave 100 guineas for this very copy.	55	13	0

(45) Bibliotheca Ratcliffiana; or, 'A Catalogue of the elegant and truly valuable Library of John Ratcliffe, Esq. late of Bermondsey, deceased. The whole collected with great judgment and expense, during the last thirty years of his life: comprehending a large and most choice collection of the rare old English *black letter,* in fine preservation, and in

Thirty years have been considered by Addison (somewhere in his Spectator) as a pretty accurate period for the passing away of one generation and the coming on of another. We have brought down our researches to within a similar period of the present times; but as Addison has not made out the proofs of such assertion, and as many of the relatives and friends of those who have fallen victims to the BIBLIOMANIA, since the days of Ratcliffe, may yet be alive; moreover, as it is the part of humanity not to tear open wounds which have been just closed, or awaken painful sensi-

elegant bindings, printed by CAXTON, LETTOU, MACHLINIA, the anonymous St. Albans Schoolmaster, Wynkyn de Worde, Pynson, Berthelet,[235] Grafton, Day,[236] Newberie,[237] Marshe,[238] Jugge,[239] Whytchurch,[240] Wyer,[241] Rastell,[242] Coplande[243], and the rest of the *Old English Typographers:* several missals and MSS. and two Pedigrees on vellum, finely illuminated.' The title page then sets forth a specimen of these black-lettered gems; among which our eyes are dazzled with a galaxy of Caxtons, Wynkyn de Wordes, Pynsons, &c. &c. The sale took place on March 27, 1776.

If ever there was a *unique* collection, this was one – the very essence of Old Divinity, Poetry, Romances, and Chronicles! The articles were only 1675 in number, but their intrinsic value amply compensated for their paucity.

The following is but an inadequate specimen.

		£.	s.	d.
No. 1315.	Horace's Arte of Poetrie, Pistles and Satyres, by Drant.[244] 1567. *First English edition.*	0	16	6
No. 1821.	The Sheparde's Calender, 1579.[245]			
	Whetstone's Castle of Delight, 1576 [246]	1	2	0

bilities which have been well nigh laid to rest; so, my dear Sir, in giving you a further account of this fatal disorder, I deem it the most prudent method *not to expatiate* upon the subsequent examples of its mortality. We can only mourn over such names as BEAUCLERK,[247] CROFTS,[248] PEARSON,[249] LORT,[250] MASON,[22] FARMER,[184] STEEVENS,[185] WOODHOUSE,[251] BRAND,[252] and REED,[187] and fondly hope that the list may not be increased by those of living characters!

		£.	s.	d.
No. 1392.	The Pastyme of the People,[253] printed by Rastell. Curious wood cuts. A copy of this book is not now to be procured. I have known £40 offered for it, and rejected with disdain	7	7	0
No. 1403.	Barclay's Shyp of Folys, printed by Pynson, 1508, *first edit.* fine copy [254]	2	10	0
No. 1426.	The Doctrinal of Sapyence, printed by CAXTON, 1489	8	8	0
No. 1427.	The Boke, called Cathon, DITTO, 1483. *Purchased by Dr. Hunter,* and now in his Museum	5	5	0
No. 1428.	The Polytyque Boke, named Tullius de Senectute, in Englyshe, by CAXTON, 1481. *Purchased for his Majesty*	14	0	0
No. 1429.	The Game of Chesse Playe. 1474	16	0	0
No. 1665.	The Boke of Jason, printed by CAXTON	5	10	0
No. 1669.	The Polychronicon of Ranulph Higden, printed by CAXTON, 1482. *Purchased by Dr. Hunter*	5	15	6

We are, in the SECOND place, to describe the SYMP-TOMS OF THE DISEASE.

The ingenious Peignot,[255] in the first volume of his 'Dictionnaire de Bibliologie,' p. 51, defines the Biblio-mania (46) to be 'a passion for possessing books; not so much to be instructed by them, as to gratify the eye by looking on them. He who is affected by this mania knows books only by their titles and dates, and is rath-er seduced by the exterior than interior.'! This is, per-haps, too general and vague a definition to be of much

		£. s. d.
No. 1670.	Legenda Aurea, or the Golden Legende 1483	9 15 0
No. 1674.	Mr. Ratcliffe's MS. Catalogues of the *rare old black letter,* and other curious and uncom-mon books, 4 vol.	7 15 0

This would have been the most delicious article to *my* palate. If the present owner of it were disposed to part with it, I could not find it in my heart to refuse him compound interest for his money. As is the wooden frame-work to the bricklayer in the con-struction of his arch, so might Mr. Ratcliffe's MS. Catalogues be to me in the compilation of a certain *magnum opus!*

The memory of such a man ought to be dear to the *'black lettered dogs'* of the present day; for he had [mirabile dictu!] *upwards of* THIRTY CAX-TONS![256]

If I might hazard a comparison between Mr. James West's and Mr. John Ratcliffe's collections, I should say that the former was more exten-

benefit in the knowledge, and consequent prevention, of the disease: let us, therefore, describe it more certainly and intelligibly.

Symptoms of this disease are instantly known by a passion for I. *Large Paper Copies:* II. *Uncut Copies;* III. *Illustrated Copies;* IV. *Unique Copies;* V. *Copies printed upon Vellum;* VI. *First Editions;* VII. *True Editions;* VIII. *A general desire for the Black Letter.* We will describe these symptoms more particularly

I. *Large Paper Copies.* These are, a certain set of limited number of the work printed in a superior manner, both in regard to ink and press work, on paper of a larger size, and better quality, than the ordinary copies. Their price is enhanced in proportion to their beauty and rarity. In the note below (47) are specified a few works which have been published in this manner, that the sober collector may avoid approaching them.

---

sive, the latter more curious: Mr. West's, like a magnificent *champagne,*[257] executed by the hand of Claude or Both, and enclosing mountains, and meadows, and streams, presented to the eye of the beholder a scene at once extensive, luxuriant and fruitful: Mr. Ratcliffe's, like one of those delicious pieces of scenery, touched by the pencil of Rysdæl or Hobbima, exhibited to the beholder's eye a spot equally interesting, but less varied and extensive. The sweeping foliage and rich pasture of the former, could not, perhaps, afford greater gratification than did the thatched cottage, abrupt declivities, and gushing streams of the latter. To change the metaphor – Mr. West's was a magnificent repository, Mr. Ratcliffe's a choice cabinet of gems.

This (48) symptom of the Bibliomania is, at the present day, both general and violent, and threatens to extend still more widely. Even modern publications are not exempt from its calamitous influence; and when Mr. Miller,[258] the bookseller, told me with what eager-

---

(46) There is a short, but smart and interesting, article on this head in Mr. D'Isræli's *Curiosities of Literature*, vol. I. 10. 'Bruyere has touched on this mania with humour; of such a collector (one who is fond of superb bindings only) says he, as soon as I enter his house, I am ready to faint on the stair case from a strong smell of morocco leather. In vain he shews me fine editions, gold leaves, Etruscan bindings, &c.[259] – naming them one after another, as if he were shewing a gallery of pictures'! Lucian has composed a biting invective against an ignorant possessor of a vast library. One who opens his eyes with an hideous stare, at an old book, and after turning over the pages, chiefly admires the date of its publication'!

(47) 1. *Lord Bacon's Essays*, 1798, 8vo.of which it is said only five copies were struck off on royal folio. In Lord Spencer's, and the Cracherode, collection I have seen a copy of this exquisitively printed book; the text of which, surrounded by such an amplitude of margin, in the language of Ernesti [see his critique on Havercamp's Sallust] 'natat velut cymba in oceano.'

2. *Twenty Plays of Shakspeare* published by Steevens from the old quarto editions, 1766, 8vo. 6 vols. Of this edition there were only twelve copies struck off on large paper. See Bibl. Steevens, No. 1312.

3. *Dodsley's collection of Old Plays*, 1780, 8vo, 12 vols, only six copies printed on large paper. See Bibl. Woodhouse, No. 198.

4. *The Grenville Homer*. Græce, 1800, 4to. 4 vols. Fifty copies, with plates, were struck off on large paper, in royal quarto. A copy of this kind was purchased at a sale in 1804, for £99 15s.

ness the large paper copies of Lord Valentia's Travels[260] were bespoke, and Mr. Evans shewed me that every similar copy of his new edition of 'Burnett's History of his own Times,'[50] was disposed of I could not help elevating my eyes and hands, in token of commiseration at the prevalence of this Symptom of the BIBLIO-MANIA!

II. *Uncut Copies.* Of all the symptoms of the Bibliomania, this is probably the most extraordinary. It may be defined in a passion to possess books of which the edges have never been sheared by the binder's tools. And here, my dear Sir, I find myself walking upon doubtful ground: – your UNCUT HEARNES rise up in 'rough majesty' before me, and almost 'push me from my stool.' Indeed, when I look around in my book-lined tub, I cannot but be conscious that this symptom of the disorder has reached my own threshold; but when it is known that a few of my bibliographical books are left with the edges uncut *merely to please my friends* (as one must sometimes study their tastes and appetites as well as one's own), I trust that no very serious

5. *Sandford's Genealogical History,* &c. 1707, fol. Mr. Arch of Cornhill purchased a copy of this work on large paper, at the late sale of Baron Smyth's[261] books, for £46. If the largest paper of Clarke's Cæsar be excepted, this is the highest priced single volume on large paper, that I just now recollect.

6. *Hearne's Works* on large paper.

conclusions will be drawn about the probable fatality of my own case. As to uncut copies, although their
inconvenience [an uncut lexicon to wit!] and defor-
mity must be acknowledged, and although a rational
man can want for nothing better than a book *once well
bound*, yet we find that the extraordinary passion for
collecting them, not only obtains with full force, but
is attended with very serious consequences to those
'qui n'ont point des pistoles' (to borrow the language of
Clement; vol. vi. p. 36).[84] I dare say an uncut *first Shakespeare*, as well as an uncut *first Homer* (49) would produce a little annuity!

III. *Illustrated Copies.* A passion for books illustrated or adorned with numerous prints, representing
characters or circumstances mentioned in the work,
is a very general and violent symptom of the Bibliomania, which has been known chiefly within the last
half century. The origin, or first appearance, of this
symptom has been traced by some to the publication
of Granger's 'Biographical History of England;'[48] but
whoever will be at the pains of reading the preface of

Something relating to Hearne will be found in the note at page 9
ante. Here it will be only necessary to observe that, the Hernëan rage for
Large Paper is quite of recent growth, but it promises to be giant-like.
When the duplicates of a part of Mr. Woodhull's[229] library, in 1803, were
sold, there was a fine set of copies of this kind; but the prices, comparatively with those now offered, were extremely moderate. Mr. Otridge,[262]
the bookseller, told me an amusing story of his going down to Liverpool,

this work, will see that Granger sheltered himself under the authorities of Evelyn,[263] Ashmole,[264] and others; and that he alone is not to be considered as responsible for all the mischief which this passion for
collecting prints has occasioned. Granger, however,
was the first who introduced it in the form of a treatise, and surely 'in an evil hour' was this treatise published – although its amiable author must be acquit-
ted of 'malice prepense.' His History of England, (50)
seems to have sounded the tocsin for a general rum-
mage after, and slaughter of, old prints: venerable philosophers and veteran heroes, who had long reposed
in unmolested dignity within the magnificent folio
volumes which recorded their achievements, were instantly dragged from their peaceful abodes to be inlaid
by the side of some spruce, modern engraving, within an ILLUSTRATED GRANGER! Nor did the madness
stop here. Illustration was the order of the day; and
Shakspeare (51) and Clarendon[265] (52) became the next
objects of its attack. From these it has glanced off in
a variety of directions, to adorn the pages of humbler
wights; and the passion, or rather this symptom of the
Bibliomania, (53) yet rages with undiminished force. If

many years ago, and accidentally purchasing from the library of the late
Sir Thomas Hanmer,[189] a *magnificent set of Large Paper Hearnes* for about
40 Guineas. Many of these are now in the choice library of his Grace the
Duke of Grafton. The copies were catalogued as *small* paper. Was there
ever a more provoking blunder?!

judiciously (54) treated, it is, of all the symptoms, the least liable to mischief. To possess a series of well executed portraits of illustrious men, at different periods of their lives, from blooming boyhood to phlegmatic old age, is sufficiently amusing (55); but to possess *every* portrait, *bad, indifferent, and unlike,* betrays such a dangerous and alarming symptom as to render the case almost incurable!

(48) Analogous to Large Paper Copies are tall Copies; that is, copies of the work published on the ordinary size paper and not much cut down by the binder. The want of *margin* is a serious grievance complained of by book collectors; and when there is a contest of margin-measuring, with books never professedly published on large paper, the anxiety of each party to have the largest copy, is better conceived than described! How carefully, and how adroitly, are the golden and silver rules then exercised!

(49) 'Un superbe exemplaire de cette édition princeps a vendu, chez M. de Cotte, en 1804, la somme de 3601 livres; mais il faut ajouter que cet exemplaire très-precieux est de la plus belle conservation; on dirait qu'il sort dessous presse. De plus, il est peut-être *l'unique dont les marges n'ont pas été rognées ni coupées!*[66]

Peignot's *Curiosités Bibliographiques,* lxv–vi.

(50) It was first published in two quarto volumes, 1766 ; and went through several editions in octavo. The last is, I believe, of the date of 1804; to which three additional volumes were published by William Noble, in 1806; the whole seven volumes form what is called an excellent library work.

(51) About two or three years ago there was an extraordinary set of prints disposed of, for the illustration of Shakspeare, collected by a gentleman in Cornwall, with considerable taste and judgment. Lord Spencer's

There is another mode of illustrating copies by which this symptom of the Bibliomania may be known: it consists in bringing together, from different works, [by means of the scissars, or otherwise by transcription] every page or paragraph which has any connection with the character or subject under discussion. This is a useful and entertaining mode of illustrating a favourite author; and copies of works of this nature, when executed by skilful (56) hands, should he preserved in public repositories. I almost ridiculed the idea of an ILLUSTRATED CHATTERTON, in this way, till I saw Mr. Haslewood's copy, in twenty-one volumes, which rivetted me to my seat

IV. *Unique Copies.* A passion for a book which has any peculiarity about it, by either, or both, of the fore-

---

beautiful octavo illustrated Shakspeare, bequeathed to him by the late Mr. Steevens, has been enriched, since it came into the library of its present noble possessor, with many a rare and many a beauteous specimen of the graphic art.

(52) I have heard of an illustrated Clarendon (which was recently in the metropolis), that has been valued at 5000 Guineas!'a good round sum !'

(53) One of the most striking and splendid instances of the present rage for illustration may be seen in Mr. Miller's own copy of the Historical Work of Mr. Fox,[267] in two volumes, imperial quarto. Exclusively of a great variety of Portraits, it is enriched with the original drawing of Mr Fox's bust from which the print, attached to the publication, is taken; and has also many original notes and letters by its illustrious author. Mr.

going methods of illustration – or which is remarkable for its size, beauty, and condition – is indicative of a rage for *unique copies,* and is unquestionably a strong prevailing symptom of the Bibliomania. Let me therefore urge every sober and cautious collector not to be fascinated by the terms '*Matchless, and Unique;*' which, 'in slim Italicks' (to copy Dr. Ferriar's happy expression) are studiously introduced into Booksellers' catalogues to lead the unwary astray. Such a Collector may fancy himself proof against the temptation; and will, in consequence, *call only to look at* this unique book, or set of books; but, when he views the morocco binding, silk water-tabby lining, blazing gilt edges – when he turns over the white and spotless leaves – gazes on the amplitude of margin – on a rare and lovely print introduced – and is charmed with the soft and coaxing

Walter Scott's edition of Dryden has also received, by the same publisher, a similar illustration. It is on large paper, and most splendidly bound in blue morocco, containing upwards of 650 portraits.

(54) The fine copy of Granger, illustrated by the late Mr. Bull, is now in the library of the Marquis of Bute, at Luton. It extends to 37 atlas folio volumes, and is a repository of almost every rare and beautiful print, which the diligence of its late, and the skill, taste, and connoisseurship of its present, noble owner have brought together.

(55) In the Memoirs of Mr. Thomas Hollis there is a series of the portraits of Milton (not executed in the best manner) done in this way; and a like series of Pope's portraits accompanies the recent edition of the poet's works by the Rev. W. L. Bowles.

manner in which, by the skill of Herring or Mackinlay, (58) 'leaf succeeds to leaf' – he can no longer bear up against the temptation – and confessing himself vanquished, purchases, and retreats – exclaiming with Virgil's shepherd ——

Ut vidi, ut perii – ut me malus abstulit error![268]

V. *Copies printed upon Vellum.* A desire for works printed in this manner is an equally strong and general symptom of the Bibliomania; but as these works are rarely to be obtained of modern (59) date, the collector is obliged to have recourse to specimens, executed three

(56) Numerous are the instances of the peculiar use and value of copies of this kind, especially to those who are engaged in publications of a similar nature. Oldys's interleaved Langbaine[269] is re-echoed in almost every recent work connected with the belles-lettres of our country. Oldys himself was unrivalled in this method of illustration; if, besides his Langbaine, his copy of 'Fuller's Worthies'[172] [once Mr. Steevens's, now Mr. Malone's. See Bibl. Steevens, n°. 1799] be alone considered! This Oldys was the oddest mortal that ever scribbled for bread.[269] Grose, in his *Olio*,[31] gives an amusing account of his having 'a number of small parchment bags inscribed with the names of the persons whose lives he intended to write; into which he put every circumstance and anecdote he could collect, and from thence drew up his history.' See Noble's *College of Arms,* p. 420.

Of illustrated copies in this way, the Suidas of Kuster,[270] belonging to the famous D'Orville,[271] is a memorable instance. This is now in the Bodleian library. I should suppose that one Narcissus Lutrell,[272] in Charles the Second's reign, had a number of like illustrated copies. His collection of contemporaneous literature must have been immense, as we may conclude from the account of it in Mr. Walter Scott's Preface to his recent edition of Dryden's works.[273] Luckily for this brilliant poet and editor,

centuries ago, in the printing offices of Aldus, Verard, and the Juntæ. Although the Bibliotheque Imperiale, at Paris, and the library of Count Macarty,[274] at Toulouse, are said to contain the greatest number of books printed upon vellum, yet, those who have been fortunate enough to see copies of this kind in the libraries of his Majesty,[275] the Duke of Marlborough,[276] Earl Spencer,[21] Mr. Johnes,[277] and the late Mr. Cracherode,[175] (now in the British Museum) need not travel on the Continent for the sake of being convinced of their exquisite beauty and splendor. Mr. Edwards's[180] *unique* copy (he will forgive the epithet) of the first Livy, upon

a part of Luttrell's collection had found its way into the libraries of Mr Bindley[151] and Mr. Heber,[278] and from thence was doomed to shine, with renew'd lustre, by the side of the poetry of Dryden.

(58) At page 11, note – the reader has been led to expect a few remarks upon the luxuriancy of modern book-binding. Mr. Roscoe,[58] in his Lorenzo de Medici, vol. ii. p. 79. edit. 8vo. has defended the art with so much skill, that nothing further need be said in commendation of it. Admitting every degree of merit to our present fashionable binders, and frankly allowing them the superiority over De Rome, Padaloup, and the old school of binding, I cannot but wish to see revived those beautiful portraits, arabesque borders, and sharp angular ornaments, that are often found on the outsides of books bound in the 16th century, with calf leather, upon oaken boards. These brilliant decorations almost make us forget the ivory crucifix, guarded with silver doors, which is frequently introduced in the interior of the sides of the binding. Few things are more gratifying to a genuine collector than a fine copy of a book in its *original binding!*

vellum, is a Library of itself! – and the recent discovery
of a vellum copy of Wynkyn De Worde's reprint of *Juliana Barnes's book*, (60) complete in every respect, [to
say nothing of his Majesty's similar copy of Caxton's
Doctrinal of Sapience, 1489,[279] in the finest preservation]
are, to he sure, sufficient demonstrations of the prevalence of this symptom of the Bibliomania in the times
of our forefathers; so that it cannot be said, as some
have asserted, to have appeared entirely within the last
half century.

VI. *First Editions*. From the time of Ancillon (61)
to Askew, there has been a very strong desire expressed for the possession of original or first published

---

(59) The modern books, printed upon vellum, have in general not succeeded; whether from the art of preparing the vellum, or of printing
upon it, being lost, I will not presume to determine. The reader may be
amused with the following prices for which a few works, executed in this
manner, were sold in the year 1804:

		£	s.	d.
No. 250.	Virgilii Opera, 1789, 4to.[280]	33	12	0
251.	Somervile's Chase, 1796, 4to.[281]	15	4	6
252.	Poems by Goldsmith and Parnell, 1795, 4to.[282]	15	15	0
253.	The Gardens, by Abbe Delille, 1798, 4to.[283]	14	3	6
254.	Castle of Otranto, printed by Bodoni, 1791, 4to.[284]	13	2	6
260.	La Guirlande Julie, 1784, 8vo.[285]	37	17	6
263.	Economy of Human Life, 1795, 8vo.[286]	15	15	0

editions of works, as they are in general superintend-
ed and corrected by the author himself; and, like the
first impressions of prints, are considered more valuable. Whoever is possessed with a passion for collecting books of this kind, may unquestionably he said to
exhibit a strong symptom of the Bibliomania: but such
a case is not quite hopeless, nor is it deserving of severe
treatment or censure. All bibliographers have dwelt on
the importance of these editions, for the sake of col-
lation with subsequent ones, and detecting, as is frequently the case, the carelessness displayed by future
(62) editors. Of such importance is the *first edition of
Shakspeare* (63)[287] considered, that a fac-simile reprint

See '*Catalogue of a most splendid and valuable Collection of Books, Superb
Missals, &c.* sold by Mr. Christie, on April 24, 1804. But the reader should
procure the Catalogue of Mr. Paris's Books, sold in the year 1790, which,
for the number of articles, is unrivalled. The eye is struck, in every page,
with the most sumptuous copies on VELLUM AND LARGE PAPER!

(60) See page 5, ante, for some account of this curious work.

(61) There is a curious and amusing article in Bayle [English edition, vol.
i, 672, &c.] about the elder ANCILLON,[288] who frankly confessed that he
'was troubled with the BIBLIOMANIA, or disease of buying books.' Mr.
D'Israeli[289] says, that he 'always purchased *first editions,* and never waited
for second ones,' – but I find it, in the English Bayle, note D, 'he chose
the best editions.' The manner in which Ancillon's library was pillaged by
the Ecclesiastics of Metz (where it was considered as the most valuable
curiosity in the town) is thus told by Bayle: 'Ancillon was obliged to leave
Metz: a company of Ecclesiastics, of all orders, came from every part, to

of it has been published with success. In regard to the Greek and Latin Classics, the possession of these original editions is of the first consequence to editors who are anxious to republish the legitimate text of an author. Wakefield, I believe, always regretted that the first edition of Lucretius had not been earlier inspected by him, When he began *his* edition, the Editio Princeps was not (as I have understood) in the library of Earl Spencer – the storehouse of almost every thing that is exquisite and rare in ancient classical literature!

It must not however be forgotten, that if first editions are, in some instances, of great importance, they are in many respects superfluous, and an incumbrance to the shelves of a collector; inasmuch as the labours of subsequent editors have corrected their errors, and superseded, by a great fund of additional matter, the necessity of consulting them. Thus, not to mention other instances, (which present themselves while noticing the present one) all the fine things which Colomiés [290]and Reimannus[291] have said about the rarity of La Croix du Maine's[292] Bibliotheque, published in 1584, are now unnecessary to be attended to, since the ample

lay hands on this fine and copious library, which had been collected with the utmost care during forty years. They took away a great number of the books together, and gave a little money, as they went out, to a young girl, of twelve or thirteen years of age, who looked after them, that they might have it to say they had *paid for them*. Thus Ancillon saw that valuable col-

and excellent edition of this work by De La Monnoye and Juvigny, in six quarto volumes, 1772, has appeared. Nor will any one be tempted to hunt for Gesner's Bibliotheca of 1545–8,[293] whatever may be its rarity, who has attended to Morhof's[85] and Vogt's[294] recommendation of the last and best edition of 1583.

VII. *True Editions.* Some copies of a work are struck off with deviations from the usually received ones, and though these deviations have neither sense nor beauty to recommend them, [and indeed are principally *defects!*] yet copies of this description are eagerly sought after by collectors of a certain class! This particular pursuit may therefore be called another, or the seventh, symptom of the Bibliomania. The note below (64) will furnish the reader with a few anecdotes relating to it.

lection dispersed, in which, as he was wont to say, his chief pleasure and even his heart was placed!' – Edit. 1734.

(62) An instance of this kind may be adduced from the *first edition* of Fabian, printed in 1516; of which Messrs. Longman, Hurst, and Co. have now engaged a very able editor[295] to collate the text with that of the subsequent editions. 'The Antiquary,' says the late Mr. BRAND, 'is desired to consult the edition of Fabian, printed by Pynson, in 1516, because there are others, and I remember to have seen one in the Bodleian Library at Oxford, with a continuation to the end of Queen Mary, 1559, in which *the language is much modernised.*' Shakspeare, edit. 1803, vol. xviii. p. 85–6.[296]

(63) A singular story is 'extant' about the purchase of the late Duke of Roxburgh's fine copy of the first edition of Shakspeare.[297] A friend was bidding for him in the sale-room: his Grace had retired to a distance,

VIII. Books printed in the *Black Letter*. Of all symptoms of the Bibliomania, this eighth symptom (and the last which I shall notice) is at present the most powerful and prevailing. Whether it was not imported into this country from Holland, by the subtlety of Schelhorn[298] (65) (a knowing writer upon rare and curious books) may be shrewdly suspected. Whatever be its origin, certain it is, my dear Sir, that books printed in the black letter are now coveted with an eagerness unknown to our collectors in the last century. If the spirits of West, Ratcliffe, Farmer and Brand, have as yet held any intercourse with each other, in that place 'from whose bourne no traveller returns,' what must be the surprise of the three former, on being told by the

to view the issue of the contest. Twenty guineas and more were offered, from various quarters, for the book; a slip of paper was handed to the Duke, in which he was requested to inform his friend whether he was 'to go on bidding' – his Grace took his pencil, and wrote underneath, by way of reply —

——————— lay on, Macduff!
And d——d be he who first cries, 'Hold, enough!'

Such a spirit was irresistible, and bore down all opposition. His Grace retired triumphant, with the book under his arm.

(64) *Cæsar. Lug. Bat.* 1635, 12mo. *Printed by Elzevir.*[299]

In the Bibliotheca Revickzkiana[300] we are informed that the true Elzevir edition is known by having the plate of a Buffalo's head at the beginning of the preface, and body of the work: also by having the page

latter, of the prices given for some of the books in his library, as mentioned below!? (66)

A perusal of these articles may probably not impress the reader with any lofty notions of the superiority of the black letter; but this symptom of the Bibliomania is, nevertheless, not to be considered as incurable, or wholly unproductive of good. Under a proper spirit of modification it has done, and will continue to do, essential service to the cause of English literature. It guided the taste, and strengthened the judgment, of Tyrwhitt[301] in his researches after Chaucerian lore.

---

numbered 153, which *ought* to have been numbered 149! A further account is given in my introduction to the Classics, vol. i. 228.

Horace: Londini, 1733, 8vo. 2 vol. Published by Pine.[302]

The *true* edition is distinguished by having at page 108, vol. ii. the *incorrect* reading 'Post Est,' – for 'Potest.'

Virgil. Lug. Bat. 1636, 12mo. Printed by Elzevir.

The *true* edition is known, by having at plate 1, before the Bucolics, the following latin passage *printed in red ink.* 'Ego vero frequentes a te litteras accipi' – Consult De Bure, No. 2684.

Idem. Birmingh. 1763, 4to. Printed by Baskerville.

A particular account of the *true* edition will be found in the second volume of my 'Introduction to the Classics' p. 337 – too long to be here inserted.

Boccaccio Il Decamerone, Venet. 1527. 4to.

Consult De Bure, No. 3667: Bandini, vol. ii. 24: [who however is extremely laconic upon this edition, but copious upon the anterior one of 1516] and Haym. vol. iii. p. 5, edit. 1803. Bibl. Paris. No. 408. Clement. (vol. iv. 352) has abundance of references, as usual, to strengthen his assertion in calling the edition 'fort rare.' The reprint or spurious edition has always struck me as the prettier book of the two.

It stimulated the studies of Farmer and of Steevens, and enabled them to twine many a beauteous flower round the brow of their beloved Shakspeare. It has since operated, to the same effect, in the labours of Mr. Douce, (67) the PORSON[303] of old English and French Literature; and in the editions of Milton and Spenser, by my amiable and excellent friend Mr. Todd, the public have had a specimen of what the *Black Letter* may perform, when temperately and skilfully exercised.

I could bring to your recollection other instances; but your own copious reading and exact memory will better furnish you with them. Let me not however omit remarking that the beautiful pages of the *'Minstrelsy of the Scottish Border'* and *'Sir Trestrem'* exhibit, in the notes, [now and then thickly studded with black letter references] a proof that the author of 'The Lay' and 'Marmion'[304] has not disdained to enrich his stores

(65) His words are as follows: 'Ipsa typorum ruditas, ipsa illa atra crassaque literarum facies *belle tangit sensus,' &c.*[305] Was ever the black letter more eloquently described? See his *Amœnitates Literariæ*, vol. i. p. 5.

(66) £. s. d

282   A Boke of Fishing with Hooke and Line, A Boke of Engines and Traps to take Polcats, Buzzards, Rats, Mice, and all other Kinds of Vermine and Beasts whatsoever, with cuts, very rare, 1600[306]   3 3 0

454   A Quip for an upstart Courtier; or, a quaint Dispute between Velvet Breeches and Cloth Breeches, &c. 1620[307]   2 16 0

of information by such intelligence as black lettered books impart. In short, though this be also a strong and general symptom of the Bibliomania, it is certainly not attended with injurious effects when regulated by prudence and discretion. An undistinguishable voracious appetite, to swallow every thing printed in the

475 A Checke, or Reproofe of Mr. Howlet's untimely screeching in her Majesty's Ear. *Black letter.* 1581.   o 12 o
As a *striking conclusion,* I subjoin the following.[310]

6479 Pappe with an Hatchett, *alias,* a Fig for my God-sonne, or, crake me this Nutt, or, a Countrie Cuffe, that is, a sound Box of the Eare for the Idiot Martin, to hold his Peace: seeing the Patch will take no warning; written by one that dares call a Dog a Dog. *Rare.* Printed by Anoke and Astile.[311]   1 8 o

(67) In the criticisms on Mr. Douce's *'Illustrations of Shakspeare and Ancient Manners,'* it has not, I think, been generally noticed that this work is distinguished: 1. For the singular diffidence and urbanity of criticism, as well as depth of learning, which it evinces: 2. For the happy illustrations, by means of wood cuts; Let any one, for instance, read a laboured disquisition on the punishment of 'the boots' – and only glance his eye on the plate representing it [vol. i. p. 34.]: from which will he obtain the clearer notions? 3. For the taste, elegance, and general correctness with which it is printed. The only omission I regret, is, that Mr. Douce did not give us, at the end, a list of the works, alphabetically arranged, with their dates, which he consulted in the formation of his own. Such a 'BIBLIOTHECA SHAKSPEARIANA' might, however, have been only a fresh stimulus to the increase of the black-letter symptom of the *Bibliomania.* How Bartholomæus[308] and Batman[309] have risen in price since the publication of Mr. Douce's work, let those, who have lately smarted for the increase, tell!

black letter, can only bring on inconquerable disease, if not death, to the patient!

Having in the two preceding divisions of this letter discoursed somewhat largely upon the History and Symptoms of the Bibliomania, it now remains, according to the original plan, to say a few words upon the Probable Means of its Cure. And, indeed, I am driven to this view of the subject from every laudable motive; for it would be highly censurable to leave any reflecting mind impressed with melancholy emotions concerning the misery and mortality that have been occasioned by the abuse of those pursuits, to which the most soothing and important considerations ought to be attached. Far from me, and my friends, be such a cruel, if not criminal, conduct! Let us then, my dear Sir, seriously discourse upon the

III. Probable Means of the Cure of the Bibliomania. *He* will surely be numbered among the philanthropists of his day, who has, more successfully than myself, traced and described the ravages of this disease, and fortified the sufferer with the means of its cure. But, as this is a disorder of quite a recent date, and as its characteristics, in consequence, cannot be yet fully known or described, great candor must be allowed to that physician who offers a prescription for so obscure and complicated a case. It is in vain that

you search the works [ay, even the best editions] of
Hippocrates and Galen for a description of this malady; nor will you find it hinted at in the more philosophical treatises of Sydenham[312] and Heberden.[313] It
had, till the medical skill of Dr. Ferriar first noticed it
to the public, escaped the observations of all our pa-
thologists. With a trembling hand, and fearful apprehension, therefore, I throw out the following suggestions for the cure, or mitigation, of this disorder:

In the *first place*, the disease of the Bibliomania is
materially softened, or rendered mild, by directing our
studies to *useful* and *profitable* works – whether these
be printed upon small or large paper, in the gothic, roman, or italic type! To consider purely the *intrinsic* ex-
cellence, and not the exterior splendor or adventitious
value, of any production, will keep us perhaps wholly
free from this disease. Let the midnight lamp be burnt
to illuminate the stores of antiquity – whether they be
romances, or chronicles, or legends, and whether they
be printed by Aldus or by Caxton – if a brighter lustre
can thence be thrown upon the pages of modern learning! To trace genius to its source, or to see how she has
been influenced or modified, by 'the lore of past times'
is both a pleasing and a profitable pursuit. To see how
Shakspeare has here and there plucked a flower, from
some old ballad or popular tale, to enrich his own un-
perishable garland – to follow Spenser and Milton in

their delightful labyrinths midst the splendor of Italian literature – are studies which stamp a dignity upon our intellectual characters! But, in such a pursuit, let us not overlook the wisdom of modern times, nor fancy that what is only ancient can be excellent. We must remember that Bacon, Boyle, Locke, Taylor, Chillingworth, Robertson, Hume, Gibbon, and Paley, are names which always command attention from the wise, and remind us of the improved state of reason and acquired knowledge during the two last centuries.

In the *second place,* the reprinting of scarce and intrinsically valuable works is another means of preventing the propagation of this disorder. Amidst all our present sufferings under the BIBLIOMANIA, it is some consolation to find discerning and spirited booksellers republishing the valuable Chronicles of Froissart, Holinshed, and Hall, (68) and the collections known by the names of 'The Harleian Miscellany'[314] and 'Lord Somers's Tracts.'[315] These are noble efforts, and richly deserve the public patronage.

In the *third place,* the editing of our best ancient authors, whether in prose or poetry, (69) is another

(68) The republication of these Chronicles is to be followed by those of Grafton and Fabian. Meanwhile, Hakluyt's Voyages, (projected by Mr. Evans), and Fuller's Worthies (by Messrs. Longman, Hurst, and Co.) will form admirable acquisitions to these treasures of past times.

means of effectually counteracting the progress of the Bibliomania, as it has been described under its several symptoms.

In the *fourth place*, the erection of Public Institutions (70) is a very powerful antidote against the prevalence of several symptoms of this disease.

In the *fifth place*, the encouragement of the study of Bibliography, (71) in its legitimate sense, and towards its true object, may be numbered among the most

---

(69) The recent Variorum editions of Shakspeare, of which some yet prefer that of Steevens, 1793, 15 vols. 8vo. – Mr. Todd's editions of Milton and Spenser; Mr. G. Chalmers's edition of Sir David Lyndsay's works; Mr. Gifford's edition of Massinger; and Mr. Octavius Gilchrist's, of Bishop Corbett's poems, exemplify the good effects of this *third means of cure.*

(70) The Royal,[316] London,[317] Surry,[318] and Russel[319] Institutions have been the means of concentrating, in divers parts of the metropolis, large libraries of *useful* books; which, it is to be hoped, will eventually suppress the establishment of what are called *Circulating Libraries* – vehicles, too often, of insuferable nonsense, and irremediable mischief!

(71) 'Unne bonne Bibliographie,' says Marchand, 'soit générale soit particulière, soit profane soit écclésiastique, soit nationale, provinciale, ou locale, soit simplement personnelle, en un mot de quelque autre genre que ce puisse être, n'est pas un ouvrage aussi facile que beaucoup de gens se le pourroient imaginer; mais, elles ne doivent néanmoins nullement prévenir contre celle-ci. Telle qu'elle est, elle ne laisse pas d'être bonne, utile, et digne d'être recherchée par les amateurs de l'Histoire Littéraire.' *Diction. Historique,* vol. i. p. 109.[320]

'Our nation,' says Mr. Bridgman, 'has been too inattentive to bibliographical criticisms and enquiries; for generally the English reader is obliged to resort to foreign writers to satisfy his mind as to the value

efficacious cures for this destructive malady. To place competent Librarians over the several departments of a large public Library, or to submit a library, on a more confined scale, to one diligent, enthuiastic, well informed, and well bred Bibliographer (72) or Librarian, [of which in this metropolis we have so many examples] is doing a vast deal towards directing the channels of literature to flow in their proper courses.

Thus briefly and guardedly have I thrown out a few suggestions, which may enable us to avoid, or mitigate the severity of, the disease called The Bibliomania.

---

of authors. It behoves us to consider that there is not a more useful or a more desirable branch of education than a *knowledge of books;* which, being correctly ascertained and judiciously exercised, will prove the touchstone of intrinsic merit, and have the effect of saving many spotless pages from prostitution.' *Legal Bibliography.* p. v. vi.

(72) Peignot, in his *Dictionnaire de Bibliologie,* vol. i. 50, has given a very pompous account of what ought to be the talents and duties of a Bibliographer. It would be difficult indeed to find such things united in one person! De Bure, in the eighth volume of his *Bibliographie Instructive,* has prefixed a 'Discourse upon the Science of Bibliography and the duties of a Bibliographer' which is worth consulting: but I know of nothing which better describes, in few words, such a character, than the following: 'In eo sit multijuga materiarum librorumque notitia, ut saltem potiores eligat et inquirat: fida et sedula apud exteras gentes procuratio, ut eos arcessat; summa patientia ut rarè venalis expectet: peculium semper præsens et paratum, ne, si quando occurrunt, emendi occasio intercidat; prudens denique auri argentique contemptus, ut pecuniis sponte careat quæ in bibliothecam formandam et nutriendam sunt insumendæ. Si fortè vir

Happy indeed shall I deem myself, if, in the description of its symptoms, and in the recommendation of the means of cure, I may have snatched any one from a premature grave, or lightened the load of years that are yet to come!

You, my dear Sir, who, in your observations upon society, as well as in your knowledge of ancient times, must have met with numerous instances of the miseries which 'flesh is heir to', may be disposed perhaps to confess that, of all species of afflictions, *the present one* under consideration has the least moral turpitude attached to it. True, it may be so: for, in the examples which have been adduced, there will be found neither Suicides, nor Gamesters, nor Profligates. No woman's heart has been broken from midnight debaucheries: no marriage vow has been violated: no child has been compelled to pine in poverty or neglect: no patrimony has been wasted, and no ancestor's fame tarnished! If men have erred under the influence of this disease, their aberrations have been marked with an excess arising from intellectual fervor, and not from a desire of baser gratifications.

literatus eo felicitatis pervenit ut talem thesaurum coaceraverit, nec solus illo invidiose fruatur, sed usum cum eruditis qui vigilias suas utilitati publicæ devoverunt, liberaliter communicet; &c.' *Bibliotheca Hulsiana.* vol. i. Præfat. p. 3. 4.[321]

If, therefore, in the wide survey which a philosopher may take of the 'Miseries of Human Life' (73) the prevalence of this disorder may appear to be less mischievous than that of others, and if some of the most amiable and learned of mortals seemed to have been both unwilling, as well as unable, to avoid its contagion, you will probably feel the less alarmed if symptoms of it should appear within the sequestered abode of Hodnet! (74) Recollecting that even in remoter situations its influence has been felt – and that neither the pure atmosphere of Hafod nor of Sledmere, (75) has completely subdued its power – you will not be disposed to exclaim with violence, at the intrusion of Bibliomaniacs ——

(73) In the ingenious and witty work so entitled, I do not recollect whether the disappointment arising from a *cropt* or a *dirty* copy has been classed among *'The Miseries of Human Life.'* [322]

(74) *Hodnet Hall,* Shropshire. The country residence of Mr. Heber.

(75) *Hafod,* in South Wales, the seat of Thos. Johnes, Esq. M. P. the translator of the Chronicles of Froissart and Monstrelet, and of the Travels of De Broquiere and Joinville. The conflagration of part of his mansion and library, two years ago, which excited such a general sympathy, would have damped any ardor of collection but that of Mr. Johnes – his Library has arisen, Phoenix-like, from the flames!

Sledmere, in Yorkshire, the seat of Sir Mark Masterman Sykes, Bart. M. P. The library of this amiable and tasteful Baronet reflects distinguished credit upon him. It is at once copious and choice. [323]

(76) Pope's *'Prologue to the Satires'.* v. 7–10.

What walls can guard me, or what shades can hide?
They pierce my thickets, through my grot they glide?
By land, by water, they renew the charge,
They stop the chariot, and they board the barge. (76)

Upon the whole, therefore, attending closely to the symptoms of this disorder as they have been described, and practising such means of cure as have been recommended, we may rationally hope that its virulence may abate, and the number of its victims annually diminish. But if the more discerning part of the community anticipate a different result, and the preceding observations appear to have presented but a narrow and partial view of the mischiefs of the BIBLIOMANIA, my only consolation is, that, to advance *something* upon the subject is better than to preserve a sullen and invincible silence. Let it be the task of more experienced bibliographers to correct and amplify the foregoing outline!

Believe me,

My dear Sir,

Very sincerely

Your's &c.

THOMAS FROGNALL DIBDIN.

Kensington, May 16, 1809.

POSTSCRIPT

On re-considering what has been written, it has struck me that a SYNOPSIS of this disease, after the manner of BURTON, as prefixed to his '*Anatomy of Melancholy,*' may be useful to some future pathologist. The reader is, accordingly, presented with the following one:

SYNOPSIS

APPENDIX

THE
BIBLIOMANIA,
AN
EPISTLE,
TO RICHARD HEBER, ESQ.

BY JOHN FERRIAR, M. D.

HIC, INQUIS, VETO QUISQUAM FAXIT OLETUM.
PINGE DUOS ANGUES.[324]

Pers. Sat. 1. *l.*108.

WHAT wild desires, what restless torments seize

The hapless man, who feels the book-disease,

If niggard Fortune cramp his gen'rous mind,

And Prudence quench the Spark by heaven assign'd!

With wistful glance his aching eyes behold

The Princeps-copy, clad in blue and gold,

Where the tall Book-case, with partition thin,

Displays, yet guards the tempting charms within:

So great Facardin view'd, as sages* tell,

Fair Crystalline immur'd in lucid cell.   10

Sages. Count Hamilton[325] in *Quatre Facardins,* and Mr. M. Lewis, in his
Tales of Romance.[326]

Not thus the few, by happier fortune grac'd,

And blest, like you, with talents, wealth and taste,

Who gather nobly, with judicious hand,

The Muse's treasures from each letter'd strand.

For you the Monk illum'd his pictur'd page,   15

For you the press defies the Spoils of age;

FAUSTUS for you infernal tortures bore,

For you ERASMUS* starv'd on Adria's shore.

The FOLIO-ALDUS loads your happy Shelves,

And dapper ELZEVIRS, like fairy elves,   }20

Shew their light forms amidst the well-gilt Twelves:

In slender type the GIOLITOS[327] shine,

And bold BODONI[328] stamps his Roman line.

For you the LOUVRE opes its regal doors,

And either DIDOT[329] lends his brilliant stores: 25

With faultless types, and costly sculptures bright,

IBARRA's Quixote[330] charms your ravish'd sight:

LABORDE[331] in splendid tablets shall explain

Thy beauties, glorious, tho' unhappy SPAIN!

O, hallowed name, the theme of future years,   30

Embalm'd in Patriot-blood, and England's tears,

---

* See the *Opulentia Sordida,* in his Colloquies, where he complains so
feelingly of the spare Venetian diet.

Be thine fresh honours from the tuneful tongue,

By Isis' streams which mourning Zion sung!

But devious oft' from ev'ry classic Muse,

The keen Collector meaner paths will choose: 35

And first the Margin's breadth his soul employs,

Pure, snowy, broad, the type of nobler joys.

In vain might HOMER roll the tide of song,

Or HORACE smile, or TULLY charm the throng;

If crost by Pallas' ire, the trenchant blade   40

Or too oblique, or near, the edge invade,

The Bibliomane exclaims, with haggard eye,

'No Margin!' turns in haste, and scorns to buy.

He turns where PYBUS[9] rears his Atlas-head,

Or MADOC's[11] mass conceals it veins of lead.   45

The glossy lines in polish'd order stand,

While the vast margin spreads on either hand,

Like Russian wastes, that edge the frozen deep,

Chill with pale glare, and lull to mortal sleep.*

* It may be said that Quintilian recommends margins; but it is still with
a view to their being occasionally occupied: Debet vacare etiam locus, in
quo notentur quæ scribentibus solent extra ordinem, id est ex aliis quam
qui sunt in manibus loci, occurrere. Irrumpunt enim optimi nonnumquam
Sensus, quos neque inserere oportet, neque differre tutum est.[332]

Inst. Lib. x. C. 3.

He was therefore no *Margin-man,* in the modern sense

Or English books, neglected and forgot,   50
Excite his wish in many a dusty lot:
Whatever trash *Midwinter* gave to day,
Or *Harper*'s rhiming sons, in paper gray,
At ev'ry auction, bent on fresh supplies,
He cons his Catalogue with anxious eyes: 55
Where'er the slim Italics mark the page,
Curious and rare his ardent mind engage.
Unlike the Swans, in Tuscan Song display'd,
He hovers eager o'er Oblivion's Shade,
To snatch obscurest names from endless night,   60
To give COKAIN[333] or FLETCHER* back to light.
In red morocco drest he loves to boast
The bloody murder, or the yelling ghost;
Or dismal ballads, sung to crouds of old,
Now cheaply bought for thrice their weight in gold.   65
Yet to th' unhonour'd dead be Satire just;
Some flow'rs† 'smell sweet, and blossom in their dust.'

* *Fletcher.* A translator of Martial.[334] A very bad poet, but *exceedingly scarce.*

> † Only the actions of the just
> Smell sweet, and blossom in the dust.
>   SHIRLEY.[335]
> Perhaps Shirley had in view this passage of Persius:
> Nunc non é tumulo, fortunataque favilla
> Nascentur Violæ?[336]   Sat. i. *l.* 37

'Tis thus ev'n SHIRLEY boasts a golden line,
And LOVELACE[337] strikes, by fits, a note divine.
Th' unequal gleams like midnight-lightnings play,   70
And deepen'd gloom succeeds, in place of day.

But human bliss still meets some envious storm;
He droops to view his PAYNTER's[338] mangled form:
Presumptuous grief, while pensive Taste repines
O'er the frail relics of her Attic Shrines!
O for that power, for which magicians vye,
To look through earth, and secret hoards descry!
I'd spurn such gems as Marinel* beheld,
And all the wealth Aladdin's cavern held,
Might I divine in what mysterious gloom   80
The rolls of sacred bards have found their tomb:
Beneath what mould'ring tower, or waste champain,
Is hid MENANDER,[339] sweetest of the train;
Where rests ANTIMACHUS'[340] forgotten lyre,
Where gentle SAPPHO's[341] still seductive fire;   85
Or he,† whom chief the laughing Muses own,
Yet skill'd with softest accents to bemoan
Sweet Philomel,‡ in strains so like her own.

    * Faërie Queen.   † Aristophanes.
    ‡ See his exquisite hymn to the Nightingale, in his Ορνιθες.[342]

The menial train has prov'd the Scourge of wit,

Ev'n OMAR[343] burnt less Science than the spit.   90

Earthquakes and wars remit their deadly rage,

But ev'ry feast demands some fated page.

Ye towers of Julius,* ye alone remain

Of all the piles that saw our nation's stain.

When HARRY's sway opprest the groaning realm,   95

And Lust and Rapine seiz'd the wav'ring helm.

Then ruffian-hands defaced the sacred fanes,

Their saintly statues, and their storied panes;

Then from the chest, with ancient art embost,

The Penman's pious scrolls were rudely tost;   100

Then richest manuscripts, profusely spread,

The brawnt Churl's devouring Oven fed:

And thence Collectors date the heav'nly ire,

That wrapt Augusta's domes in sheets of fire.†

Taste, tho' misled, may yet some purpose gain,   105

But fashion guides a ‡book-compelling train.

Once, far apart from Learning's moping crew,

The travell'd beau display'd his red-heel'd shoe,

* Gray.

† The fire of London.

‡ Cloud-compelling Jove. ————Pope's Iliad.

Till ORFORD[34] rose, and told of rhiming Peers,

Repeating *noble* words to polish'd ears;*   110

Taught the gay croud to prize a flutt'ring name,

In trifling toil'd, nor 'blush'd to find it fame.'[344]

The letter'd fop now takes a larger scope,

With classic furniture, design'd by HOPE,[13]

(HOPE, whom Upholst'rers eye with mute despair,   115

The doughty pedant of an elbow-chair;)

Now warm'd by ORFORD, and by GRANGER[48] school'd,

In Paper-books, superbly gilt and tool'd,

He pastes, from injur'd volumes snipt away,

His *English Heads,* in chronicled array.   120

Torn from their destin'd page, (unworthy meed

Of knightly counsel, and heroic deed)

Not FAITHORNE's[345] stroke, nor FIELD's own types[346] can save

† The gallant VERES, and one-eyed OGLE brave.

Indignant readers seek the image fled,   125

And curse the busy fool, who *wants a head.*

---

*———— gaudent prænomine molles
      Ariculæ.
                          JUVENAL.[347]

† The gallant Veres, and one-eyed Ogle. Three fine heads, for the sake of
which, the beautiful and interesting Commentaries of Sir Francis Vere
have been mutilated by Collectors of English portraits.[348]

Proudly he shews, with many a smile elate,

The scrambling subjects of the *private plate;*

While Time their actions and their names bereaves,

They grin forever in the guarded leaves.[349]   130

Like Poets, born, in vain Collectors strive

To cross their Fate, and learn the art to thrive.

Like Cacus,[350] bent to tame their struggling will,

The tyrant-passion drags them backward still:

Ev'n I, debarr'd of ease, and studious hours,   135

Confess, mid' anxious toil, its lurking pow'rs.

How pure the joy, when first my hands unfold

The small, rare volume, black with tarnish'd gold!

The Eye skims restless, like the roving bee,

O'er flowers of wit, or song, or repartee,   140

While sweet as Springs, new-bubbling from the stone,

Glides through the breast some pleasing theme unknown.

Now dipt in *Rossi's terse and classic style,

His harmless tales awake a transient smile.

Now BOUCHET's motley stores my thoughts arrest,   145

With wond'rous reading, and with learned jest.

* Generally known by the name of Janus Nicius Erythræus. The allusion
is to his Pinacotheca.[351]

Bouchet,* whose tomes a grateful line demand,
The valued gift of Stanley's lib'ral hand.
Now sadly pleased, through faded Rome I stray,
And mix regrets with gentle Du Bellay;†   150
Or turn, with keen delight, the curious page,
Where hardy ‡Pasquin braves the Pontift's rage.

But D———n's strains should tell the sad reverse,
When Business calls, invet'rate foe to verse!
Tell how 'the Demon claps his iron hands,'   155
'Waves his lank locks, and scours along the lands.'[352]
Though wintry blasts, or summer's fire I go,
To scenes of danger, and to sights of woe.
Ev'n when to Margate ev'ry Cockney roves,[353]
And brainsick poets long for shelt'ring groves,   160
Whose lofty shades exclude the noontide glow,
While Zephyrs breathe, and waters trill below,§

---

* Les Serées de Guillaume Bouchet,[354] a book of uncommon rarity. I posses a handsome copy by the kindness of Colonel Stanley.[355]

† *Les Regrets,* by Joachim du Bellay, contain a most amusing and instructive Account of Rome, in the 16th Century.[356]

‡ Pasquillorum Tomi duo.[357]

§ Errare per lucos, amœnæ,
Quos et aquæ subeunt et auræ.
                                        Horat.[358]

Me rigid Fate averts, by tasks like these,

From heav'nly musings, and from letter'd ease.

Such wholesome checks the better Genius sends,   165

From dire rehearsals to protect our friends:

Else when the social rites our joys renew,

The stuff'd Portfolio would alarm your view,

Whence volleying rhimes your patience would o'ercome,

And, spite of kindness, drive you early home.   170

So when the traveller's hasty footsteps glide

Near smoking lava, on Vesuvio's side,

Hoarse-mutt'ring thunders from the depths proceed,

And spouting fires incite his eager speed.

Appall'd he flies, while rattling show'rs invade,   175

Invoking ev'ry Saint for instant aid:

Breathless, amaz'd, he seeks the distant shore,

And vows to tempt the dang'rous gulph no more.

FINIS.

MANCHESTER,
APRIL, 1809.

Notes to the Text

1. In 1775, Captain Dibdin was hired to carry troops and freight for the East India Company from Tillicherry to Bombay. Every aspect of the arrangement was unsatisfactory; he was required to carry twice the specified number of troops without sufficient water, and when he landed the Governor and Council refused to pay the bill. To add to his troubles, his ship foundered soon after this mission.

Despite his earlier problems with the 'Honourable' East India Company, Captain Dibdin was prevailed upon to carry urgent correspondence to England via Cairo for George Stratton, Governer of Fort St George, Madras, and the Nabob of Arcot. It seems to have been T. F. Dibdin's understanding (and quite possibly his father's) that this commission was on behalf of the Governor of Madras, Lord Pigot, for Dibdin describes Stratton as Pigot's 'right-hand counsellor' [Dibdin 1836, p. 18]. In fact, however, Stratton and the Nabob were plotting Pigot's downfall [Feiling 1954, p. 168] [Christie 1958, p. 204]. Captain Dibdin was assured by Stratton and the Nabob that he would be paid for this service, although the latter refused to sign a contract as it was 'beneath the dignity of a prince' to do so [Dibdin 1836, p. 19].

However, Captain Dibdin only got as far as Juddah before he was struck by lightning in the thigh and fell seriously ill. He despatched his second officer, George Romaine, who fulfilled the contract by sailing to Suez and travelling

overland to Cairo where he delivered the packet to a Mr
George Baldwin. Despite their assurances, neither the Nabob nor Stratton paid the outstanding amount of 7,000 star
pagodas and Captain Dibdin was forced to sell his ship to
pay Romaine.

2. An area rich in literary associations. Anthony Trollope's
sister Cecilia was married to John Tilley there by Dibdin
on 11 February 1839 [Hall 1991, p. 61]. Mr Dombey lived in
'the shady side of a tall, dark, dreadfully genteel street in
the region between Portland-place and Bryanstone-square'
[Dickens 1848, p. 16] and 'the breaking of the engagement
with the Marquis of Farintosh was known in Bryanstone
Square' [Thackeray n.d., p. 432].

3. There have been many attacks on Dibdin's accuracy,
mostly posthumous and many, if not unfounded, then at
least unsubstantiated. 'As a bibliographer,' wrote one com-
mentator, 'his inaccuracies and absurdities have long been a
by-word' [O'Dwyer 1967, p. 41]. Likewise, William Blades
remarked that 'the Doctor's bibliography is very incorrect'
[Blades 2004, p. 13].

It is certainly true that Dibdin made mistakes, especially
in his later works. In *Reminiscences*, Richard Gough is called
John [Dibdin 1836, p. 973] and Isaac D'Israeli is also John
[ibid., index p. 20].

4. Even this is a bit harsh, although it is true that he was the
founder of the Roxburghe Club which, in its early days, had
a rather dilettantish reputation.

5. There are, it is true, some useful additions, such as a detailed account of the sale of Brand's library.

6. Imagine, if you will, how many entries that august institution must have under the letter L, and the letter D.

7. John Ferriar (1761–1815), physician and active member of the Manchester Literary and Philosophical Society. As well as his essay on Sterne and his *Bibliomania* (see Appendix), he wrote an essay on Massinger which was incorporated into Gifford's edition of the dramatist's works. His 'Illustrations of Sterne' point to Sterne's borrowings from *Anatomy of melancholy* and elsewhere, but it was clear that Sterne was intentionally plagiarising while writing about plagiarism. Ferriar recognised that, as Christopher Ricks puts it, 'there could hardly be a more witty or more telling illustration of the point which Sterne was so concerned to make' [Sterne 1967, p. 25]. See the p. xxvi for more on Dr Ferriar.

8. Francis Quarles (1592–1644), poet. Dibdin published an edition of Quarles's *Judgement and mercy for afflicted souls* under the pseudonym Reginalde Wolfe in 1807.

9. Charles Small Pybus (1766–1810), Member of Parliament for Dover. In 1800 he published *The sovereign. Addressed to His Imperial Majesty Paul Emperour of all the Russias* [Pybus 1800]. A satire on the poem by 'Caroline Petty Pasty' was published in the same year [Pasty 1800].

10. Thomas Bensley (1760–1835) was one of the finest printers of the age. Through a partnership with Gottlob Koenig (1774–1833), he was also responsible for persuading John Walter II to introduce steam presses at *The Times* in 1814 [Dyas 2001].

11. Robert Southey's *Madoc* was published in 1805.

12. Southey encouraged White (1785–1806) during his brief life and published *The remains of Henry Kirke White* in 1807. Byron wrote rather unctuously 'His poems abound in such beauties as must impress the reader with the liveliest regret that so short a period was allotted to talents, which would have dignified even the sacred functions he was destined to assume' [Byron 1809, p.64].

13. Thomas Hope (1769?–1831), wealthy art collector. He purchased a house in Duchess Street, Cavendish Square, London, in about 1796 which he had furnished to his own designs. These were illustrated in his *Household furniture and interior decoration,* published in 1807. His novel *Anastasius, or memoirs of a Greek* (1819) was widely believed to be Byron's work when it first appeared. In a letter of 22 July 1820, Byron told John Murray that he thought the novel 'good but no more written by a Greek – than by a Hebrew' [Byron 1997, p. 138]. He later told Lady Blessington 'he would have given his two most approved poems to have been the author of *Anastasius*' [ibid., f.n.].

14. Johann Friedrich Gronov (1611–71), German classical scholar.

15. Bernard de Montfaucon (1655–1741), French academic. His *Palæographia Græca* (1708) and *Bibliotheca bibliothecarum manuscriptorum nova* (1739) were outstanding contributions to the study of Greek literature.

16. Vitruvius, the Roman author of *De architectura;* the great English architect Inigo Jones (1573–1652); the Scottish architect James Gibbs (1682–1754); and the English architect Sir William Chambers (1723–96).

17. Edward Jenner (1749–1823), inventor of smallpox vaccination. 'Illustrious name, revered by nations, and which was of great value to our city' (Lucan, *Pharsalia*, xi, 203–4). This same quotation was used by Edmund Burke to refer to Lord Chatham in his speech on American taxation, 19 April 1774.

Jenner, his friend John Ring and the Rev. Thomas Pruen persuaded Dibdin to write a poem entitled 'Vaccinia' to promote smallpox vaccination [Dibdin 1836, p. 200].

18. Although Sir Richard Burton's famous English translation did not appear until 1885, the tales had been available in translations of Antoine Galland's edition since 1705.

19. Robert Burton (1577–1640) published *Anatomy of melancholy* in 1621. This work influenced Milton's *L'allegro* and *Il penseroso* which, in turn, provided the basis for Charles Jennes's libretto for Handel's *L'allegro, il penseroso ed il moderato*. If Burton himself borrowed, he was in good company. Shakespeare's *Romeo and Juliet* draws upon Arthur Brooke's *The tragicall historye of Romeus and Iuliet*, which he translated from Pierre Boiastuau's translation of a story by Matteo Bandello. That, in turn, was a reworking of Luigi da Porto's retelling of a story by Masuccio Salernitano.

20. Dame Juliana Barnes or Berners (b. 1388?), said to have been prioress of Sopwell Nunnery near St Albans. The treatise on hunting and hawking was credited to her by the printer known as the St Albans Schoolmaster in *The Boke of Saint Albans* (1486) and in Wynkyn de Worde's edition of 1496. Blades tells how a copy of the *Boke of Saint Albans* was bought by a pedlar in 1844 (with a number of other books) for 9*d* [Blades 2004, p.23].

21. George John Spencer (1758–1834), second Earl Spencer, was First Lord of the Admiralty 1794–1801 and Home Secretary 1806–7. He was an avid and discerning book-collector. Dibdin, who became a close friend, compiled *Bibliotheca Spenceriana*, a catalogue of his holdings of fifteenth-century printed books and rare first editions [Spencer 1814–15].

Dibdin tells us that he spent three years almost completely working at Spencer House, plus another year cataloguing the books at Althorp and the library of the Duke di Cassano which Spencer bought in 1820 [Dibdin 1836, pp. 496, 549]. The whole Spencer Collection is now in the John Rylands Library, Manchester.

22. William Mason (1725–97) was a friend of Thomas Gray, whose *Life and letters* he published in 1775, and Horace Walpole. Mason destroyed much of the correspondence from Gray to Richard West but not his love poems to him. Wilmarth Lewis says that Mason was

> the least agreeable of Walpole's major correspondents. When it became clear that he would never be a bishop and that he could amass in church preferments only the modern equivalent of about £12,000 a year, he grew even more rancorous and bitter. It was hateful to him to have to 'go morning and afternoon to see the ancient maiden gentlewomen and decayed tradesmen... mumble their matins and their vespers' in York Minster'
> [Lewis 1961, p. 177].

23. Wynkyn de Worde (d. 1535), Caxton's assistant, thought to have been born in Wörth in Lorraine. It is likely that he met Caxton in Cologne and moved to England with him in 1476. His presence in England by 1480 is attested by a deed among the muniments of Westminster Abbey. He inherited Caxton's business in 1491 and continued to produce

books at Caxton's house in Weſtminſter until 1500 or 1501 when he moved to Shoe Lane, Fleet Street [Moran 2003, pp. 8–21].

Although he reprinted a number of Caxton's titles, such as the *Morte darthur* (to which he added illuſtrations), *The golden legend* and *The Canterbury tales,* he brought out many new titles including grammars and music books. One of his moſt intereſting publications was *Oratio de laudibus et vtilitate trium linguarum,* the text of a leĉture delivered at Cambridge by Robert Wakefield, the Arabic and Hebrew scholar who was appointed the firſt Regius Professor of Hebrew in 1540 [Toomer 1996, p.45] and had previously been Professor of Hebrew at Tübingen [Goldschmidt 1955, p.55]. De Worde's edition (variously dated to 1524 and 1528) was the firſt book in England to use italic type (although according to Talbot Baines Reed [Reed 1955, p. 46], the firſt use was in de Worde's edition of Lucian's *Complures dialogi* in 1528). The main text is in roman and there is also some Greek type. There is some Hebrew (the firſt in an English printed book) but it is in the form of crude woodcuts. The author complained that the third part of the book could not be printed because the printer had no Hebrew type [Plomer 1925, p. 90].

One of de Worde's texts, William Lily's Latin grammar, was so popular that it was ſtill in use at Eton in 1860 [Steinberg 1996, p. 63]. His colophon incorporated a sun with a face, not unlike depiĉtions of Sul Minerva, and this emblem is now used by the Wynkyn de Worde Society.

24. Strangely, Dibdin proceeds to italicise many words of Old English origin: hart, hare, horse, wolf, mo, buck and doe.

25. Sir Samuel Egerton Brydges (1762-1837), published *Censura literaria,* 1805–9. He moved to Lee Priory near

Canterbury in 1810 where the printers John Johnson and John Warwick founded a private press in 1813. Brydges told Dibdin that he merely provided copy and that printers ran the business at their own risk [Oswald 1928, p. 270].

26. Joseph Haslewood (1769–1833), collector and editor of materials relating to the English stage from the Tudor period onwards. He published *The secret history of the green rooms* in 1790. The British Library holds a number of dramatic tracts, poems, handbills, ballads, etc., collected by him. Haslewood is referred to as BERNARDO in later editions of *Bibliomania*.

27. Thomas Thornton (1757–1823) whose *A sporting tour through the Northern parts of England, and great part of the highlands of Scotland* was published in 1804. After purchasing an estate in France, he styled himself Prince de Chambord and Marquis de Pont.

28. Tipu (also Tippoo, Tipoo) Sultan (1749–1799), ruler of Mysore, made peace with the British in 1784 but provoked a war by his invasion of Travancore, a state under British protection. He was defeated by Cornwallis in 1792 and forced to cede territory. He entered into an alliance with the French in 1798 which prompted the British, in alliance with the Nizam of Hyderabad, to attack him, and he was killed at the Siege of Seringapatam in 1799. His remarkable automaton of a tiger mauling a British soldier to gruesome sound effects is now in the Victoria & Albert Museum.

A catalogue of his library was compiled by Charles Stewart, Professor of Oriental Languages at the East India Company's Haileybury College [Stewart 1809].

29. Frederick the Great was not just a collector of snuff boxes but also a keen snuff-taker. Contemporary accounts invariably comment on how much snuff had accumulated on his waistcoats. Six of his elaborate snuff boxes are in the Gilbert Collection at Somerset House in London.

30. Possibly Charles Chauncey (1706–77), physician and collector.

31. Francis Grose (1731?–91) published *Antiquities of England and Wales* between 1773 and 1787. He was very interested in both dialect and slang, publishing *A classical dictionary of the vulgar tongue* in 1785 and *A provincial glossary* [Grose 1787]. *The Olio* [Grose 1792] which is attributed to him was published posthumously and may not be his work. Samuel Rawle (1771–1860) was a distinguished engraver of topographical prints.

32. Amongst White's treasures was a music manuscript dating from about 1505 called the 'Fairfax book'. It was partly transcribed by Dr Burney, and John Stafford Smith (whose music for 'Anacreon in Heaven' provided the tune for the 'Star spangled banner') included material from it in *A collection of English songs* [Smith 1779]. The book is now in the British Library (Add. MS 5465).

33. Charles Burney (1726–1814), father of the novelist Fanny Burney (Madame d'Arblay), published his *History of music* in five volumes between 1776 and 1798.

34. Horace Walpole (1717–97), fourth Earl of Orford, founded the Strawberry Hill Press (also known as the Officina Arbuteana, or the Elzevierianum) in 1757. He published

his *Anecdotes of painting in England* in 1762 and his famous gothic novel *The castle of Otranto* in 1764.

35. Joseph Warton (1722–1800), minor poet and headmaster of Winchester College who was forced into retirement by the protests of his pupils. It is said that when he came to a difficult passage in Greek he would allow the boy construing to get through it as best he could, and hide his own ignorance by raising his voice and complaining of noises [Clarke 1959, p. 48].

36. William Lisle Bowles (1762–1850) published an edition of Pope's works in 1806. His own writing included *Fourteen sonnets* [Bowles 1789].

37. Thomas Herbert (1656–1733), eighth Earl of Pembroke, a Whig politician and a collector of books and antiques. 'We may consider the Pembroke Library as the oldest now existing of those of Private Collectors; and especially of collectors of rank' [Dibdin 1817, iii, p. 287]. Locke dedicated his *Essay concerning human understanding* to him.

38. Michael Maittaire (1668–1747), French refugee, was a classical scholar, schoolmaster at Westminster School, librarian and typographer.

39. Samuel Palmer (d. 1732), printer, and author of *The general history of printing* [Palmer 1732].

40. Nicolas Jenson (1420–80), French printer working in Venice from about 1469. He was renowned for the high quality of his roman types. Pembroke's collection contained quite a few Jensons, including the first book from

the press, Cicero's *Epistolæ ad Atticum*, the very handsome 1470 edition of Eusebius's *De evangelica præparatione* and a copy of the 1472 Macrobius on vellum [Dibdin 1817, iii, pp. 288–91].

41. William Caxton (1421?–91?). Despite his lack of typographical flair, his position as first English printer made (and makes) him a must for serious collectors of 𝕭𝕝𝕒𝕔𝕜𝕝𝕖𝕥𝕥𝕖𝕣. Pembroke's library included two different Caxton editions of de Cessolis's *Game and playe of the chesse*, a copy of the *Liber festivalis*, Cicero's *De senectute*, a copy of the first edition (1480) of *Cronicles of Englond* and 'Socrates Sayings, Caxton, 1477, fol.' which is presumably the *Dictes or sayengis of the philosophres* [Dibdin 1817, iii, pp. 288–91].

42. The lines are from Alexander Pope's 'Epistle iv to Richard Boyle, Earl of Burlington'.

43. Thomas Hearne (1678–1735), antiquary who republished many of the old English chronicles. He was appointed Architypographus at the University Press, Oxford, in 1714/5. This grand title disguised a rather menial role, the real running of the Press being handed to Stephen Richardson. Hearne resigned a few months later [Carter 1975, pp. 145–6].

44. Richard Mead (1673–1754), English physician and book-collector. Queen Anne and Alexander Pope were among his patients.

45. Sir Hans Sloane (1660–1753), English physician, naturalist and President of the Royal Society whose library (some 30,000 printed volumes, plus many manuscripts), herbarium and other collections formed the basis of the British

Museum. He was one of those who employed the services of John Bagford as book-collector [Reed 1952, p. 179].

46. Few would argue with Steinberg's description of Aldus Manutius (Teobaldo Manucci/Aldo Manuzio 1450–1515) as 'the greatest printer of sixteenth-century Venice' [Steinberg 1996, p. 34]. Indeed, his fine press-work and elegant setting mark him out as one of the finest printers of any era. At the same time, his books had mass-market appeal, as he and his successors produced many reasonably-priced small octavos to high editorial standards. His introduction of the first italic type, cut by Francesco Griffo, while allowing more economical production (thanks to the narrower characters), further enhanced the beauty of his books.

Erasmus approached Aldus in 1507 to print his *Adagia* and subsequently spent eight months in Venice, much of it at the Aldine printing house [Huizinga 1952, pp. 63–4].

47. Pope's 'Epistle iv to Richard Boyle' contains this reference to l'Abbé du Süeil, an eighteenth-century Paris bookbinder. Sometimes spelt Seuil.

48. Rev. James Granger (1723–1776) published in 1769 *A biographical history of England, from Egbert the Great to the Revolution* [Granger 1769], with blank pages for the reception of engraved portraits. This embellishment is known as Grangerising and has been responsible for the wholesale destruction of many handsome volumes.

49. Mark (not William) Noble (1754–1827) published *A history of the College of Arms* [Noble 1804] and *A biographical history of England, from the Revolution to the end of George I's reign; being a continuation of the Rev. J. Granger's work* [Noble 1806].

50. Gilbert Burnet (1643–1715), Bishop of Salisbury, published volume 1 of *The history of my own times* in 1724 and volume 2 in 1734. A new edition was published in 1809.

51. Thomas Hearne's *Ductor historicus* was partly responsible for introducing Gibbon to the Greek and Roman historians, as he readily acknowledged [Gibbon 1814, i, p. 41] but he describe Hearne as:

> … poor in fortune, and indeed poor in understanding. His minute and obscure diligence, his voracious and undistinguishing appetite and the coarse vulgarity of his taste and style, have exposed him to the ridicule of idle wits. Yet it cannot be denied that Thomas Hearne has gathered many gleanings of the harvest; but if his own prefaces are filled with crude and extraneous matter, his editions will be always recommended by their accuracy and use. [Gibbon 1814, iii, p.567]

52. John Leland or Leyland (1506?–52), successively chaplain and librarian to Henry VIII. He travelled throughout England between 1535 and 1543 in his capacity as the King's antiquarian but he descended into madness in 1550 and his planned book on the 'History and antiquities of this nation' was not published in his lifetime. Much of the material he collected was later published by Hearne.

53. Peter Langtoft (d. 1307?) wrote a French verse chronicle of England. It was translated into English by Robert Mannyng of Brunne.

54. Edward Rowe Mores (1730–78) published *A dissertation upon English typographical founders and founderies* [Mores 1778]. It was probably printed by Mores himself at his private press at Low Leyton.

55. Alfred of Beverley, a sacristan at Beverley, Yorkshire, wrote a chronicle in about 1143. It is of little historical value, being a compilation of Geoffrey of Monmouth and Simeon of Durham.

56. John Hudson (1662–1719), English classicist. Dibdin praises his 1696 edition of Thucydides [Dibdin 1808, ii, 293]. He was appointed to head the Bodleian Library in 1701. Although Hearne described him as 'one that will do any thing for Money,' he gave nearly six hundred books from his own collection to the Bodleian and encouraged others to do likewise [Sutherland & Mitchell 1986, pp. 414, 728].

57. Antoine-Augustin Renouard (1765–1853) published this history of the Aldine Press [Renouard 1803] in 1803 not 1804. Dibdin calls it a 'very useful and popular work' [Dibdin 1817, ii, p. 203]. Many years later, Renouard published a history of the printing establishment of the Estienne family [Renouard 1838].

58. William Roscoe (1753–1831) was a lawyer, banker, botanist, book-collector and author. Among his many works were *The life of Lorenzo de' Medici* [Roscoe 1795], *The butterfly's ball* [Roscoe 1807], *The life and pontificate of Leo the Tenth* [Roscoe 1805], *Observations on penal jurisprudence, and the reformation of criminals* [Roscoe 1819] and *A brief statement of the causes which have led to the abandonment of the celebrated system of penitentiary discipline, in some of the United States* [Roscoe 1827].

He purchased the Johann Reinhold Forster Herbarium in 1799 for the Liverpool Botanic Garden which opened in 1802 [Roscoe 1802]. He was President of the Liverpool Society for the Abolition of Slavery, an address to which was published [Roscoe & Hodgson 1823]. Somehow, he also found time to edit a new edition of Pope's works [Pope 1824].

59. Antoine Michel Padeloup (1685–1758), the most distinguished member of a family of French bookbinders, was binder to the French court from 1733 to 1744. He is particularly associated with the development of *dentelle* borders [Glaister 1960, p. 293].

60. Nicolas Denis Derome (1731–88), a French binder renowned for his *dentelle* borders [Glaister 1960, p. 102].

> There's Eve, – not our first mother fair, –
> But Clovis Eve, a binder true;
> Thither does Bauzonnet repair,
> Derome, Le Gascon, Padeloup!
> But never come the cropping crew
> That dock a volume's honest size,
> Nor they that 'letter' backs askew,
> Within that Book-man's Paradise! [Lang 1890, p. 75].

Dibdin complained that he was 'a GREAT CROPPER,' and added that 'a greater heresy can scarcely be conceived' [Dibdin 1817, ii, p.497].

61. John Baumgarten (1771?–82), German bookbinder working in Duchy Lane, Strand, London.

62. Roger Payne (1739–97) bookbinder first employed by the bookseller Thomas Osborne, and then for Thomas Payne (no relation). 'His appearance bespoke either squalid wretchedness or a foolish and fierce indifference to the received opinion of others' [Dibdin 1817, ii, p. 512].

His intemperate habits, the squalor in which he lived, and the quaint diffuseness of his bills have perhaps falsely enhanced his reputation; but credit is undoubtedly due to him for the introduction of new designs which had a marked influence on binding in France as well as in England. His favourite leathers were brown russia, dark blue or red straight-grain, and olive smooth morocco, while he had a marked and often unhappy partiality for green headbands and purple endpapers. Among his best patrons were Lord Spencer, Sir Richard Colt Hoare, and the Rev. C. M. Cracherode.   [Howe 1950, p. 110]

Dibdin says that his great merit 'lay in his *taſte* – in his choice of ornaments; and especially in the working of them,' but adds that:

his favourite colour was *olive*, which he called *Venetian*... He was fond of what he called 'purple paper,' the colour of which was as violent as its texture was coarse. It was liable also to change, and become spotty; and as a harmonising colour with olive, it was odiously discordant.   [Dibdin 1817, ii, p. 516]

63. Chriſtian Samuel Kalthoeber (fl. 1782–1815), German bookbinder and executor of Baumgarten whose premises he took over [Howe 1950]. 'Latterly, Mr. Kalthoeber hath worked in the premises of Mr. Otridge the bookseller, and his flat-backed oſtavos quickly shew the quarter whence they derive their embellishments' [Dibdin 1817, ii, p. 520].

64. Charles Hering (fl. 1799–1812), bookbinder in St Martin's Street, Leiceſter Square. His brother, John, was also a bookbider [Howe 1950, p. 46]. Dibdin describes Charles as

... a worthy, industrious and extremely skilful binder... His workmanship or style of binding was rather sound and substantial, than elegant and classical: but for a good thumping folio, or quarto...

you could not do better than employ the said Charles Hering.
[Dibdin 1817, ii, p. 525]

65. L. Staggemeier:

Of Mr. Staggemeier's bibliopegistic skill I wish to speak with all
possible respect and good nature. This binder hath a quick and
clever way of putting octavos into a comely garb, and his choice of
ornaments is by no means disparaging to his taste. The Royal Institution Library possesses the 'ne plus ultra' of Mr. Staggemeier's
skill. It is the *Didot Horace* of 1799; in blue morocco and embel-
lished with ornaments cut after antique models.
[Dibdin 1817, ii, p. 520]

Dibdin goes on to indicate that the book described above
was a gift from Thomas Hope and that the binding was
made to his specifications.

66. John Mackinlay was a bookbinder in Bow Street between 1774 and 1808. Dibdin says that 'the backs of Mr.
Mackinlay's smaller volumes are too frequently heavy and
tasteless' [Dibdin 1817, ii, p. 519].

67. Stephen Gosson (1554–1624), actor and playwright turned
puritan critic of plays and poetry. 'We must not contrast his
plays as "art" with his pamphlet as "theology," ' says C. S.
Lewis; 'in the *School* he is still the artist, still indeed the
commercial artist, catering for a well established taste in
rhetoric' [Lewis 1954, p. 395]. Lewis argues that Gosson was
not a puritan at all.

68. By Admiral Sir John Mennes (1599–1671) who encouraged Pepys to appreciate Chaucer's *Troilus and Criseyde* and
Canterbury Tales [Tomalin 2003, p. 48].

69. It is so rare that at the time of writing (early 2004) a copy is being offered for sale by the bookseller John W. Doull of Halifax, Nova Scotia, for the equivalent of £857.14.

70. John Bagford (1650–1716). William Blades wrote of him that 'it is a serious matter when Nature produces such a wicked old biblioclaſt as John Bagford, one of the founders of the Society of Antiquaries, who, in the beginning of the laſt century, went about the country, from library to library, tearing away title pages from rare books of all sizes' [Blades 2004, p. 48]. One of Bagford's less harmful aĉtivities was the colleĉtion of early trade cards.

71. Robert Harley (1661–1724), firſt Earl of Oxford, managed to combine book-colleĉting on a monumental scale with a dazzling political career. His son Edward, the second Earl, added subſtantially to his library. It was later sold to the nation and now forms the Harleian Colleĉtion of the British Library.

72. John Moore (1646–1714) was a noted book-colleĉtor. George I bought his colleĉtion in 1715 and presented it to the University of Cambridge. Consiſting of an eſtimated 28,965 books and 1,790 manuscripts, it almoſt trebled the size of the University library.

73. Humphrey/Humfrey Wanley (1672–1726), Anglo-Saxon scholar, librarian and palæographer. Samuel Pepys gave Wanley, then a draper's apprentice, a letter of introduĉtion to Thomas Smith, the Cottonian Librarian [Workman 1992, p. 17].
    Wanley was Secretary to the Society for Promoting Chriſtian Knowledge before becoming Librarian to Rob-

ert Harley, fir&t Earl of Oxford. He designed a new Anglo-Saxon fount for an Old English grammar but complained:

> I did what was required in the most exact and able manner that I could in all respects. But it signified little; for when the alphabet came into the hands of the workman (who was but a blunderer), he could not imitate the fine and regular stroke of the pen; so that the letters are not only clumsy, but unlike those that I drew. This appears by Mrs. Elstob's *Saxon Grammar*.   [Reed 1952, p. 148]

He published his *Catalogus librorum septentrionalium* in 1705 [Wanley 1705].

74.

> An imposing tome, it sets on a single page the Hebrew text of the Old Testament, the Septuagint (the ancient Greek translation of the Hebrew), the Vulgate, a new Latin translation, and, at the bottom, Aramaic commentaries on the Hebrew. Its blocks of text, orderly and varied, spread across the page like quilting squares' [Cahill 1997].

The Complutensian Polyglot was originally planned by Cardinal Ximenes de Cisneros (1437–1517) who did not live to see it completed, although one element of it, the fir&t printed Greek New Te&tament, was produced in 1514 [Metzger 1992, p. 96]. However, it was not immediately available for sale and the fir&t Greek New Te&tament to appear on the market was that of Desiderius Erasmus [Metzger 1992, p. 98]. The printer, appointed to the new University of Alcalá (Latin name Complutum) by Cardinal Ximenes, was Arnão Guillén de Brocar. The finished Bible, in Hebrew, Chaldee, Greek and Latin, was issued in 1522 [Steinberg 1996, pp. 45–6].

75. *The hi&torical antiquities of Hertfordshire* [Chauncy 1700] was fir&t published in 1700 and is &till frequently quoted in

local histories. Sir Henry Chauncy (1632–1719) was reluctantly involved in one of the last English witch trials, that of Jane Wenham [Anon 1712]. A number of pamphlets were published claiming scriptural authority for and against the existence of witches. This debate must have proved a boon to the English book trade. Indeed, a J. Baker printed both *The belief of witchcraft vindicated* [G. R. & A. M. 1712] and *The impossibility of witchcraft* [Anon 1712a].

76. Joseph Ames (1689–1759) published his *Typographical antiquities* in 1749. He was considered eccentric for dropping the long s (ſ) which did not generally start to disappear until Bell's Shakespeare of 1785 [Reed 1952, p. 47]. Dibdin published a much-enlarged edition [Ames 1810–19].

77. Benjamin Moseley (1742–1819) wrote many letters to the *Morning herald* and a tract on rabies. A former Surgeon General in Jamaica, he published *A treatise on tropical diseases* in 1787. He was a rather old-fashioned doctor and opposed smallpox vaccination.

78. Richard de Bury (1281–1345), Bishop of Durham.

> Although from our youth upwards we had always delighted in holding social commune with learned men and lovers of books, yet when we prospered in the world and made acquaintance with the King's majesty and were received into his household, we obtained ampler facilities for visiting everywhere as we would, and of hunting as it were certain most choice preserves, libraries private as well as public, and of the regular as well as of the secular clergy...Besides all the opportunities mentioned above, we secured the acquaintance of stationers and booksellers, not only within our own country, but of those spread over the realms of France, Germany, and Italy, money flying forth in abundance to

anticipate their demands; nor were they hindered by any distance or by the fury of the seas, or by the lack of means for their expenses, from sending or bringing to us the books that we required. [Richard de Bury 1996, chap. 8]

79. Johannes Scotus Erigena, a ninth-century Irish philosopher. He moved to France in about 845 to take over the Palatine Academy at the request of Charles the Bald. His *De divisione naturæ* was placed on the *Index librorum prohibitorum* in 1681.

80. Nennius wrote *Historia Brittonum* in the late eighth century. It became one of the sources of Arthurian romance.

81. Sir William Dugdale (1605–86), Garter King-of-Arms, was author of several important historical works including *Monasticon Anglicanum* between 1655 and 1673.

82. Jacques François Paul Aldonce de Sade (1705-1778) (Abbé de Sade) published his *Memoires pour la vie de François Pétrarque* in 1764. The Abbé, Vicar-General of Toulouse, was uncle of the Marquis de Sade and was responsible for his upbringing.

83. The first printed edition of the *Philobiblon* (without the third i) was actually published in Cologne in 1473.

84. David Clément (1701–60), *Bibliothèque curieuse historique et critique* [Clément 1750–60].

> … he is sometimes ridiculously minute in a pompous account of editions which are in every one's hands, and which he gravely pronounces 'extrément rare!' but his enthusiasm, indefatigability, and research, and his having had access to many of the most celebrated

libraries abroad, render the perusal of his volumes at once a duty
and a pleasure.   [Dibdin 1808, p. 370]

85. Daniel Georg Morhof (1639–91) was appointed Professor of Poetry at the University of Roſtock in 1660, Professor
of Eloquence and Poetry at the University of Kiel in 1665
and Professor of Hiſtory there in 1673. He published *Un-
terricht von der Teutschen Sprache und Poesie* in 1682. Dibdin
[Dibdin 1808, i, p. xii] recommends the fourth edition of his
Polyhiſtor literarius, philosophicus, et praſticus [Morhof 1747].

86. Josse Bade (1462-1535) Latinised his name to Jodocus
Badius Ascensius (from Aasche near Brussels). He was
a classiciſt who turned to printing, firſt in Lyon, then in
Paris. As well as many classics and the *Philobiblon,* he published the firſt Paris edition of Sebaſtian Brant's *Das Narrenschiff* and a French translation of that, *La nef des folz du
monde* [Putnam 1962, ii, p. 13].

87. Melchior Goldaſt von Heimingsfeld (1578–1635), Swiss
Calviniſt lawyer, philologiſt and hiſtorian in his *Philologi-
carum epiſtolarum centuria una diversorum* [Goldaſt 1674].
Some of Goldaſt's library found its way into the possession
of Queen Chriſtina of Sweden and is now in the Vatican
[Hall 1913, p. 341].

88. I have been unable to identify this edition. There were
several printers by the name of Hummius. Johannes Nico-
laus Hummius of Frankfurt was printing in the second half
of the seventeenth century.

89. John Bale (1495–1563), Bishop of Ossory and author of
what may be considered the firſt hiſtory play, *Kynge Johan.*
His moſt important work is a hiſtory of British writers,

IlluStrium maioris Britanniæ scriptorum [Bale 1548]. He was
a leading supporter of the English Reformation and made
many enemies with his attacks on those who did not support
his views, such as 'pompouse popyshe bisshops' [Bale 1544].

90. Henry Wharton (1664–95) published his two-vol-
ume *Anglia sacra* in 1691, in which he colleɛted together
many fascinating documents on the hiſtory of the English
church.

91. William Cave (1637–1713), Anglican divine whose extensive writing on church hiſtory included *EcclesiaStici*
[Cave 1683].

92. *A catalogue of the bishops of England* by Francis Godwin
(1562–1633), Bishop of Hereford [Godwin 1601].

93. These have now been moved to the Bodleian Library.

94. Antoine Vérard (d. 1513), French printer. Caxton adopted type originally used by him in about 1490 and Wynkyn
de Worde continued its use. Steinberg says that Vérard was
'a pioneer in introducing Renaissance forms in his book-
ornaments' [Steinberg 1996, p. 38].

95. Guillaume EuStace (fl. 1500–1535), French publisher who
sometimes worked with Philippe Pigouchet. He published
an edition of Froissart's chronicles [Froissart 1513], a copy of
which was owned by William Hunter.

96. Philippe Pigouchet (1486–1512), French bookseller and
printer renowned for his woodcuts. In a book of hours he
produced, every page had an appropriate border composed

of 'delicately executed miniature engravings on wood, or on metal handled the same way that the wood blocks were, each separated by set figures and ornamental designs, and varied by woodland and hunting scenes' [Winship 1926, p. 58].

97. Henry Howard (1517?–47), Earl of Surrey, was a friend and disciple of Thomas Wyatt. Howard's translation of books II and IV of the *Æneid* is the earliest known example of English blank verse and one of the earliest English translations of that work [Virgil 1963. p. 1].

98. Sir Thomas Wyatt (1503?–42), poet. He was imprisoned in the Tower of London in 1536 and there witnessed the execution of Anne Boleyn, with whom he was rumoured to have had an affair.

99. John Colet (1467?–1519), Dean of St Paul's and founder of St Paul's School. Samuel Knight (1675–1746) published his biography in 1724. Aubrey relates that:

> … after the Conflagration (his Monument being broken) his coffin which was Lead, was full of liquor which conserved the body. Mr. Wyld and Ralph Greatorex tasted it, and 'twas of a kind of insipid tast, something of an Ironish tast…   [Aubrey 2000, p. 85]

100. Sir Thomas More (1478–1535), Henry VIII's Lord Chancellor who was executed for opposing the King's break with Rome. His *Utopia* (1516) was seen through the press by his friend Erasmus.

101. The great Reformation scholar Desiderius Erasmus (1466?–1536) was responsble for the first readily available printed edition of the New Testament in Greek. Cardinal

Ximenes's was actually printed *before* but published *after* it [Metzger 1992, p. 98]. Erasmus's edition was used by the editors of the King James Bible and by Tyndale. Erasmus made several visits to England and was for a while Professor of Divinity and Greek at Cambridge University. Erasmus described hunting in libraries as 'by far the most enjoyable sport' [Schoeck 1990, p. 45]. Erasmus sold his library in 1525 to the Polish nobleman Jan Laski (Johannes a Lasco) for 300 crowns [Ibid., p. 297].

102. An absurd assertion. Henry VIII was a very well-read man with substantial libraries and 'of his possessions books are the one category to have survived in great qualtity' [Carley 2000, p. xxiii]. Many were undoubtedly 'fine'. Moreover, his wish to prove the supremacy of the Crown over the Church led him to collect many English chronicles and Anglo-Saxon laws [ibid., p. xxxv].

103. George Frederick Nott (1767–1841), divine and author. The works of Surrey and Wyatt referred to did not appear until 1815–16. Nott's library of 12,500 volumes was sold 11–25 January 1842.

104. Roger Ascham (1515–68), tutor to the Princess Elizabeth, Latin secretary to Queen Mary and tutor to Elizabeth again upon her accession. He was author of a number of interesting books including *The scholemaster* [Ascham 1570] and *Toxophilus* [Ascham 1545].

105. Guillaume Budé (1467–1540), French academic who wrote *Commentarii Græcæ linguæ*. Dibdin calls him 'one of the earliest and brightest ornaments of Lexicography' [Dibdin 1808, ii. p. 383].

106. Members of the Estienne family (Latinised as Stephanus, Anglicised as Stephens) of distinguished Parisian printers founded by Henri Estienne (d. 1520) who were renowned not only for the fine printing and typography of their publications, but also for the highest academic standards.

Robert Estienne (1503–59) was a noted scholar and he was appointed 'Regius in Græcis Typographus' [Reed 1952, p. 52]. His Greek New Testaments were used as sources by the translators of the King James Bible. He carried a wide range of types, including some very fine Greeks by Claude Garamond and Sephardic and Rabbinical Hebrew, one possibly by Estienne himself. An account of his type holdings has recently been published [Vervliet 2004].

Robert's influence on his native language was significant, as he published his *Dictionaire Francois–Latin* in 1540 and *Traicté de la grammaire Francoise* in 1557. The former tended to promote etymological rather than phonetic spellings [Rickard 1989, 92–94]. His publications often brought him into conflict with the Church authorities and he moved to Geneva in 1550.

Robert's son Henri continued the printing business in Geneva and contributed further to the discussions on the French language with his *De la precellence du langage François* (1579).

107. Jakob Faber Stapulensis (Jacques Lefèvre d'Etaples) (1450–36), French Catholic theologian whose ideas were influential in the Reformation. He translated the Bible into French.

108. Adrien Turnèbe (1512–65), French classical scholar who worked with Guillaume Morel on the production of Greek books at the Imprimerie Royale. It is said that his father

was a Scotsman whose surname, Turnbull, was rendered as Tournebœuf in French and later contracted to Turnèbe.

109.

> The vast, golden, renowned, lovely apparatus by which I desire with all my heart to give glory to the true brilliance of the British is collected together in my house. But the wicked stepmother, Fortune, is envious of this happy undertaking of mine. And so, lest all the labours of many nights should perish in one short hour, o Cranmer (outstanding representative of pious people!), I am forced to beg your kindness...

110.

> But alas the sad turn of human affairs! Alas the deplorable and most unfortunate fate of this excellent man!

William Camden (1551–1623) was possibly the greatest of all the English chroniclers. One modern historian has commented that Camden's dedication to historical evidence, both written and physical, was later 'incorporated into historiography so thoroughly that modern historians tend to forget to whom they owe this debt' [Arnold 2000, p. 42].

> Mr Camden much studied the Welch language, and kept a Welsh servant, to improve him [in] that language for the better understanding of our Antiquities.   [Aubrey 2000, p. 68]

Camden's biographer, Thomas Smith (1638–1710), was a noted orientalist in his youth and known as 'Rabbi Smith'. His *Diatriba de Chaldaicis paraphrastis* of 1662 was 'significant not for its novelty (it was hardly original) but for the wide range of sources that a young bachelor of arts of two years' standing was able to marshal' [Tyacke 1997, p. 470]. He later worked as librarian of the Cotton collection and kept up a correspondence with Hearne and Wanley.

111. John Stow(e) (1525?–1605), tailor, chronicler and editor of Lydgate and Chaucer. His *Summarie of Englyshe chronicles* was published in 1565.

When his house was searched for Papiſt literature, it was reported that:

> He hath a great store of folishe fabulous bokes of olde prynte as of Sir Degory Tryamore, &c. He hath also a great sorte of old written English Chronicles both in parchement and in paper, some long, som shorte. He hath besides, as it were, miscellanea of diverse sortes both touching phisicke, surgerye, and herbes, with medicines of experience, and also touching old phantasticall popishe bokes prynted in the olde tyme, with many such also written in olde Englisshe on parchement. All which we have pretermytted to take any inventarye of. We have only taken a note of such bokes as have been lately putt forth in the realme or beyonde the Seas for defence of papistrye: with a note of som of his own devises and writinges touching such matter as he hath gathered for Chronicles, whereaboute he seemeth to have bestowed much travaile. His bokes declare him to be a great favourer of papistrye.
> [Clode 1875, ii. 299-302]

112. William Lambarde (1536–1601) published a number of intereſting books including *Perambulation of Kent* [Lambarde 1576] and *Archaionomia* [Lambarde 1568], a collection of Anglo-Saxon laws. Some of his papers were purchased by the Folger Shakespeare Library in 1924 [Lambarde 1962, p. 3].

113. Polydore Vergil or Virgil (1470?–1555?), a native of Urbino, came to England as a subcollector of Peter's Pence. He wrote the magiſterial *Anglicæ hiſtoriæ libri XXVI* [Vergil 1534] and was the firſt editor of Gildas's *De excidio et conqueſtu Britanniæ* [Gildas 1525].

He was deeply unpopular with many English historians for questioning the historical basis of Arthurian myth and the idea that London had been founded by Brutus. After the Reformation, his position as a papal representative confirmed English prejudices against him. There seems to be no basis for the accusations by Bale, Caius and others that he destroyed his source material [Hay 1952, pp. 158–60].

114. John Caius (1510–73) was a distinguished physician and the refounder of what is now Gonville and Caius College, Cambridge. His *De antiquitate Cantabrigiensis Academiæ* [Caius 1568] contains what purports to be a charter granted to Cambridge University by King Arthur in AD 531.

115. Nicholas of Lyra (c.1270–1349), outstanding biblical scholar whose works influenced Luther. His *Postilla super totam Bibliam* was printed in Rome by Sweynheim and Pannartz in 1471–2.

116. Johannes von Sturm (1507–89), humanist and educational reformer. who founded the Strasbourg Gymnasium in 1538.

117. Sebastianus Greyff or Gryphius (1493–1556) published George Rataller's translation of these works in Lyon [Sophocles 1550].

> His editions of ancient authors rivalled those of the Aldus and Stephanus presses. For his critical editions of the classical physicians, Hippocrates and Galen, Gryphius obtained no less an editor than François Rabelais. [Steinberg 1996, p. 42]

118. Hieronymus Wolf (1516–80), humaniſt. Wolf edited a number of editions of Isocrates. Dibdin ranks that published by Henri Eſtienne in 1570 as the beſt [Dibdin 1808, ii p. 5]. Wolf was Reċtor of the Gymnasium at Augsburg and Direċtor of Augsburg Public Library.

119. John Singleton Copley (1738–1813), talented American-born painter living in London from 1775. He painted portraits of both Paul Revere and Lord Cornwallis. *The offer of the crown to Lady Jane Grey* was exhibited in 1808.

120. The British Inſtitution, Pall Mall, was built by Alderman John Boydell to house his Shakespeare Gallery. When he ran into financial difficulties in 1805, he held a lottery in which William Tassie, a gem engraver, won much of the colleċtion and the building. Tassie employed Chriſtie's to auċtion the colleċtion in the subsequent year and the lease was bought for £4,500. Two exhibitions were held every year, one of old maſters, the other of contemporary painters. It closed in 1867 and was demolished in 1868. [Jackson n.d.].

121. William Cecil (1520–98), firſt Baron Burleigh or Burghley, Secretary of State (1550–53) and Lord Treasurer (1572–98). Many of his manuscripts remain at Hatfield House but moſt of his books were sold in 1687 [Cecil 1687].

122. Martin Borrhaus or Cellarius (1499–1564), a leading Proteſtant academic who published a book on Ariſtotle's *Rhetoric* [Borrhaus 1551]. Martin Luther met Borrhaus and Marcus Stübner when they were ſtudents at Wittenberg and told Spalatin that he had uncovered Satan, who was indeed motivating these men. During the meeting, Borrhaus 'foamed and growled and raged... so that I could not

get a word in edgewise' [Edwards 1975, p. 25]. According to Borrhaus, there were 2,665,886,746 devils in Hell [Pettegree 2000, p.17].

123. Written by William Vallans (fl. 1578–90), a Hertfordshire salt merchant and antiquary, to publicise his home town of Ware. It was included in Hearne's edition of Leland [Leland 1710–12].

124. For an interesting discussion on portraits of Queen Elizabeth, see [Cooper 2003].

125. Robert Laneham, in *A letter: whearin, part of the entertainment vntoo the Queenz Maiesty, at Killingwoorth Castl, in Warwik Sheer in this soomerz progress 1575. iz signified: from a freend officer attendant in the Coourt, vntoo hiz freend a citizen and merchaunt of London,* describes Cox's library at length (see below).

126. Captain Cox (fl. 1575).

But aware, kéep bak, make room noow, heer they cum! And fyrst, captin Cox, an od man I promiz yoo: by profession a Mason, and that right skilfull, very cunning in fens, and hardy az Gawin; for hiz tonsword hangs at his tablz éend: great ouersight hath he in matters of storie: For, az for king Arthurz book, Huon of Burdeaus, The foour suns of Aymon, Beuys of Hampton, The squyre of lo degrée, The knight of courtesy, and the Lady Faguell, Frederik of Gene, Syr Eglamoour, Sir Tryamoour, Sir Lamwell, Syr Isenbras, Syr Gawyn, Olyuer of the Castl, Lucres and Eurialus, Virgil's life, The castle of Ladiez, The wido Edyth, The King & the Tanner, Frier Rous, Howleglas, Gargantua, Robinhood, Adambel, Clim of the clough, & William of Cloudesley, The Churl & the Burd, The seauen wise Masters, The wife lapt in a Morel's skin, The sak full of nuez, The seargeaunt that became a Fryar, Skogan, Collyn cloout,

The Fryar & the boy, Elynor Rumming, and the Nutbrooun maid,
with many moe then: I rehearz héere: I beléeue hee haue them all
at hiz fingers endz.   [Laneham 1907, pp. 28–30]

127. Joseph Ritson (1752–1803), a notoriously ill-tempered
vegetarian. Scott consulted him while writing his *Border
minstrelsy*. Ritson criticised the editorial techniques of many
contempories, and was particularly scathing about Bishop
Percy's textual accuracy. He published *Ancient metrical romances* in 1802. Yale University holds many of his papers.

128. John Harington (fl. 1550) and his son Sir John Harington (1560–1612). Elizabeth I banned Sir John from court
for corrupting her ladies with his partial translation of
Oriosto's *Orlando furioso*, telling him he could only return
when he had translated all of it. The completed work was
published in 1591. Henry Harrington (1755–91), a descend-
ant of Sir John, compiled *Nugæ antiquæ* from family papers,
mostly relating to Sir John. The first volume appeared in
1769, the second in 1775.

129. Thomas Park (1759–1834), engraver and antiquary. He
expanded Walpole's *Catalogue of the royal and noble authors*
[Walpole 1806].

130. Thomas Mathias or Matthias (1754?–1835), satirist and
Italian scholar, was private tutor to Spencer Percival, the
only British Prime Minister to be assassinated. He attacked
many contemporary writers in *The Pursuits of literature: or
what you will: a satirical poem in dialogue*, the first part of
which appeared in 1794.

131. Filippo Giunta (Felipe Junta) published an edition of
the *Decameron* in Florence in 1516.

132. Nicola Francesco Haym (1679–1730) published *Notizia de' libri rari nella lingua Italiana* in London in 1726. Subsequent editions were called *Biblioteca Italiana, o sia notizia de'libri rari nella lingua Italiana*. Haym wrote the librettos for Handel's *Amadigi di Gaula, Flavio, Giulio Cesare, Ottone, Radamisto* and *Teseo*.

133. Pellegrino Antonio Orlandi (1660–1727) published *Abecedario pittorico*, one of the earlieśt art bibliographies, in 1704. In 1722 he published his hiśtory of printing, *Origine e progressi dell'arte impressoria* [Orlandi 1722]. Dibdin says that 'copies *on śtrong writing-paper* are rather valuable' [Dibdin 1808, i, p. xvi].

134. Angelo Maria Bandini (1726–1803) published *Specimen literaturæ Florentinæ sæculi XV* in 1747–51. He was appointed Librarian of the Biblioteca Medicea Laurenziana in 1757 in which capacity he catalogued the collećtions extensively.

135. Samuel Paterson (1728–1802), aućtioneer, bookseller and cataloguer. He was a friend of Dr Johnson, Horace Walpole, William Bowyer and Richard Gough. The great breadth of his knowledge is displayed in the *Bibliotheca Croftsiana* [Crofts 1783] and similar aućtion catalogues.

In *Joineriana*, he described how to deal with 'saucy authors, who dare to print upon their own account'. If an author asks for his books,

> be sure you say, there's none bound! – And, if he would take it in sheets – tell him the rat-catchers are in the warehouse, and you dare not go in for fear of disturbing them – but he may have one a week hence, if he'll call. [Paterson 1772, p.55]

136. In fact, Paterson's entry reads '3976 BOCCACCIO (GIOV.) *Il Decamerone*, 4to. fine Tit. (this I take to be *la vera Ediz. di Giunta* Fior. 1527)' [Crofts 1783].

137. Henry John Todd (1763–1845) published his 8-volume edition of Spenser's work in 1805. William Wordsworth wrote to Sir Walter Scott on 7 November that year,

> Like you, I had been sadly disappointed with Todd's Spencer [sic]; not with the Life which I think has a sufficient share of merit; though the matter is badly put together; but three parts of four of the Notes are absolute trash. That style of compiling notes ought to be put an end to.'   [Wordsworth 2000, i, p. 641]

138. Jacques Georges de Chauffepié published his supplement to Bayle's Dictionary in 1750.

139. Isaac Vossius (1618–89), Dutch scholar and book-collector. Vossius was librarian to Queen Christina of Sweden and bought her library on her abdication in 1654. It included the *Codex argentius* which had been plundered during the Swedish occupation of Prague in 1648. This was subsequently bought by Count Magnus Gabriel De La Gardie and presented to the University of Uppsala. Thanks to the influence of John Pearson, later Bishop of Chester, Vossius was appointed canon of Windsor in 1670 and spent the rest of his life in England.

He left his library jointly to his nephew Gerard John Vossius and his niece Attia Vossius, advising them to contact the Dutch Ambassador and follow his advice regarding the sale. It was bought by the University of Leiden [Bruce & Nichols 1863, p. 149].

140. Georg Wolfgang Panzer (1729–1805), German bibliographer whose works included *Annalen der älteren Deutschen Literatur* [Panzer 1788] and *Annales typographici ab artis inventæ origine ad annum MD* [Panzer 1793–1802] which Dibdin called 'this very elaborate and valuable production, which comprehends a complete and systematic account of all books printed from the origin of the typographical art to the year 1536' [Dibdin 1808, i, p. xix].

141. 'It is certainly an unusual way to add to books!' (exclaims the author) 'It is perfectly clear that the author has done this so that he should get the same price for the first and second books, or editions, and that both are equally necessary for readers.'

142. William Savage (1770–1843), a fine English printer. He printed the first edition of *Bibliomania* and the first volume of Dibdin's edition of *Typographical antiquities* [Ames 1810]. He wrote *Practical hints on decorative printing* [Savage 1822], *On the preparation of printing ink* [Savage 1832] and *A dictionary of the art of printing* [Savage 1841]. Savage invented new, oil-free inks which were said to cause less damage to the paper. Nonetheless, Dibdin's own publications, including the first volume of *Typographical antiquities*, are very subject to foxing, a fact which Blades attributed to the failure of the paper-makers to neutralise their bleach correctly [Blades 2004, p. 13].

Savage also revived the chiaroscuro technique in which many wood blocks are used to lay down solid areas in a range of shades. One illustration in *Practical hints* required 29 blocks. Despite falling out with Coleridge over the publication of *The friend* [Coleridge 2000, iii, p. 140], he was appointed printer to the Royal Institution in 1815.

143. Richard Smith or Smyth (1590–1675). His library was auctioned in 1682 and fetched £1,414 12s 11d. He had the strange idea of compiling the obituaries of everyone with his name [Smyth 1849].

144. Thomas Baker (1656–1740). As a non-juror, he was deprived of his fellowship of St John's College, Cambridge, although he was allowed to retain his rooms. He amassed many manuscripts for a proposed history of the University which were bequeathed to Edward, Earl of Oxford, and are now in the British Library's Harley collection.

145. Richard Gough (1735–1809), antiquary, bibliographer and topographer, bequeathed more than 3,700 volumes to the Bodleian Library, including many connected with Old English literature and over 200 pre-Reformation service books of the English Church [Bodleian Library n.d.].

146. Thomas Osborne (d. 1767) and Charles Rivington proposed to Samuel Richardson 'a little volume of Letters, in a common style' which, although published after *Pamela,* was undoubtedly the inspiration for that hugely successful epistolatory novel [Dobson 1902, pp. 18, 19]. Dr Johnson was employed by Osborne to catalogue the Harleian collection. On one occasion,

> Osborne offensively reproved him for negligence, and Johnson knocked him down with a folio. The book with which the feat was performed (*Biblia Græca Septuaginta,* fol. 1594, Frankfort) was in existence in a bookseller's shop at Cambridge in 1812, and should surely have been placed in some safe author's museum.
> [Stephen 1878, p. 27]

If only this editor could lay his hands on that Greek Septuagint and Becky Sharp's Dictionary, his library would be
complete!

147. Thomas Rawlinson (1681–1725), friend of Joseph Ames
and John Bagford. He was the son of Sir Thomas Rawlinson, Lord Mayor of London.

148. John Bridges (1666–1724), Solicitor of the Customs and
collector of topographical manuscripts, tracts, etc.

149. Anthony Collins (1676–1729,) a leading English deist.
John Locke wrote to him

> Sir I forgot you had an estate in the Country, a Library in Town,
> Friends every where, amongst which you are to while away as
> pleasantly I hope as any one of this our planet a large number of
> years...'   [Locke 1976, viii, p. 189]

Locke appointed Collins his executor and in his will he
left:

> to my good Freind Mr. Anthony Collins of the Middle Temple
> my Plautus in folio of Lambins edition *Gesneri Bibliotheca auc-*
> *ta per Simlerum Kerckringii Spicilegium anatomicum, Catalogus li-*
> *brorum bibliothecæ Raphælis Trichett du Fresne Bibliotheca Thuana et*
> *Bibliotheca Heinseana* and Witsens Map of Tartary that hangs up
> in my Study.   [Locke 1976, viii, p. 420]

150. Charles Townley (1737–1805), a wealthy collector of
antiquities. His Roman sculptures were purchased after
his death by the British Museum for £20,000. Zoffany
painted a rather extraordinary picture of Townley (to be
seen at Townley Hall Art Gallery), with his friends, Baron
d'Hancarville (Pierre François Hugues), Thomas Astle and

the Hon. Charles Greville, looking rather uncomfortable among the marbles.

151. James Bindley (1737–1818) Commissioner of the Stamp Duties and a book-collector. He is LEONTES in later editions of *Bibliomania*. In his edition of Dryden's works, Edmund Malone wrote:

> My warmest acknowledgments are also due to my friend James Bindley, Esq., First Commissioner in the Stamp-Office, whose urbanity, classical taste, and various knowledge, are only exceeded by his great liberality in the communication of the very curious materials for literary history, and the illustration of temporary allusions, which his valuable library contains. By the aid of some very rare tracts and poems in his possession, several of which are wanting in my own Collection, I have been enabled to throw some new light on our author's history, as well as on many of his writings; as I have more particularly mentioned in the proper places.
>
> [Malone 1800, i, p. v]

152. Edmund Malone (1741–1812), Shakespearian scholar who wrote *An attempt to ascertain the order in which the plays of Shakespeare were written*, 1778. It was Malone who uncovered Ireland's forgeries. He is MARCELLUS in later editions of *Bibliomania*.

153. Francis Douce (1757–1834) published *Illustrations of Shakespeare* in 1807. He was Keeper of Manuscripts at the British Museum 1807–11. He bequeathed over 19,000 volumes of printed books (including 479 incunabulæ) to the Bodleian [Bodleian Library n.d.]. He is PROSPERO in later editions of *Bibliomania*.

154. Robert Masters (1713–98). As well as his life of Baker [Masters 1748], he also wrote a history of Corpus Christi College, Cambridge [Masters 1753].

155. Brian Walton (1600?–61), Bishop of Chester. Editor, with Edmund Castell, of the *English polyglot Bible* (1654–57), an early example of subscription publishing. It was placed in the *Index librorum probibitorum*.

156. Edmund Castell (1606–85), Semitic scholar. His *Lexicon polyglotton*, which had been influenced by his work with Walton, was published in 1669.

157. John Nourse (1705–80) was Henry Fielding's bookseller, supplying him with the law books he required. He also found Fielding a house in Essex Street [Battestin 2000, p. 109]. His papers in the British Library (MS. Addl. 38729), containing many author agreements, are a valuable source of information on author–publisher relations in the eighteenth century [Feather 1981].

158. 'When an oak tree falls, everyone gets wood,' or, as Dibdin put it, 'an oak of no ordinary size has fallen, to afford almost every man a faggot for his fire' [Dibdin 1836, p. 442].

159. John Nichols (1745–1826) was apprenticed to the printer William Bowyer the Younger in 1757. Bowyer encouraged Nichols to write. In 1765 he entrusted Nichols with the task of negotiating with the Chancellor of Cambridge University the abortive proposal that Bowyer should take over the running of the University Press.

160. John Locke (1632–1704), English philosopher whose influential works reflected and reinforced the move towards greater religious toleration in England after the Glorious Revolution.

In his last letter to Collins, of 23 August 1704, he wrote, 'The knowledg I have of your vertue af all kinds secures the trust which by your permission I have placed in you,' and near the end he adds, 'May you live long and happy in the enjoyment of health, freedom, content and all those <blesseings> which providence has bestowed on you and your virtue intitles you to' [Locke 1976, viii, pp. 418–9].

Locke showed himself to be quite interested in the finer points of bibliopegy when he wrote to Collins in June 1703:

> In the parts of good binding besides folding beating and sowing well I count strong pastboards and as large margents as the paper will possibly afford, and for lettering I desire it should be upon the same leather blackd, and barely the name of the author as in this case Vossius.   [Locke 1976, viii, p. 7–8]

161. Samuel Clarke (1675–1729), theologian. Dibdin praises his edition of Homer and says:

> No one seems to have united, in a more successful degree, the qualifications of a good and a great man: of a consummate theologian, accomplished scholar, and rigidly upright moral character. [Dibdin 1808, i, pp. 381–2].

162. Melchior Pfintzing's *Die... Geschichten des... Ritters Herr Tewrdannckhs* was actually printed in 1517, not 1527, by Hans Schoensperger, Nuremberg. Mead's copy is now in Glasgow University Library. The book was a very elaborate production. As well as 118 woodcuts, it boasted a Fraktur typeface based on the handwriting of Vinzenz Rockner, secretary to the Emperor Maximillian. This type was

so complex, with many flourishes, that a long discussion raged about whether the book had been printed from wood blocks rather than moveable metal type. Vogt, Fournier and Papillon favoured the former, Dibdin the latter [Dibdin 1817, i, p. 206]. In this, Dibdin was correct.

163. Henry Winstanley (1644–1703), Charles II's Clerk of Works at Audley End near Saffron Walden. He issued a set of 24 plans and views of the house.

164. Martin Folkes (1690–1754), scientist and antiquarian. He was appointed President of the Royal Society in 1741 and of the Society of Antiquaries in 1756.

165. Richard Rawlinson (1690–1755), antiquary and non-juror divine, was the brother of Thomas Rawlinson (whose library sale is mentioned on pp. 32–3). Like Dibdin, he went to St John's College, Oxford. He endowed a chair in Anglo-Saxon at Oxford and he left his papers and collection of seals to the Bodleian Library. It was one of the greatest bequests in the history of the Bodleian. It was not finally sorted and numbered until the nineteenth century when it was found to consist of 1,900 printed books and some 5,000 volumes of manuscripts [Sutherland & Mitchell 1986, p. 736]. To the Ashmolean Museum he gave a model of a Venetian gondola, an Indian palanquin, and a white fox from Muscovy. He had previously mounted a successful campaign to abolish access fees to the Museum [Sutherland & Mitchell 1986, p.652].

166. Samuel Baker (1711?–78), bookseller and auctioneer. He held his first auction, of the books of Sir John Stanley, in 1744. The auction house he founded became known as

Leigh & Sotheby after passing to his nephew John Sotheby and Baker's partner George Leigh. Now it is known simply as Sotheby's.

167. Robert Fabyan (d. 1513), London merchant, member of the Drapers' Company. He published his *New chronicles of England and France* in 1516.

168. Edward Hall (d. 1547). The firﬆ edition of his chronicle was published by Jacques Berthelot in 1542.

169. Richard Grafton (d. 1572?) published a number of English Bibles and the firﬆ *Book of common prayer* in 1549. He published Hardyng's chronicle in 1543 and republished Hall's in 1548.

170. Admiral Antonio de Ulloa (1716–1795) was captured by the British in 1745 and brought to England as a prisoner. His scientific abilities were much appreciated there and he was swiftly appointed a Fellow of the Royal Society. It is entirely appropriate that a copy of his *Relacion hiﬆorica del viage a la America meridional* [Juan & Ulloa 1748] should have been in Folkes's library since it was Folkes, then President of the Royal Society, who was responsible for Ulloa's release and return to Spain. In 1766, he was appointed Governor of 'Florida Ocidentale' (i.e. Louisiana) where he banned slave trading [Fabel 1988, p. 30].

171. *Museo de las medallas desconocidas espanolas* by Vincencio Juan de Laﬆanosa (1607–1684).

172. Thomas Fuller (1608–61). The work of publishing *The hiﬆory of the worthies of England* was completed in 1662 by his son John.

173. *Les edifices antiques de Rome* [Desgodetz 1682] by Antoine Babuty Desgodetz (1653-1728), with its many accurate engravings, was, with Vitruvius's and Palladio's works, one of the most important sources consulted by neo-classical architects.

While in Italy, Robert Adam thought of producing a new edition:

> Desgodetz's book is almost entirely out of print. Neither in England, France or Italy can one get a copy of it under double price. Several have thought of reprinting it but neither had the talents, the money nor the courage. As I am on the spot where these antiquities are, have Clérisseau's assistance and other conveniences, in course of conversation with Wood and Ramsay the thought struck me that it would be a good scheme for me.
> [Fleming 1962, p. 170]

174. William Hunter (1718–83), anatomist. He left his collections to the University of Glasgow, where his books were absorbed into the existing library and the artefacts now make up the Hunterian Museum. His youngest brother, John, also worked as an anatomist and also built up an impressive collection.

175. Clayton Morduant Cracherode (1730–99), reclusive book-collector. He left all his prints, drawings, coins, gems and books, except his Complutensian Polyglot (which went to Shute Barrington) and a Homer first edition (to Cyril Jackson), to the British Museum. These two works also went to the museum in due course.

176. Richard Laughton (1668?–1723) tutor at Clare College, Cambridge, and ardent supporter of Newtonian philosophy.

177. John Henley (1692–1756), orator. Pope called him the 'zany of thy age' (*Dunciad,* iii, 205–6).

178. James Jurin (1684–1750), physician, Secretary of the Royal Society and editor of *Philosophical transactions.* He wrote a series of papers on the success of smallpox vaccination as well as *Geometry no friend to infidelity,* a defence of Newton and other British mathematicians, under the pseudonym 'Philalethes Cantabrigiensis' [Jurin 1734].

179. Thomas Birch (1705–66), Secretary of the Royal Society (1752–65), an industrious biographer.

180. George Edwards (1694–1773), an outstanding naturalist who has been called 'the father of British ornithology'. He not only wrote and illustrated his books *A natural history of uncommon birds* [Edwards 1751] and *Gleanings of natural history* [Edwards 1758], but also etched the plates and coloured them himself. *Gleanings* is unusual for having parallel English and French texts. He was a friend of Sir Hans Sloane.

181. Heinrich Aldegrever (1502–61), painter and engraver.

182. Lewis Theobald (1688–1744), dramatist and editor of Shakespeare. In 1726, the year after the publication of Pope's edition of Shakespeare, he published *Shakespeare restored: a specimen of many errors, as well committed as unamended, by Mr. Pope in his late edition of this poet...* Theobald's own edition of Shakespeare was published in 1733.

183. William Warburton (1698–1779), Bishop of Gloucester. He corresponded with Theobald and later accused him of stealing his ideas. He published his own edition of Shake-

speare's works in 1747 He also published *A vindication of Mr. Pope's essay on man* in 1715 and *The alliance between church and state* in 1736.

184. Richard Farmer (1735–97), Master of Emanuel College, Cambridge. He published *Essay on the learning of Shakespeare* in 1767. It was said that he loved three things: old port, old clothes and old books. Nichols records that the catalogue of his books (sold in 1798) ran to 379 pages. The 8,155 books fetched £2,210 [Nichols & Bentley 1812, ii, 649]. He was a close friend of Thomas Percy who wrote:

> Dear Farmer, I haunt you upon Paper like your Evil Genius; and break in upon your Philosophical and Tutorial persuits with my old ballads; as Punch interrupts the most solemn scenes of the puppet-show with his impertinent ribaldry. [Percy 1944, vol. ii, p. 66]

185. George Steevens (1736–1800) reprinted many of Shakespeare's plays from the quarto editions in 1766 (ironically in octavo). These he had mostly borrowed from Garrick's library. In Steevens's collection was a second folio of Shakespeare 'with notes and alterations of the scenes, by King Charles the First; together with that Monarch's name and motto, Dum spiro spero, in his own hand-writing' [Nichols & Bentley 1812, ii, p.658].

186. George Chalmers (1742–1825), prolific Scottish writer on politics and economics. Amongst his works was a biography of Thomas Paine, written under the pseudonym Francis Oldys of the University of Pennsylvania. He also compiled a history of printing in Scotland. He was fooled by Ireland's Shakespeare forgeries and, after they were exposed, published a pamphlet on how they might have been

genuine, while acknowledging that they were not. He is
AURELIUS in later editions of *Bibliomania*.

187. Isaac Reed (1742–1801), a friend of Boswell's. He had a
fine collection of old books, mostly drama, and published a
variorum edition of Shakespeare in 1803.

188. Dr Johnson's edition of Shakespeare appeared in 1765.

189. Sir Thomas Hanmer (1677–1746) published a sumptuous edition of Shakespeare, based upon Pope's, in 1744.

190. Pierre des Maizeaux (1673–1745), editor and biographer of Bayle. His family, being protestants, left France
for Switzerland after the revocation of the Edict of Nantes.
He studied at the Lyceum in Berne and then in Geneva.
On his way to England, he met up with French refugees in
Holland, including Bayle to whom he offered his services.
Bayle hesitated, but, having quelled the young man's 'excessive obsequiousness', agreed. Des Maizeaux subsequently
served as an intermediary between Bayle and Jacob Tonson
concerning the English edition of the *Dictionnaire*.
    He published a *Life of Mr. Bayle* anonymously in 1708
and was instrumental in the publication of Bayle's correspondence. Des Maizeaux became an English citizen in
1708 [Broome 1955].

191. Pierre Bayle (1647–1706) founded *Nouvelles de la répub-
lique des lettres,* an early literary and philosophical journal,
in 1684. His most important work was his *Dictionnaire historique et critique* published in 1696.

192. William Lowndes (1652–1724), Secretary to the Treasurer. He foolishly proposed debasement of the silver coinage.

193. Patrick Blair (d. 1728) Scottish physician and botaniſt. After imprisonment during the 1715 rebellion, he moved briefly to London before settling in Boſton, Lincolnshire.

194. Joseph Addison (1672-1719) told in the *Speʠator*, 23 April 1710, how he accidentally left his notes in Lloyd's coffee house. Before he could retrieve them, they were read out to everyone's amusement. There is, indeed, a similarity with the contents of Henley's library:

MINUTES.

Sir Roger de Coverley's country seat—Yes, for I hate long speeches—Query, if a good Christian may be a conjurer—Childermas-day, Salt-seller, Housedog, Screech-owl, Cricket—Mr. Thomas Inkle of London, in the good ship called the Achilles. Yarico—*Ægrescitque medendo*—Ghosts—The Lady's Library— Lion by trade a taylor—Dromedary called Bucephalus—Equipage the Lady's *summum bonum*—Charles Lilly to be taken notice of—Short face a relief to envy—Redundancies in the three professions—King Latinus a recruit—Jew devouring an ham of bacon—Westminster-abbey—Grand Cairo—Procrastination— April Fools—Blue Boars, Red Lions, Hogs in armour—Enter a King and two Fidlers *solus*—Admission into the Ugly Club— Beauty how improveable—Families of true and false humour— The parrot's school-mistress—Face half Pict half British—No man to be an hero of a tragedy under six foot—Club of Sighers— Letters from Flower-pots, Elbow-chairs, Tapestry figures, Lion, Thunder—The Bell rings to the puppet-show—Old Woman with a beard married to a smock faced Boy—My next coat to be turned up with blue—Fable of Tongs and Gridiron—Flower Dyers—The Soldier's Prayer—Thank ye for nothing, says the Gally-pot—Pactolus in stockings, with golden clocks to them—Bamboos, Cudgels, Drum-sticks—Slip of my Landlady's eldest daughter—The black mare with a star in her forehead—The barber's pole—Will Honeycombe's coat-pocket—Cæsar's behaviour and my own in parallel circumstances—Poem in patch-work—*Nulli grævis est percussus* Achilles—The Female Conventicler—The Ogle-master. [Addison 1804, i, pp. 118–9]

195. James Dormer (d. 1741) of Roucham Park, Oxfordshire. His estate, including a fine library, was inherited by his first cousin, Sir Clement Cottrell, who adopted the additional name Dormer. We are told that George Steevens bought many books at the sale of the library in 1764 'where he got the French translation of Xenephon's Works by Pyramus de Candale, Cologn, 1613, bound in Morroco and gilt leaves, worth 40*l*. and upwards, for 12*l*. 12*s*' [Nichols & Bentley 1812, ii, 658].

196. Joseph 'Consul' Smith (1682–1770). His library was a major component of George III's library, now the British Library's 'King's Library'. Smith was also a great collector of Canaletto's paintings.

197. James West (1704?–72) managed to combine legal and political careers with serious book-collecting. He was a barrister, MP for St Albans, Secretary to the Treasury and, from 1769 until his death, President of the Royal Society.

198. Giovanni Battista Pasquali (1702–84) ran a printing house in Venice for Consul Smith. Amongst the most famous productions of the press were engravings of Canaletto's views of Venice and a facsimile of Palladio's *Four books of architecture*.

199. 'What brought Sir Visto's ill got wealth to waste? | Some dæmon whisper'd, "Visto! have a taste."' Pope, 'Epistle IV to Richard Boyle, Earl of Burlington', 15–16.

200. I have deleted an '8vo,' which has obtruded itself here in the original text.

201. John Cuthell (1744?–1828), bookseller in Holborn. He was convicted of seditious libel in 1799 for publishing the Rev. Gilbert Wakefield's pamphlet criticising the Pitt administration

202. If only Jupiter would restore to me those bygone years! Virgil, *Æneid*, viii, 560.

203. William Fletewode, Recorder of London. George Whetstone, a relation, dedicated his *Promos and Cassandra* to him in 1578 [Hardison 1968, p. 218].

204. John Lettou, believed to be Lithuanian, founded the first London (as opposed to Westminster) press in 1480. He went into partnership with William de Machlinia in 1482 and in that year published the first printed book of English law, Sir Thomas Littleton's *Tenores novelli*, a treatise on land tenures.

205. William de Machlinia (fl. 1481-1486) published the first legal year books as well as a wide range of other works in English and Latin, including the twelfth-century *Vision of the monk of Eynsham* (incorrectly referred to as the 'monke in the abbey of Euishamme', i.e. Evesham, in Machlinia's edition) describing the torments to be heaped upon homosexuals and others in Purgatory, an English translation of Terence and a *Treatise on the pestilence*. In *Bibliophobia* Dibdin says of Machlinia's *Fructus temporum*, 'It is, typographically speaking, a "frightful" book' [Dibdin 1832, p. 7].

206. The anonymous printer known as the St Albans Schoolmaster used types which seem to have been supplied by Caxton [Hellinga 1982, pp. 75–6].

207. Richard Pynson (d. 1530), London printer of Norman origin. He appears to have studied at the University of Paris. His printing office was originally in the parish of St Clement's, but he moved to a house within Temple Bar at the corner of Chancery Lane and Fleet Street in 1500 [Duff 1905, pp.126–7]. Pynson became Printer to the King in 1508. In 1509 he printed Petrus Gryphus's *Oratio*, the first use of roman type in England [Reed 1952, p. 40].

208. Anthony Askew (1722–74), physician, classicist and book-collector. He was physician to St Bartholomew's and Christ's Hospitals and Registrar to the College of Physicians. Although mostly remembered as a classicist, he seems to have been highly regarded by his medical colleagues. When John Radcliffe, physician to William and Mary, retired, he passed his gold-headed cane to Richard Mead who then passed it to Askew, like a staff of office [Dubos 1959, p. 121].

209. Andrew Maunsell (d. 1596), a bookseller in St Paul's Churchyard, at the sign of the 'Brasen Serpent'. He produced *The catalogue of printed books* in 1595. The first part was of religious works, the second of scientific books and the third (which was never produced) was intended to be of humanities.

210. Claude Gros de Boze (1680–1753), French numismatist whose library contained many rare block books and incunabula. He issued a catalogue of his collection in 1745 and

a sale catalogue of over 2,723 lots was produced after his death in 1753. The whole library was bought by two collectors called de Cotte and Boutin who sold some of the incunabula to Gaignat.

211. Louis Jean Gaignat (d. 1768), an official at the Palais de Justice in Paris. His remarkable book collection was sold in 1769. The *Whitehall evening post* for 15 August 1769 reported that William Hunter paid a thousand guineas at the sale. Almost a third of Hunter's final holdings of fifteenth-century books (now in the University of Glasgow Library) were acquired from the Gaignat sale [Weston 2003].

The Gutenberg 42-line Bible on vellum bequeathed to the British Library in 1846 by Thomas Grenville had also belonged to Gaignat.

212. John Hardyng (1378–1465), English chronicler who, as a boy, was in the service of Harry Hotspur. He later fought at Agincourt.

213. Raphael Holinshed (d. c. 1580), English chronicler whose work supplied much of the material for Shakespeare's plays.

214. That is, Richard Gough (see note 145).

215. Daniel Lysons (1762–1834) started writing his *Environs of London* [Lysons 1796] while he was a curate in Putney. In 1806 he published the first four volumes of *Magna Britannia* [Lysons & Lysons 1806] with his brother Samuel (1763–1819). Samuel also published several other volumes, notably *Reliquiæ Britannico-Romanæ* [Lysons 1801–17].

216. John Burges (1745–1807), a physician who collected *materia medica*.

217. William Herbert (1718–95), bibliographer. He spent time in India where he 'wore the usual Oriental habit, and... suffered his beard to grow "as long as it would"' [Ames 1810–19, i, 95]. On his return, he devoted many years to updating Ames's *Typographical antiquities* which he published between 1785 and 1790. It was his edition which Didbdin augmented and expanded.

218. David Garrick (1717–79), the celebrated actor, who had been a pupil of Dr Johnson's. He had a large library, including a collection of Shakespeare quartos.

219. Probably Robert Dodd (1748–1816), marine artist, engraver and print-seller.

220. Peter Elmsley (1736–1802), bookseller in the Strand and elsewhere [Maxted n.d.].

221. Thomas Payne (1719–99), a well-loved bookseller, known universally as 'honest Tom Payne'.

> Mr. Payne supported the character of an *honest* man to the last; and, without the modern flash of wealth, which, ostentatiously exposed in a fine shop, has involved so many traders of all descriptions in difficulties and ruin, he acquired that fortune which enabled him to bring up two sons and two daughters with credit... [Nichols & Bentley 1812, vi, p. 440]

222. There were numerous Richardsons in the London book trade at this date.

223. John Chapman (1704–89), Anglican divine. His library was sold by Leigh & Sotheby, 4–14 April 1785.

224. Probably George Wagstaff I (d.1784), bookseller specialising in blackletter books. He was based in Brick Lane, Spitalfields, 1766–83 [Maxted n.d.].

225. *A brefe chronycle concernynge the examinacyon and death of the blessed martyr in Christ syr Iohan Oldecastell*, 1544. Sir John Oldcastle (1378?–1417) was executed for his support of the Lollards. Shakespeare used his name, but not the details of his life, for the character now known as Sir John Falstaff. He was forced to change the name after pressure from Oldcastle's descendants.

226. Henry Hills and William du Garde described themselves on the title page of *The government of the Commonwealth of England, Scotland, & Ireland* [Cromwell, 1654] as 'printers to His Highness the Lord Protector'.

227. Stanesby Alchorne (d. 1800), Assay Master at the Royal Mint. Much of his library is now in the John Rylands Library, Manchester. Alchorne was a keen collector of plants as well as books. He was a member of the Society of Apothecaries and wrote 'A Catalogue of the Fifty Plants, from Chelsea garden, presented to the Royal Society, by the Worshipful Company of Apothecaries for the year 1771' [Alchorne 1773]. The genus *Alchornea* is named after him.

228. George Leigh (d. 1815), bookseller and auctioneer. Leigh was in partnership with Samuel Baker and, after his death in 1778, with Baker's nephew, John Sotheby. The company is now known as Sotheby's.

229. Michael Wodhull (1740–1816), wealthy book-collector. Dibdin says that no better bibliographer existed in either England or France, 'Indeed, respecting the French school of editions and printers, during the xvith century, it may be doubted whether Mr Wodhull's equal could be found' [Dibdin 1817, iii, p.365]. He is ORLANDO in later editions of *Bibliomania*.

230. Isaac Gosset (1735?–1812), classicist and book-collector. He helped Dibdin to prepare the second edition of his *Introduction to the classics*.

231. Louis César de La Baume Le Blanc, Duc de La Vallière (1708–80). His library of 50,000 volumes was said to be the largest private collection in existence at the time. Earl Spencer bought his copy of the Sweynheym and Pannartz Apuleius (1469). At one time, the Duke owned the original manuscript of Montausier's *La guirlande de Julie*.

232. Chrétien François de Lamoignon (1735–89). 'Of all tasteless and terrific styles of binding,' demands Dibdin, 'what equalleth the relieure à la Lemoignon?' [Dibdin 1817, ii, p. 497].

233. John Ratcliffe (d. 1776) bought old books to use as wrapping paper for his chandlers shop, but started reading, collecting and dealing in them.

> Mr. Ratcliffe used to give coffee and chocolate every Thursday morning to Book and Print Collectors. Dr. Askew, Messieurs Beauclerk, Bull, Crofts, Samuel Gillam, West, &c. &c. used to attend, when he would produce some of his latest purchases. He generally husbanded them, and only produced a few at one time. He would exultantly say 'There, there is a curiosity! – what think you of

that' – though probably at the same time he had more than two or three copies in his possession. [Nichols & Bentley 1812, pp. 456–7]

Dibdin tells us that Ratcliffe 'hath a vehement love of green calf' [Dibdin 1817, ii, p. 505].

234. Nicole Gilles, *Annales et croniques de France*.

235. Thomas Berthelet, printer and bookbinder to Henry VIII. There was rivalry between him and the Raſtell family who were related by marriage to Sir Thomas More. In effeſt More and the King were fighting a propaganda war by proxy [Warner 1998]. His printing house was in Fleet Street 'nere to ye cundite at ye signe of Lucrece' [Duff 1905, p. 11].

236. John Day (1522–84), one of the great Elizabethan printers whose motto was 'Arise, for it is Day'. Archbishop Parker was his patron and Day published Parker's English translation of the Psalms. Day was one of the firſt English music printers and the firſt printer to produce an Anglo-Saxon type (for Parker's edition of Ælfric's *A teſtimonie of antiquitie*, 1567). He was also the firſt English printer to use a Garamond pica roman [Fergusson 1989, p. 12]. Day was the original printer of Foxe's *Martyrs*.

237. Ralph Newberie (fl. 1590), a Fleet Street printer. He published Richard Hakluyt's *The principall nauigations, voiages and discoueries of the English nation* with George Bishop in 1589 and Holinshed's *Chronicles* in 1587 with Bishop and others.

238. Thomas Marshe (fl.1554–84), printer. Began work in 1554 at the Prince's Arms (also called the King's Arms) in Fleet Street [Duff 1905, p. 100].

239. Richard Jugge (fl. 1531–71), Old Etonian printer. He and John Cawood were jointly printers to Elizabeth I. In 1568 he printed the first edition of the *Bishops' Bible* [Duff 1905, p. 82].

240. Edward Whytchurch or Whitchurch (d. 1562), publisher. He and Richard Grafton caused the first complete English Bible to be printed at Antwerp in 1537. They also paid for Coverdale's corrected *New Testament* to be printed in Paris in 1538. With the help of Thomas Berthelet, they then set up a press in London. From the end of his partnership with Grafton in about 1541, he operated from various addresses in Old Jewry until he took over what had once been Wynkyn de Worde's office at the Sun in Fleet Street. He published a number of important books including the Prayer Book and *Paraphrases of Erasmus* [Duff 1905, p. 169].

241. There were at least three printers of this name. John Wyer printed Bale's *Ymage of both churches* in 1550. Richard published *The rekenynge and declaration of the fayth of Huldrike Zwyngly* in 1548 and *Debate betwene the heraldes of Englande and Fraunce* in 1550. He also published *A christen sentence: and true iudgement of the moste honorable sacrament* (1548?). His shop was in St Paul's churchyard. Robert started printing in about 1529 at Charing Cross. He printed a large number of popular books and a few important ones such as *Defence of peace* [Duff 1905, pp. 175–6].

242. William Rastell and his father John, as noted elsewhere, were rival publishers to the King's Printer, Thomas Berthelet. William had a shop in St Bride's Churchyard.

John, an Oxford-educated barrister, was married to Sir Thomas More's sister Elizabeth. In 1517 he fitted out a ship to explore the New World with his chief printer as second-in-command, but they only made it as far as Waterford in Ireland. Later he designed the banqueting hall for the Field of the Cloth of Gold [Smith 1938, p. 431].

243. Robert Coplande (fl. 1508–47), printer, author and translator. In his translation of *Kyng Appolyn of Thyre* (1510) he says that he gladly follows 'the trace of my mayster Caxton'. Wynkyn de Worde left him ten marks in his will. A translation of *Le compost et kalendrier des bergiers*, probably by him, was published as *The kalender of shepeherdes* by Wynkyn de Worde in 1516 (dated 1508) and again in 1528. William Coplande, possibly his younger brother, was also a printer and published Robert's *Jyl of Braintfords Testament*.

244. Thomas Drant (1540?–78?). Both Spenser and Gabriel Harvey scorned the rules he formulated for writing quantitative verse, what Harvey referred to as 'Dranting of verses' [Mukherjee 2000].

245. This is *The shepheardes calender* [Spenser 1579] by Edmund Spenser (1552?–99).

246. *The castle of delight* was the first of a four-part miscellany, *The rocke of regard*, by the puritan George Whetstone (1544?–1587?).

247. Topham Beauclerk (1739–80), great-great-grandson of Charles II and Nell Gwyn. He was a friend of Dr Johnson and a renowned book-collector. His library 'to the number of upwards of thirty thousand volumes, in most languages, and upon almost every branch of science and polite literature' was sold by auction in 1781 by Samuel Paterson. He

also had an observatory at Muswell Hill and a chemical laboratory [Dibdin 1817, iii, p. 312].

J. Dalby said that he 'made it a rule never to lend a book to any person whatever. Mr. Gibbon was the only exception; who, I remember, when he was writing the Roman History, had the Byzantine authors a volume at a time' [Dibdin 1817, iii, p. 313].

248. Thomas Crofts (1722–81) accumulated a magnificent library including 'several thousand articles' of Italian literature and an almost complete set of Aldines [Crofts 1783, p. v]. The auction in 1783 consisted of 8,360 lots, from oriental history to Americana and Iberian poetry. There were also several Shakespeare quartos and other quartos attributed to Shakespeare (*Sir John Olde-Castle*, *A Yorkshire tragedy*) [Crofts 1783, pp. 260–1].

249. Major Thomas Pearson (1740?–81), whose library was sold in 1788 [Pearson 1788]. Dibdin writes of the 'bibliomaniacal Major' whose bird emblem on the backs of his books was recommendation enough [Dibdin 1817, ii, 505]. The manuscript of Middleton's *The witch* was amongst his possessions and was bought in 1788 by George Steevens for £2 14s. Malone bought it in 1800 for £17 10s and, with most of Malone's collection, it passed to the Bodleian Library in 1821 [Middleton 1950, p. v]. Also in the sale were Webbe's *Discourse of English poetrie* (1586), Puttenham's *Art of English poesie* (1589), *The castell of laboure* printed by Pynson (1505?), *England's Helicon* (1600), *The example of virtu* and the *Lyf of St. Ursula* printed by Wynkyn de Worde and ancient songs and ballads 'chiefly collected by Robert Earl of Oxford, and purchased at the sale of the library of James West, Esq., in 1773' [Dibdin 1842, pp. 403–6].

250. Michael Lort (1725–90) antiquary.

> There was also Mr. Lort, who is reckoned one of the most learned
> men alive; – he is also a Collector of Curiosities, alike in Literature &
> natural History: his manners are somewhat blunt & odd, & he is, all
> together, out of the common Road, without having chosen a better
> path.   [Burney 1994, pp. 111–2]

His library 'contained a great number of books rarely met with elsewhere; particularly of rare Tracts on the subjects of British Antiquities, and of curious Books and Pamphlets of every description…' [Nichols & Bentley 1812, ii, p. 605].

251. Probably John Woodhouse whose library was auctioned in 1803 by Leigh, Sotheby and Son [Woodhouse 1803].

252. John Brand (1744–1806), Secretary of the Society of Antiquaries. He was commissioned by Thomas Saint, proprietor of the *Newcastle courant,* to write a history of Newcastle upon Tyne [Sweet 1997]. The sale of his library took place in two parts, the first in May–June 1807, the second in February 1808 [Brand 1807].

253. *Pastyme of the people* was John Rastell's own work, 'a dull history book with very quaint woodcuts' [Smith 1938, p. 430].

254. Alexander Barclay (1475?–1552) translated Sebastian Brant's *Das Narrenschiff* into English, largely basing his text on Jacob Locher's Latin version, *Stultifera navis,* but drawing upon a French translation and the German original as well [Berdan 1920]. Pynson's edition was dated 1508 in error and was actually published in 1509. Wynkyn

de Worde published a translation by Henry Watson in the same year [Steinberg 1996]. This was presumably the same Henry Watson who was Wynkyn de Worde's apprentice [Plomer 1925].

255. Etienne Gabriel Peignot (1767–1849) published his *Dictionnaire raisonné de bibliologie* in 1802 and *Essai de curiosités bibliographiques* in 1804.

256. There are more like fifty Caxtons listed but it seems likely that some have been listed more than once. There are two individual *Polychronicon* lots and one lot of two copies, for instance. One of the two copies of the catalogue in the Wellcome Library (shelfmark 11389/B) bears the annotation 'he had upwards of thirty Caxtons' at the top of the first page.

257. That is, 'champaigne', an open landscape.

258. William Miller (1769–1844), a London publisher and bookseller for whom William Bulmer printed Valentia's *Travels* in 1809.

259.

> James Edwards of Halifax, invented a style of ornamenting calf by means of ordinary book stamps loaded with acid. The result is not unpleasing, and such books are known as 'Etruscan,' because many of the designs are of classical feeling – little urns, the Greek fret and the like. But Edwards' little acid burnt designs are only used as accessories; there is plenty of gold work and ordinary blind work upon them as well.   [Davenport 1930, p. 201]

260. George, Viscount Valentia (1769–1844).

261. Probably Sir Sidney Stafford Smyth. 'Baron' here does not indicate a member of the peerage but a judge of the Court of the Exchequer.

262. James Otridge (d. 1824) was a bookseller in the Strand, as was his father, William, before him [Maxted n.d.].

263. John Evelyn (1620–1706), one of the great English diarists. Like John Aubrey, he was one of the less scientifically-minded Fellows of the Royal Society.

264. Elias Ashmole (1617–92), antiquary, now remembered for founding the University of Oxford's Ashmolean Museum. Evelyn was scathing about Ashmole's plans to present the University of Oxford with John Tradescant's 'Ark': 'our *Alma Mater* men will be forc'd to play the Apes; You heare they talke already of founding a Laboratorie, have beg'd the Reliques of old Tradescant, to furnish a Repository' [Hunter 1981, pp. 146–7].

265. Edward Hyde, Earl of Clarendon (1609–74). His *History of the rebellion* was immensley profitable to Oxford University Press and helped pay for the conſtruction of its Clarendon Building. The Press ſtill uses the Clarendon Press imprint on many of its scholarly publications. A House of Lords decision of 1774 removed perpetual copyright in printed works, but an Aɛt of 1775 allowed the Press to preserve it in a few special cases and they chose to do so with this book [Carter 1975, pp. 367–9]. A new, illustrated edition was published in 1807 and, in 1816, Samuel Woodburn published a set of plates for Grangerising both Granger and Clarendon [Woodburn 1816].

266.

> A superb copy of this first edition sold, at M. de Cotte's, in 1804, for 3,601 *livres;* but it should be added that this very precious copy is in the finest condition; one might say that it is fresh off the press. Moreover, it is perhaps the *only one of which the margins have been neither trimmed nor cut.*

267. William Miller had published the first edition of Charles James Fox's *History* [Fox 1808] with a single plate (a portrait of Fox). Dibdin is referring to Miller's own Grangerised copy.

268. 'How I saw [you], how I perished! | How an awful madness swept me away!' Virgil, *Eclogues,* VIII, 41–2.

269. William Oldys (1696–1761), poet, antiquary and bibliographer. He worked with Dr Johnson on the Catalogue of the Harleian Library for the bookseller Osborne. He published anonymously *The British librarian* from January to June 1737 and subsequently reissued it as a single volume [Oldys 1737]. He annotated his interleaved copy of *An account of the English dramatick poets* by Gerard Langbaine (1656–1692) and this later became the basis of Theophilus Cibber's *Lives of the poets.*

270. Ludolf Kuster (1670-1716), a classical scholar from Westphalia. He published an edition of Suidas's Greek lexicon which was printed by the University Press, Cambridge [Suidas 1705]. Dibdin says that Kuster's edition is the best [Dibdin 1808, ii, 394].

271. Jacob Philipp (Jacques Philippe) D'Orville (1696–1751), Professor of History, Eloquence and Greek at the Univer-

sity of Amsterdam. His manuscripts are now in the Bodleian Library.

272. Narcissus Luttrell (1657–1732), English diarist and antiquary. He amassed a large collection of ballads, pamphlets and broadsides, now in the British Library. He dated these items with what modern scholarship has shown to be dates of publication, not purchase, thus providing valuable information [Parks 1999, p. 10]. His collection of seventeenth-century book sale catalogues is also in the British Library. While MP for Saltash, he compiled a parliamentary diary [Luttrell 1972]. He also kept a record of contemporary events over nearly forty years [Luttrell 1857]. The Luttrell Psalter is not named after him, but Sir Geoffrey Luttrell.

273. Walter Scott published both a life of the dramatist John Dryden, and a collected edition of his works (including the biography) in 1808.

274. The catalogue of the fabulous library of Justin, Comte de MacCarthy Reagh, (1744–1811) was published by the de Bures [MacCarthy Reagh 1815, 1817] and sold in 1817. Among its treasures was a Gutenberg Bible on vellum (the Grenville copy), now in the British Library. Dibdin gives some details of the sale in his *Bibliographical decameron* [Dibdin 1817, pp. 162–80].

275. George III's magnificent library was given to the nation by George IV in 1823 and is now the centrepiece of the British Library in St Pancras, its beautifully tooled bindings displayed in a towering column of glass and bronze.

276. George Spencer (1739–1817), sixth Earl of Sunderland and the fourth Duke of Marlborough.

277. Hafod House, which included an octagonal library designed by John Nash [Davis 1960, p. 10], burnt down in 1807. Thomas Johnes (1748–1816) founded a private press at Hafod which was active from 1803 to 1810. An edition of Froissart's *Chronicles* was the first publication of the Hafod Press [Glaister 1960, p.167]. Johnes bought Alchorne's library in 1813 [Dibdin 1817, iii, p. 83].

278. Richard Heber (1773–1833) came from a wealthy landed family. His half-brother Reginald was Bishop of Calcutta. He showed an interest in books from an early age, first only Greek and Latin classics, but later diversifying into English plays and poems. He was a close friend of Dibdin's and is referred to as ATTICUS in later editions of *Bibliomania*.

Of all Dibdin's close acquaintances, Heber was the one most clearly suffering from book madness. At the time of his death, he had eight houses (two in London, one each at Hodnet, Oxford, Paris, Brussels, Antwerp and Ghent) all overflowing with books. This made finding his will particularly difficult; it was eventually found by Dibdin in Heber's Pimlico residence in 1834 [Dibdin 1836, pp. 443–4]. He was painted as a young boy, holding a cricket bat and ball, by the American-born artist John Singleton Copley, in 1782. The picture is now in the Yale Center for British Art.

279. 'That is written in this lytyl book,' wrote Caxton in his prologue, 'ought the prestes to lerne and teche to theyr parysshens and also it is necessary for symple prestes that understonde not the scriptures' [Blake 1975, p. 77].

280. This is presumably the edition edited by Brunck [Virgil 1789].

281. *The chase* by William Somervile (1675–1742) was originally printed in 1735 as *The chace*. The 1796 edition [Somervile 1796] was printed by Bulmer and has wood engravings by Thomas Bewick and his brother John (who died in 1795).

> The Bulmer editions in Royal quarto of Poems by Goldsmith and Parnell, 1795, and the companion volume of Somervile Chase, 1796, the first 'fine' English books illustrated with woodcuts, are typographically the most notable of the books illustrated by Bewick and his pupils. How highly Bulmer regarded the engravings may be seen from his Advertisement to the Poems where he says: 'The ornaments are all engraved on blocks of wood, by two of my earliest acquaintances, Messrs. Bewick, of Newcastle-upon-Tyne and London, after designs made from the most interesting passages in the Poems they embellish. They have been executed with great care, and I may venture to say, without being supposed to be influenced by ancient friendship, that they form the most extraordinary effort of the art of engraving upon wood that ever was produced in any age, or any country. Indeed it seems almost impossible that such delicate effects could be obtained from blocks of wood.' [Ruzicka 1943, p. 20]

Sadly, Somervile's writing fails to live up to the presentation: 'So from their kennel rush the joyous pack; | A thousand wanton gaieties express | Their inward ecstasy, their pleasing sport | Once more indulged, and liberty restored…' etc., etc.

282. Another fine Bulmer edition with Bewick wood engravings (see above).

283. A handsome edition with illustrations by Francesco Bartolozzi.

284. A book no bibliomaniac could resist: a gothic novel purporting to be translated from the Italian of 'Onuphrio Muralto' but actually written by the noted English bibliophile Horace Walpole, printed by the great Italian printer and typographer, Giambattista Bodoni.

285. A collection of madrigals [Sainte-Maure 1784]. They were compiled (and many were written) by Charles de Sainte-Maure, duc de Montausier (1610–90) for Julie d'Angennes whom he married in 1645.

286. The first part of *The economy of human life* (spelt 'œconomy' in some editions), which purports to be translated from an Indian manuscript, is sometimes attributed to Robert Dodsley (1703–64), the footman turned poet, and sometimes to Philip Dormer Stanhope, fourth Earl of Chesterfield (1694–1773). It was first published in 1750. The second part is by John Hill (1714?–75).

> No book published in the eighteenth century was issued in more separate printings than Dodsley *Œconomy*. In the fifty years that remained of the century after its publication, the *Œconomy* appeared in approximately two hundred editions, and another hundred followed in the next century.   [Solomon 1996, p. 139]

I have identified only one British octavo edition published in 1794, that printed for A. Millar, W. Law, & R. Cater, London [Dodsley 1794]. It is hard to imagine why this edition should fetch fifteen guineas, especially when Bodoni's quarto edition of *The castle of Otranto* only fetched £13 2s 6d. The popularity of *The economy of human life* with its overwhelming banality and anachronistic style ('Let not thy mirth be so extravagant as to intoxicate thy mind; nor thy sorrow so heavy as to depress thy heart...', etc.) is hard to fathom. Who, though, could resist the 1806 edition [Dodsley 1806], with Samuel Harding's drawings beautifully rendered as stipple engravings by William Gardiner?

287. A type facsimile was published in 1807 [Shakespeare 1807].

288. David Ancillon (1617–92) was a Protestant who was obliged to leave France after the revocation of the Edict of Nantes and became pastor to the French expatriate community in Berlin. His son Charles (1659–1715) was appointed 'Juge et Directeur de Colonie de Berlin' by the Elector Frederick. In 1690 he wrote *Histoire de l'établissement des francois dans les états de son altesse electorale de Brandebourg* and *La France intéressée à rétablir l'Édit de Nantes*.

289. Isaac D'Israeli (1766–1848), a prominent literary critic and father to the future British Prime Minister, Benjamin Disraeli, published the first volumes of his *Curiosities of literature* with John Murray I in 1791. Further volumes were published by John Murray II. Saintsbury wrote that:

> Isaac D'Israeli was not a good writer… But his anecdotage, though, as perhaps such anecdotage is bound to be, not extremely accurate, is almost inexhaustibly amusing, and indicates a real love as well as a wide knowledge of letters.   [Saintsbury 1896, p. 180]

Writing of his time at Oxford, Dibdin said that D'Israeli's *Curiosities of literature* 'was the companion of my evening hours and lone musings beyond midnight' [Dibdin 1836, p.87].

290. Paul Colomiès (1638–92), French librarian and writer.

> Among the learned people with whom he mixed, there was none he had closer business dealings with than Isaac Vossius and I think

that if he left for England early, before the Protestants of France
endured the harsher blows of the storm which overwhelmed the
Edict of Nantes, it was because Isaac Vossius had become Canon
of Windsor.'   [Bayle 1740, ii, p. 195]

Colomiès was appointed librarian at Lambeth Palace and
rector of Eynesford in Kent. He was naturalised in 1688.

291. Jacob Friedrich Reimann whose *Catalogus bibliothecæ
theologicæ* is mentioned by Dibdin as being 'an interesting
publication' [Dibdin 1808, i, p. xvi].

292. François Grud, Sieur de la Croix du Maine, (1552–92).
His *Bibliothèque* was published in two volumes in 1584. A
new edition, with Antoine du Verdier's complementary
Bibliothèque (1585), was published in 1772–3, with additional
matter by Jean Antoine Rigoley de Juvigny and Bernard de
La Monnoye.

293. Konrad Gesner (1516–65) was a professor at the University of Zurich. His *Bibliotheca universalis* was printed in
Zurich by Christoph Froschauer in 1545. Froschauer, a Ba-
varian by birth, was closely associated with the Reformation.
His nephew of the same name printed the 1583 edition.

294. Johann Vogt (1695–1764) in his *Catalogus historico-criticus librorum rariorum* published in Hamburg by Christian
Herold in 1753.

295. This 'very able editor' was Henry Ellis (1777–1869),
Head of the Department of Printed Books at the British
Museum. He became Principal Librarian in 1827 and was
knighted in 1828.

296. This is presumably the edition printed in that year by John Kynsgton [Fabyan 1559].

297. A copy of the First Folio, but hardly a fine copy, was given by John Ker, third Duke of Roxburghe (1740–1804), to the bookseller George Nicol in about 1790. It is now in the Folger Shakespeare Library. The Duke's library was sold at auction in 1812 [Roxburghe 1812]. As Werner Gundersheimer remarked, 'The plain truth is that the First Folio, leaving aside its indisputable cultural importance, is not a particularly rare book' [Blayney 1991, p. v]. Indeed, the Folger Shakespeare Library alone has 80 copies.

298. Johann Georg Schelhorn (1693–1773), Lutheran theologian and antiquarian. His *Amœnitates* was a rich compilation of information on printers, libraries, rare books and antiquities.

299. Leiden had been freed from Spanish rule in 1574 and the university there was founded in the following year. Louis Elzevir, a bookbinder and bookseller from Louvain, set up his publishing company in this new centre of Protestant learning in 1593. Although Louis and his successors were not great scholars like the Estiennes, the company was one of the most important academic publishers until it closed in 1791. Elzevir's typography and printing were acceptable rather than outstanding, but the firm produced cheap duodecimo classics which became very popular.

300. The library catalogue of Károly Imre Sándor, Count Reviczky (1737–93), was originally published in 1784 under the pseudonym Periergus Deltophilus [Deltophilus 1784]. A new edition was published under his own name after

his death [Reviczky 1794]. Earl Spencer bought his library which, with the rest of the Spencer collection, is now in the John Rylands Library, Manchester. Dibdin says that Reviczky, was 'an ardent and not unlearned bibliographer; but his taste, in his choice of books was far from being attic. He was infected also with the heresy of a love of "washing, cleansing and ruling"' [Dibdin 1817, iii, p. 395].

301. Thomas Tyrwhitt (1730–86), classicist, who studied for the Bar but did not practise. He turned his philological talents to the study of English literature, including Shakespeare, Chaucer and 'Rowley'. His edition of the *Canterbury tales* [Chaucer 1775–78] was so thorough and well-informed that many of his notes are incorporated into modern editions, and his edition of Rowley [Chatterton 1777] convinced nearly everyone that the poems were the work of Chatterton.

302. There is no letterpress in this edition of Horace. The whole book was engraved on copper by John Pine (1690–1756). It is said to be the finest English book of this sort [Davenport 1930, p. 118].

303. Richard Porson (1759-1808), English classical scholar, promoted a new style of Greek type. Bagster, writing to Dibdin, said 'The Greek and Roman type I think will also be admired for the delicate neatness of their execution. The Hebrew and Greek types are of the neatest form, and the latter is that of Porson...' while Talbot Baines Reed commented 'It may be doubted if the Porsonian letter would be recognized by an ancient Greek scribe as the character of his native land; but at any rate it is neat, elegant, and legible, and dispenses with all useless contractions and ligatures' [Reed 1952, pp. 333, 54–5]. See also note 317.

304. That is, Sir Walter Scott, who is SIR TRISTREM in later editions of *Bibliomania*.

305. The very crudeness of the type, that very black and rough appearance of the letters *touches the senses beautifully,* etc.

306. This short book [Mascall 1600] is actually adapted by Leonard Mascall (d. 1589) from the first part of the *Boke of Saint Albans*. It had first been published in this form ten years earlier [Mascall 1590].

307. The pamphlet [Greene 1620] is one of several editions (the first being in 1592) of this work by Robert Greene (1558?–92) who is mostly remembered for referring to Shakespeare as an 'upstart crow, beautified with our feathers' in his *Groats-worth of witte* [Greene 1592, FI verso].

308. Bartholomæus Anglicus, thirteenth-century English Franciscan whose *De proprietatibus rerum* was the most popular late medieval encyclopædia because of its 'superior organization... and its extensive extracts from Aristotle and Arabic scholars' [Mantello & Rigg 1996, p. 704]. It is suggested as a source for Shakespeare's 'Seven ages of man'.

309. Stephen Batman (d. 1584), who edited and augmented John Trevisa's English translation of Bartholomæus for the press [Bartholomæus 1582].

310. This book [Wiburn 1581], by the prominent Puritan Perceval Wiburn (d. 1606), was a response to *A brief discours contayning certayne reasons why Catholiques refuse to goe to church* by 'John Howlet', i.e. Robert Parsons (1546–1610),

director of the English Jesuit Mission. Parsons's book [Parsons 1580] was produced on the secret Greenstreet House Press he had helped to set up [Wagner 1999, p.230]. Only some eight books were issued from this press [Peck 1977].

311. An anti-Marprelate tract thought to be by John Lyly (1554?–1606).

312. Although Thomas Sydenham (1624–89) was called the 'English Hippocrates', the fact that his medical works were still being reprinted [Sydenham 1809] when *Bibliomania* appeared, 120 years after his death, is surprising.

313. William Heberden (1710–1801), English physician. Benjamin Franklin was a friend of Heberden and persuaded him to write a pamphlet on smallpox inoculation (not to be confused with vaccination which was introduced by Edward Jenner in the 1790s) to which Franklin appended his own pamphlet on the success of inoculation. The two were printed together [Franklin & Heberden 1759]. Heberden's part says 'Printed at the expence of the author, to be given away in America'.

Dr Johnson called Heberden 'the last of the learned physicians' and Fanny Burney said of him 'he knows so much of Physic, that Mrs. Thrale is never so happy as when her Husband is with him' [Burney 1994, pp. 318–9]. His work of ten years, *Commentarii de morborum historia et curatione* [Heberden 1802], was published postumously in 1802 and an English translation, believed to by his son (William Jr) was also published in that year [Heberden & Heberden 1802].

314. *The Harleian miscellany* was a selection from manuscripts and pamphlets collected by Robert Harley, first Earl

of Oxford, and his son Edward. The Harleian collection was bought by the bookseller Thomas Osborne who employed Dr Johnson and William Oldys to catalogue it and Oldys to edit the *Miscellany*, to which Johnson contributed a preface. It was published by Osborne [Harley 1744–6]. Lady Harley, wife of the fifth Earl of Oxford, had several children as the result of extra-marital affairs, and these were also known as the 'Harleian miscellany'.

315. John Somers, Baron Somers of Evesham (1651–1716), distinguished English lawyer and one of the architects of the Glorious Revolution. He was appointed Solicitor General in 1689 and Lord Chancellor in 1697. *A collection of scarce and valuable tracts* [Somers 1748] draws heavily on his collection, as does a revised edition by Sir Walter Scott [Somers 1809–15]. Swift dedicated *A tale of a tub* to Somers.

316. The Royal Institution was founded in 1799 by the exiled American royalist, Benjamin Thompson, Count Rumford (1753–1814), the inventor of a better fireplace. It is the only one of the four institutions referred to which has survived, and it continues to play an important role in British science. The great Sir Humphry Davy (1778–1829) was Professor of Chemistry at the Royal Institution and performed his electrolytical experiments there to much public amazement. Michael Faraday (1791–1867), who had been apprenticed to a bookbinder, attended one of Davy's lectures and, after demonstrating his enthusiasm and competence by writing up the lecture, was appointed Davy's assistant. Faraday went on to become one of the most innovative scientific thinkers of the nineteenth century.

Dibdin himself delivered twenty-eight lectures on 'English literature' at the Royal Institution from 1806 to 1808.

He records that there was an audience for his first talk of about 500. He also lectured there on 'The art of printing'. It fell to Dibdin to inform the audience at a meeting in December 1807 that Humphry Davy had fallen seriously ill [Dibdin 1836, pp. 230–48].

317. The London Institution, Old Jewry (and later Finsbury Circus). Richard Porson (see note 303) was the first librarian and died there in 1808. William Maltby, quoted in [Rogers 1856, p.333], remarked 'A man of such habits as Porson was little fitted for the office of Librarian to the London Institution. He was very irregular in his attendance there; he never troubled himself about the purchase of books which ought to have been added to the library; and he would frequently come home dead drunk long after midnight.'

Dibdin repeated his Royal Institution lectures on 'The art of printing' at the London Institution in 1823. He was 'much struck by the number of female Quakers in those audiences; and still more so with the evident marks of satisfaction which the specimens of ballad-poetry produced upon them' [Dibdin 1836, p. 238].

318. The Surrey Institution (commonly referred to as 'the Surry') was in Blackfriars. Coleridge gave lectures there 1812–13 [Coleridge 2000, iv, p. 925] and Hazlitt gave a number of successful lectures there, too [Grayling 2003], apparently including one on William Roscoe's *Lorenzo de' Medici* [Harling 1938, p. 29]. Rowlandson produced a print of Friedrich Christian Accum lecturing on chemistry there.

319. The Russell Institution for the Promotion of Literary and Scientific Knowledge, created by the house-builder

James Burton (1781–1837), was 'a kind of social centre, in Coram Street, combined Greek Doric columns and Roman arches in a peculiarly graceless fashion and was justifiably sat on by the critics'[Summerson 1945, p. 154]. It is one of the many clubs to which Phileas Fogg did not belong [Verne 1995, p. 7]. Coleridge toyed with the idea of lecturing there, although there is no evidence that he actually did so [Coleridge 2000, iv, pp. 925, 926].

320.

A good bibliography, be it general or specific, be it lay or ecclesiastical, be it national, regional or local, be it simply personal, in a word, of whatever type it might be, is not so easy a task as many people might imagine it to be; nonetheless, they should in no way be warned off it. It is such that it cannot fail to be good, useful, and worthy of being pursued by literary history enthusiasts.

321.

He should have a complex knowledge of books and materials so that he can, at least, choose and seek out the better ones; the trustworthy and diligent cultivation of foreigners so that he can obtain them [books]; the greatest patience to watch out for those rarely available; always in command of private funds so that, when they present themselves, he can take the opportunity to buy them; and finally, a prudent disdain for gold and silver so that he may willingly do without the money which must be expended on the formation and upkeep of a library. If, by chance, a man of letters achieves that degree of happiness which allows him to acquire such treasure, let him not enjoy it selfishly alone, but he should be willing to share its use freely with the learned people who have devoted their waking hours to the public good.

322. Rev. James Beresford (1764–1840) wrote this amusing book in 1806 under the name Timothy Testy. It went through innumerable editions [Beresford 1806].

323. Dibdin tells us that Sykes:

> ... left behind such a memorial of his ardour in the collection of BOOKS and PRINTS, considered conjointly, as has not been equalled. The amount for both sales was 36,436 *l*... Never did the owner of such treasures more enjoy them! Never was one more keen in their acquisition! Sweynheym and Pannartz, and Hollar, were the gods of his idolatry!' [Dibdin 1836, p. 321]

324.

> 'Here,' you say, 'I forbid anyone to crap.' Paint two snakes.

The prohibition is of a sort often placed on Roman religious monuments. Clearly, the Romans had a problem with vandalism long before the coming of the Vandals.

> 'Pinge duos angues' are the words of Persius obeying orders. Snakes were commonly painted or carved on sacred places to represent the Genius loci, and to protect the walls from this sort of profanation' [Juvenal & Persius 1867, p. 386]

325. *Les quatre Facardins* [Hamilton 1730] by Anthony, Count Hamilton (1646–1720), was translated by 'Monk' Lewis, who completed it.

326. Matthew Gregory Lewis MP (1775–1818), *Romantic tales* [Lewis 1808]. Lewis specialised in gothic horror. He was commonly called 'Monk' Lewis after his most successful book, *The monk: a romance* [Lewis 1796].

327. Gabriele Giolito de' Ferrari (d. 1578) took over the press started in Venice by his father, Giovanni. His great significance is as a publisher of Italian literature.

He published almost thirty editions of Ariosto's work and reprinted Petrarch and Bocaccio [Steinberg 1996, pp. 35–6]. He also published the poetess, Laura Bacio Terracina (1519–c. 1577), whom Marcantonio Passero lauded as the latest 'mostro del sesso femminile' [Shemek 1998, p. 127]

328. Giambattista Bodoni (1740–1813), great Italian printer, typographer and type designer who served as an apprentice in the press of the Propaganda Fide. He left Rome after his kind employer, Ruggeri, committed suicide. He took charge of the Stamperia Reale at Parma in 1768 and was later appointed honorary printer to Carlos III of Spain [Updike 1922, ii, pp. 163–6].

Bodoni's legacy consists of the 'Modern' founts ('Didone' in the barbarous and ill-conceived Euro-speak of the British Standard [BSI 1967]) with strong vertical stress and unbracketed serifs. The types were well suited to the simple elegance of the age but required Bodoni's high standards of presswork and typography to really shine.

329. The formidable French printing family of Didot made major contributions to printing and typography over more than a century. The most famous are Firmin (1764–1836) and Pierre l'aîné (1761–1853). Firmin's types, which are 'Modern' faces, have been lovingly recreated in seven optical sizes by Hoefler & Frere-Jones of New York.

330. Joachín Ibarra (1725–85), the Spanish contemporary (and many would say equal) of Didot and Bodoni, was printer to the Spanish court. His edition of Don Quixote,

published in 1780 for the Spanish Royal Academy, was a work of great beauty. Although influenced by Didot, Bodoni and possibly Baskerville, Ibarra produced types and typography of a distinctly Iberian character

331. Alexandre de Laborde (1773–1842), *Voyage pittoresque et historique de l'Espagne* [Laborde 1806–20], a fine-looking book printed by Pierre Didot *l'ainé*.

332.

> There needs also to be space for noting down things which occur to writers out of the ordinary, i.e. from other sources than those they are studying; for often excellent ideas interrupt us which should not be inserted but which it is not safe to discard.

333. Sir Aston Cokain (1608-84), an undistinguished poet and playwright.

334. Robert Fletcher, whose *Ex otio negotium. Or, Martiall his epigrams translated* was published in 1656.

335. James Shirley (1596–1666), poet and dramatist. The lines are from the song 'The glories of our blood and state' in his *Contention of Ajax and Ulysses*, 1659.

336. 'Now will not violets grow from the grave mound and her fortunate ashes?'

337. Richard Lovelace (1618–57/8), poet.

338. William Painter (1540?–94), who is thought to have translated Curione's 'Pasquillus ecstaticus'.

339. Menander (342–291 BC), Greek playwright. His work was mostly known from small quotations in Ferriar's time, but substantial fragments of four plays on papyrus were discovered in 1905.

340. Antimachus of Colophon (5th century BC), scholarly Greek poet. Very little of his work seems to have survived.

341. Sappho (7th century BC), Greek poetess famous for her love poetry addressed to other women. Very little of her poetry was known at the time Ferriar was writing. More fragments on papyrus were recovered in the twentieth century.

342. This is rather confusing. Aristophanes follows the traditional version of the story in which Philomela is turned into a swallow. It is her sister Prokne who is turned into a nightingale. The Latin authors reversed these roles.

343. The Caliph Omar I was said to have ordered the burning of the Library at Alexandria.

344. 'Let humble Allen, with an awkward shame, | Do good by stealth, and blush to find it fame.' Pope, *Epilogue to Satire Dialogue* 1, lines 135–6.

345. William Faithorne the elder (1616?-91) was an artist and engraver. He copied the Droeshout portrait of Shakespeare in the First Folio for the 1640 edition of *The rape of Lucrece*, and engraved many other portraits including that of Milton for *The history of Britain* (1670). His son, William Jr (1656–1710), also produced many engraved portraits.

346. Not Richard (as the Portico Library's edition suggests [Ferriar 1996, p. 30]) but John Field (d. 1668) who printed Vere's *Commentaries*. His great claim to fame was to print a 32mo Bible in Pearl type (approximately 5pt) in 1653 which was said to contain over 6,000 mistakes due to the difficuly of proofreading such small type [Reed 1952, pp. 41–2]. It is said that he used silver type, although it may have been silver-plated [Reed 1952, p. 101].

Field (who styled himself 'Printer to Parliament') and Henry Hills held the Bible monopoly under Cromwell. In 1655 he was appointed Printer to the University of Cambridge [Black 1984, p. 76].

347. 'Delicate ears rejoice at the forename.' Although Ferriar attributes this to Juvenal, it is Horace, *Satires*, II, v, 32.

348. Sir Francis Vere (1560–1609) was an English soldier whose *Commentaries* describe his military service in the Low Countries. Also included is an account of the Battle of Nieuport by Sir John Ogle (1569–1640), his friend and companion

349. Guarding is a term for inserting single leaves or pairs of leaves into a book by attaching them to strips of cloth or paper before sewing. The 'guarded leaves' here are thus the illustrations inserted to Grangerise the book.

350. Cacus or Kakos, a giant of Greek mythology.

351. Giovanni Vittorio Rossi (1577–1647) used the pen name Giano Nicio Eritreo (Latinised as Janus Nicius Erythræus). He published his *Pinacotheca*, or picture gallery, in 1643.

352. Erasmus Darwin (1731–1802), in his *Botanic garden* (first published 1791), wrote of malaria:

> Before, with shuddering limbs, cold Tremor reels,
> And Fever's burning nostril dogs his heels;
> Loud claps the grinning fiend his iron hands,
> Stamps with black hoof, and shouts along the lands;
> [Darwin 1824, p. 159]

Erasmus Darwin (grandfather of the even more famous Charles) was one of the most remarkable thinkers of the age.

353. The seaside town of Margate in Kent was an early holiday resort. It did not have the social pretensions which Brighton had acquired with the arrival of the Prince Regent.

354. Guillaume Bouchet (1513–94), a rather insignificant French author given to misogynistic comments such as 'La bigamie consiste a avoir une femme de trop; la monogamie aussi' and 'Il y a mille inventions pour faire parler les femmes, mais pas une seule pour les faire taire.'

355. Thomas Stanley (1749–1818), MP for Lancashire. He was 'a well-versed scholar, a finished gentleman, and an honest man' [Dibdin 1817, iii, 78].

356. Joachim Du Bellay (1522–1560), French poet. In *La deffence et illustration de la langue Françoyse* [Du Bellay 1549] he argued that the french language was not yet suitable for fine poetry. With *Les regrets* [Du Bellay 1558], many thought he had disproved his own thesis.

357. Pasquinades, or pasquils, were a type of satirical writing, often at the expense of the Papal authorities. They were originally attached to a statue in Rome which had been dubbed 'Pasquin'. Celio Secondo Curione published a collection of them, *Pasquillorum tomi duo*, in 1544, including his own 'Pasquillus ecstaticus' which someone, possibly William Painter, translated as *Pasquine in a traunce* [Curione 1566].

In *Pantagruel*, the library of St Victor is said to contain '*Pasquilli, doctiris marmorei, de capreolis cum chardoneta comedendis, tempore papali ab Ecclesia interdicto*' [Rabelais 1964, p. 113], i. e. Pasquin, marble doctor, on eating wild goat with cardoons, forbidden by the Church during the Papal period (a pun on *tempore Paschali*, at Easter-time).

In England, the character of Pasquin or Pasquill took up arms against the Puritans in anti-Marprelate tracts, notably *A countercuffe given to Martin Iunior*, 1589, which was formerly ascribed to Thomas Nash [Pasquill 1589].

358. 'I wander through groves where pleasant waters rise and breezes rustle.' Horace, *Odes*, III, iv, 7–8. In the 1809 edition (or BL 78.f.7 and the Portico Library copy, at least) *amœnæ* is misspelt *æmænæ*.

Select Bibliography

Addison, Joseph (1804), *The works of the Right Honourable Joseph Addison*, Thomas Tickell (ed.), London: printed for Vernor and Hood [etc.].

Alchorne, Stanesby (1773), 'A catalogue of the fifty plants, from Chelsea garden, presented to the Royal Society, by the Worshipful Company of Apothecaries for the Year 1771, pursuant to the direction of the late Sir Hans Sloane, Bart. M. D. Sec. Reg. nuper Præses: by Stanesby Alchorne, member of the said Society of Apothecaries in London', *Philosophical transactions of the Royal Society of London*, XIII, part 1, pp. 30–37.

Alchorne, Stanesby (1813), *Catalogue of a portion of the valuable library of the late Stanesby Alchorne: containing various rare books and first editions printed in the fifteenth century ... To which are added the valuable duplicates of a nobleman. The whole will be sold by auction, on Saturday, the 22nd of May by R.H. Evans*, London: printed by W. Bulmer and Co.

Ames, Joseph (1749), *Typographical antiquities; being an historical account of printing in England: with some memoirs of our antient printers, and a register of the books printed by them, from the year MCCCCLXXI to the year MDC. With an appendix concerning printing in Scotland and Ireland to the same time*, London: printed by W. Faden and sold by J. Robinson.

Ames, Joseph (1810–1819), *Typographical antiquities; or, The history of printing in England, Scotland, and Ireland: containing memoirs of our ancient printers, and a register of the books printed by them begun by the late Joseph Ames; considerably augmented by William Herbert; and now greatly enlarged, with copious notes, and illustrated with appropriate engravings comprehending the history of English literature and a view of the progress of the art of engraving in Great Britain by Thomas Frognall Dibdin*, London: William Miller [vol. 3 John Murray, vol. 4 Longman, etc.].

Anon (1712), *A full and impartial account of the discovery of sorcery and witchcraft practis'd by Jane Wenham of Walkerne in Hertfordshire. Upon the bodies of Anne Thorn, Anne Street, &c: the proceedings against her from her being first apprehended, till she was committed to gaol by Sir Henry Chauncy. Also her tryal at the assizes at Hertford before Mr. Justice Powell, where she was found guilty of felony and witchcraft, and receiv'd sentence of death for the same, March 4. 1711-12*, London: printed for E. Curll, at the Dial and Bible against St. Dunstan's Church in Fleetstreet.

Anon (1712a), *The impossibility of witchcraft: plainly proving, from Scripture and reason, that there never was a witch, and that it is both irrational and impious to believe there ever was: in which the depositions against Jane Wenham, lately try'd and condemn'd for a witch, at Hertford, are confuted and expos'd,* London: printed, and sold by J. Baker.

Aravamudan, Srinivas (1999), *Tropicopolitans: colonialism and agency, 1688-1804,* Durham, N.C: Duke University Press.

Arnold, John H. (2000), *History: a very short introduction,* Oxford: Oxford University Press.

Ascham, Roger (1545), *Toxophilvs: the schole of shootinge conteyned in tvvo bookes: to all gentlemen and yomen of Englande, pleasaunte for theyr pastyme to rede, and profitabie for theyr use to folow, both in war and peace,* London: in ædibus Edouardi VVhytchurch.

Ascham, Roger (1570), *The Scholemaster. Or plaine and perfite way of teachyng children, to vnderstand, write and speake, the Latin tong, but specially purposed for the priuate brynging up of youth in jentlemen and noble mens houses, and commodious also for such, as haue forgot the Latin tonge, and would, by themselues, without a scholemaster, in short tyme, and with small paines, recouer a sufficient habilitie, to vnderstand, write and speake Latin,* London: Iohn Daye.

Aubrey, John (2000), *Brief lives together with an apparatus for the lives of our English mathematical writers and the life of Thomas Hobbes of Malmesbury,* John Buchanan-Brown ed., Harmondsworth: Penguin Books.

Bale, John (1544), *The epistle exhortatorye of an Englyshe Christyane vnto his derelye beloued co[n]treye of Englande : against the pompouse popyshe bysshoppes therof, as yet the true members of theyr fylthye father the great Antichrist of Rome,* Henry Stalbrydge, Antwerp: A. Goinus.

Bale, John (1548), *Illvstrivm Maioris Britanniæ Scriptorvm, Hoc Est, Angliæ, Cambriæ, ac Scotiæ Summariu, in quasdam centurias diuisum, cum diuersitate doctrinaru atq; bannoru recta supputatione per omnes ætates a Iapheto sanctissimi Noah filio, ad annum domini. M.D.XLVIII,* Ipswich: per Ioannem Ouerton.

Bartholomæus Anglicus (1582), *Batman uppon Bartholome, his booke, de proprietatibus rerum, newly corrected, enlarged and ammended: with such additions as are requisite, unto every severall booke: taken foorth of the most approved authors, the like heretofore not translated in English. Profitable for all estates, as well for the benefite of the mind as the bodie,* Stephen Batman (ed.) & John Trevisa (trans), London: Thomas East.

Battestin, Martin C (2000), *A Henry Fielding companion,* Westport, CN: Greenwood Press.

Bayle, Pierre (1740), *Dictionaire historique et critique, 5e édition, revue, corrigée, et augmentée avec la vie de l'auteur, par Mr Des Maizeaux,* Pierre Des Maizeaux, Eusèbe Renaudot, & Anthelme de Tricaud (eds), Amsterdam [&c.]: chez P. Brunel [et al.].

Berdan, John M. (1920), *Early Tudor poetry,* New York: Macmillan.

Beresford, James (1806), *The miseries of human life; or, the groans of Timothy Testy, and Samuel Sensitive. With a few supplementary sighs from Mrs. Testy. In twelve dialogues,* London: William Miller.

Berners, Juliana (1486), *Here in thys boke afore ar contenyt the bokys of haukyng and huntyng with other plesuris dyuerse as in the boke apperis and also of Cootarmuris a nobull werke. And here now endyth the boke of blasyng of armys translatyt and compylyt to gedyr at Seynt Albons,* St Albans: Schoolmaster Printer.

Berners, Juliana (1496), *Book of hawking, hunting, and heraldry*, Westminster: Wynkyn de Worde.

Black, M. H. (1984), *Cambridge University Press 1584–1984*, Cambridge: Cambridge University Press.

Blades, William (2004), *Enemies of books, revised and enlarged by the author*, Nevada City, CA: eBookMall.

Blake, N. F. (1975), *Caxton's own prose*, London: André Deutsch.

Blayney, Peter W. M (1991), *The first folio of Shakespeare*, Washington, D.C: Folger Library Publications.

Bodleian Library (n.d.), Department of Printed Books (Western): 'Alphabetical guide to shelfmarks and named special collections of printed books'.

Borrhaus, Martin (1551), *Martini Borrhai Stugardiani In tres Aristotelis de arte dicendi libros commentaria / Hermolai Barbari, eorundem versio, cum græco textu capitibus suis distincto, & figuris Aristotelicam methodum indicantibus illustrato. Accessit geminus ac locuples rerum & verborum memorabilium index*, Basle: Impensis Ioannis Oporini.

Bowles, William Lisle (1789), *Fourteen sonnets, elegiac and descriptive: written during a tour*, Bath: printed by R. Cruttwell, and sold by C. Dilly, London.

Brand, John (1807), *Bibliotheca Brandiana: a catalogue of the unique, scarce, rare, curious, and numerous collection of works on the antiquity, topography, and decayed intelligence of Great Britain and Ireland, from the first invention of printing down to the present time;... being the entire library of the late Rev. John Brand, Fellow and Secretary of the Antiquarian Society, author of the History of Newcastle, Popular antiquities, &c., &c. which will be sold by auction, by order of his executors, by Mr. Stewart, at his room, no.194, Piccadilly, (opposite Albany,) on Wednesday, May 6, 1807, and thirty-six following days*, London: Stewart.

Broome, John (1955), 'Bayle's Biographer: Pierre des Maizeaux', *French Studies*, **9** (1), pp. 1–17.

Bruce, John & Nichols, John Gough (1863), *Wills from Doctors' Commons: a selection from the wills of eminent persons proved in the Prerogative Court of Canterbury, 1495-1695*, London: The Camden Society.

Brydges, Samuel Egerton (1805–1809), *Censura literaria, containing ttles, abstracts, and opinions of old English books, with original disquisitions, articles of biography, and other literary antiquities*, London: Longman, Hurst, Rees, and Orme.

BSI (1967), *Typeface nomenclature and classification: BS 2961*, London: British Standards Institution.

Bure, Guillaume-Francois de (1763–1768), *Bibliographie instructive: ou traité de la connoissance des livres rares et singuliers disposé par ordre de matieres et de facultés ... avec une table générale des auteurs, & un systême complet de bibliographie choisie*, Paris: chez Guillaume-François de Bure le jeune.

Burney, Fanny (1994), *The early journals and letters of Fanny Burney* Lars E. Troide and Stewart J. Cooke (eds), Oxford: Clarendon Press.

Byron, George Gordon Noël, Baron (1809), *English bards, and Scotch reviewers. A satire*, 2nd edn, London: printed for J. Cawthorn.

Byron, George Gordon Noël, Baron, (1977), '*Between two worlds', Byron's letters and journals vol. 7: 1820*, Lesie A. Marchand (ed.), London: John Murray.

Cæsar, Caius Julius (1635), *C. Iulii Cæsaris quæ extant ex emendatione Ios. Scaligeri*, Leiden: ex officina Elzeviriana.

Cahill, Elizabeth Kirkland (11 April 1997), 'A Bible for the Plowboy', *Comonweal*, **124**, pp. 19–20.

Caius, John (1568), *De antiquitate Cantabrigiensis academiæ libri duo: In quorum secundo de Oxoniensis quoque gymnasij antiquitate disseritur, & Cantabrigiense longè eo antiquius esse definitur. Londinensi authore. Adiunximus assertionem antiquitatis Oxoniensis academiæ ab Oxoniensi quodam annis iam elapsis duobus ad reginam conscriptam in qua docere conatur, Oxoniense gymnasium Cantabrigiensi antiquius esse. Vt ex collatione facilè intelligas, vtra sit antiquior,* London: excusum per Henricum Bynneman.

Camden, William (1691), *Gulielmi Camdeni, et illustrium virorum ad G. Camdenum epistolæ. Cum appendice varii argumenti. Accesserunt annalium regni Regis Jacobi I. apparatus, et Commentarius de antiquitate, dignitate, et officio Comitis Marescalli Angliæ. Præmittitur G. Camdeni vita,* Thomas Smith (ed.), London: impensis R. Chiswell.

Carley, James P. (2000), *The libraries of King Henry VIII,* Corpus of British medieval libraries no. 7, London: British Library in association with British Academy.

Carnegie, Andrew & Van Dyke, John Charles (1920), *Autobiography of Andrew Carnegie,* Boston, New York: Houghton Mifflin Company.

Carter, Harry (1975), *A history of the Oxford University Press, vol. 1: to the year 1790,* Oxford: Clarendon Press.

Cave, William (1683), *Ecclesiastici, or, the history of the lives, acts, death, & writings, of the most eminent fathers of the church, that flourisht in the fourth century : wherein among other things an account is given of the rise, growth, and progress of Arianism, and all other sects of that age descending from it. Together with an introduction, containing an historical account of the stage of paganism under the first Christian emperours,* London: printed by J.R. for Richard Chiswel.

Cecil, William (1687), *Bibliotheca illustris: sive catalogus variorum librorum in quâvis linguâ & facultate insignium ornatissimæ bibliothecæ viri cujusdam prænobilis ac honoratissimi olim defuncti: libris rarissimis tam typis excusis quàm manuscriptis refertissimæ: quorum auctio habebitur Londini, ad insigne ursi in vico dicto Ave-Mary-Lane, prope templum D. Pauli, Novemb. 21. 1687. Per T. Bentley, & B. Walford, bibliopolas. Lond,* London: catalogues are distributed at 6d. per catalogue, at Mr. Willis in Kings-street, Westminster [etc.].

Chatterton, Thomas (1777), *Poems supposed to have been written at Bristol by Thomas Rowley, and others, in the fifteenth century; the greatest part now first published from the most authentic copies, with an engraved specimen of one of the MSS. To which are added, a preface, an introductory account of the several pieces, and a glossary,* Thomas Tyrwhitt (ed.), London: T. Payne and Son.

Chaucer, Geoffrey (1775–1778), *The Canterbury tales: of Chaucer. To which are added, an essay upon his language and versification; an introductory discourse; and notes. In four volumes,* Thomas Tyrwhitt (ed.), London: printed for T. Payne.

Chauncy, Sir Henry (1700), *The historical antiquities of Hertfordshire. With the original of counties, hundreds or wapentakes and hamlets; the foundation and origin of monasteries, churches, and vicarages; the several honors, mannors, and parks of the nobility and gentry; and the succession of the lords each. Faithfully collected from public records, ancient manuscripts and other select authorities together with an exact transcript of Domesday-book, so far as concerns this shire, and the translation thereof in English. To which are added, the epitaphs and memorable inscriptions in all the parishe,* London: B. Griffin, S. Keble.

Christie, Ian R. (1958), *The End of North's Ministry: 1780–1782,* London: Macmillan.

Clarendon, Edward Hyde Earl of, (1702–1704), T*he history of the Rebellion and Civil Wars in England begun in the year 1641: with the precedent passages and actions that contributed thereunto, and the happy end and conclusion thereof by the King's blessed restoration and return, upon the 29th of May in the year 1660,* Oxford: printed at the Theater.

Clarke, M. L. (1959), *Classical Education in Britain, 1500-1900,* Cambridge: Cambridge University Press.

Clément, David (1750–60), *Bibliothèque curieuse historique et critique, ou catalogue raisonné de livres difficles à trouver,* Göttingen: Chez Jean Guillaume Schmid.

Clode, Charles Mathew (1875), *Memorials of the guild of merchant taylors of the fraternity of St. John the Baptist, in the city of London: and of its associated charities and institutions,* London: Harrison and sons.

Coleridge, Samuel Taylor (2000), *Collected letters of Samuel Taylor Coleridge,* Earl Leslie Griggs (ed.), Oxford: Clarendon Press.

Cooper, Tarnya (2003), 'Queen Elizabeth's public face', *History today,* **53** (5), 38–41.

Crofts, Thomas (1783), *Bibliotheca Croftsiana: a catalogue of the curious and distinguished library of the late Reverend and learned Thomas Crofts, A.M., which will be sold by auction, by Mr. Paterson, at his Great Room, No.6. King-Street, Covent-Garden, London, on Monday, April 7, 1783 and the forty-two following days,* London: Samuel Paterson.

Croix du Maine, François Grud, sieur de la (1584), *Premier volume de la bibliotheque du Sieur de la Croix-du Maine. Qui est un catalogue general de toutes sortes d'autheurs, qui ont escrit en françois depuis cinq cents ans et plus, jusques à ce jourd'huy: avec un discours des vies des plus illustres & renommez entre les trois mille qui sont compris en cet oeuvre, ensemble un recit de leurs compositions, tant imprimées qu'autrement. Dedie' et presente' au roy. Sur la fin de ce livre se voyent les desseins et projects dudit Sieur de la Croix, lesquels il presenta au Roy l'an 1583 pour dresser une bibliotheque parfaite & accomplie en toutes sortes. Dauantage se voit le Discours de ses oeuvres et compositions. Imprimé derechef sur la copie qu'il fist mettre en lumiere l'an 1579,* Paris: A. l'Angellier.

Cromwell, Oliver (1654), *The government of the Common-wealth of England, Scotland, & Ireland, and the dominions thereto belonging : as it was publickly declared at Westminster the 16. day of December 1653. in the presence of the Lords Commissioners of the Great Seal of England, the Lord Maior and aldermen of the City of London, divers of the judges of the land, the officers of state and army, and many other persons of quality, at which time and place His Highness, Oliver Lord Protector of the said Commonwealth, took a solemn oath for observing the same. Published by His Highness the Lord Protector's special commandment,* London: printed, by William du-Gard, and Henry Hills, printers to His Highness the Lord Protector.

Curione, Celio Secondo (1566), *Pasquine in a traunce: a Christian and learned dialogue (contayning wonderfull and most strange newes out of heauen, purgatorie, and hell) wherein besydes Christes truth playnely set forth, ye shall also finde a numbre of pleasaunt hystories, discouering all the crafty conueyaunces of Antechrist. Whereunto are added certayne questions then put forth by Pasquine, to haue bene disputed in the Councell of Trent. Turned but lately out of the Italian into this tongue, by W.P. Seene allowed according to the order appointed in the Queenes Maiesties iniunctions,* London: by VVylliam Seres dwelling at the weast ende of Paules at the signe of the Hedgehogge.

Darwin, Erasmus (1824), *The botanic garden, a poem, in two parts; containing the economy of vegetation and the loves of plants. With philosophical notes,* London: Jones & Company.

Davenport, Cyril (1930), *The Book: Its History and Development,* New York: Peter Smith.

Davis, Terence (1960), *The architecture of John Nash,* London: Studio.

Delille, Jacques (1798), *The gardens, a poem. Translated from the French of the abbé De Lille,* London: printed by T. Bensley.

Deltophilus, Periergus (1784), *Bibliotheca Græca et Latina, complectens auctores fere omnes Græciæ et Latii veteris, quorum opera, vel fragmenta ætatem tulerunt, exceptis tantum asceticis, et theologicis patrum nuncupatorum scriptis; cum delectu editionum tam primariarum, principum, et rarissimarum, quam etiam optimarum, splendidissimarum, atque nitidissimarum, quas usui meo paravi Periergus Deltophilus* [i.e. Count Károly Imre Sándor Reviczky], Berlin.

Desgodetz, Antoine (1682), *Les edifices antiques de Rome, dessinés et mesurés tres exactement,* Paris: chez I.B. Coignard.

Dibdin, Thomas Frognall (1797), *Poems,* London: printed for the author; sold by Booker, Bond Street, Murray & Co. Fleet Street, and J. Bliss, Oxford.

Dibdin, Thomas Frognall (1808), *An introduction to the knowledge of rare and valuable editions of the Greek and Latin classics, including an account of polyglot Bibles, editions of the Septuagint and New Testament, and lexicons and grammars,* 3rd edn, London: printed for Longmans, Hurst, Rees and Orme.

Dibdin, Thomas Frognall (1809), *The bibliomania; or, book-madness; containing some account of the history, symptoms, and cure of this fatal disease. In an epistle addressed to Richard Heber, Esq.* London: printed for Longman, Hurst, Rees, and Orme,... by W. Savage.

Dibdin, Thomas Frognall (1811), *The bibliomania; or, book madness: a bibliographical romance, in six parts. Illustrated with cuts,* London: printed for the author by J. M'Creery... and sold by Messrs. Hurst, Rees, Orme, and Brown.

Dibdin, Thomas Frognall (1817), *The bibliographical decameron ; or, Ten days pleasant discourse upon illuminated manuscripts, and subjects connected with early engraving, typography, and bibliography,* London: printed for the author, by W. Bulmer and co., Shakespeare press.

Dibdin, Thomas Frognall (1832), *Bibliophobia: remarks on the present languid and depressed state of literature and the book trade... by Mercurius Rusticus* [i.e., T. F. Dibdin], London: H. Bohn.

Dibdin, Thomas Frognall (1836), *Reminiscences of a literary life,* London: J. Major.

Dibdin, Thomas Frognall (1842), *Bibliomania; or book-madness; a bibliographical romance. Illustrated with cuts... to which are now added preliminary observations, and a a supplement including a key to the assumed characters in the drama,* London: Henry G. Bohn.

Dibdin, Thomas Frognall (2003), *Bibliomania; or book-madness: A bibliographical romance illustrated with cuts*, Great British Book Collectors and their Libraries, volume 1, Bristol: Thoemmes Continuum.

Dickens, Charles (1848), *Dombey and son*, London: Bradbury and Evans.

D'Isræli, Isaac (1807), *Curiosities of literature*, London: John Murray.

D'Isræli, Isaac (2004), *Isaac D'Isræli on books; pre-Victorian essays on the history of literature*, Spevack, Marvin, London and New Castle, DE: British Library and Oak Knoll Press.

Dobson, Austin (1902), *Samuel Richardson*, London: Macmillan.

Dodsley, Robert (1794), *The economy of human life, complete in two parts : translated from an Indian manuscript. Written by an ancient Bramin. To which is prefixed, an account of the manner in which the said manuscript was discovered ; in a letter from an English gentleman residing at China, to the Earl of ************, London: printed for A. Millar, W. Law, & R. Cater; and for Wilson, Spence, & Mawman, York.

Dodsley, Robert (1806), *The œconomy of human life, translated from an Indian manuscript, written by an ancient Bramin*, London: W. Gardiner; Vernor, Hood & Sharpe.

Dowden, Edward (1887), *The life of Percy Bysshe Shelley*, London: K. Paul Trench & Co.

Du Bellay, Joachim (1549), *La deffence et illustration de la langue Francoyse*, Paris: A. L'Angelier.

Du Bellay, Joachim (1588), *Les regrets et autres œuvres poétiques de Joach. Du Bellay*, Paris: impr. de F. Morel.

Dubos, René (1959), *Miracle of health: utopias, progress, and biological change*, New York: Doubleday.

Duff, E. Gordon (1905), *A century of the English book trade of all printers, stationers, book-binders, and others connected with it from the issue of the first dated book in 1457 to the incorporation of the Company of stationers in 1557*, London: The Bibliographical Society.

Dyas, E. (2001), 'The birth of the modern newspaper', *The Times*, 23 Nov.

Edwards, George (1751), *A natural history of uncommon birds: and of some other rare and undescribed animals, quadrupeds, fishes, reptiles, insects, &c., exhibited in two hundred and ten copper-plates, from designs copied immediately from nature, and curiously coloured after life, with a full and accurate description of each figure, to which is added A brief and general idea of drawing and painting in water-colours; with instructions for etching on copper with aqua fortis; likewise some thoughts on the passage of birds; and additions to many subjects described in this work*, London: printed for the author, at the College of Physicians in Warwick-Lane.

Edwards, George (1758), *Gleanings of natural history: exhibiting figures of quadrupeds, birds, insects, plants, etc., most of which have not, till now, been either figured or described. With descriptions of seventy different subjects, designed, engraved, and coloured after nature, on fifty copper-plate prints*, London: printed for the author, at the Royal College of Physicians.

Edwards, Mark U. (1975), *Luther and the false brethren*, Stanford, CA: Stanford University Press.

Fabel, Robin F. A (1988), *The economy of British West Florida, 1763-1783*, Tuscaloosa AL: University of Alabama Press.

Fabyan, Robert (1516), *The Chronicles of Fabyan. Prima Pars Cronecarum. For that in the accomptynge of the yeres of the worlde, etc.... Thus endeth the newe Cronycles of Englande and of Fraunce* [etc.], London: R. Pynson.

Fabyan, Robert (1559), *The chronicle of Fabian, whiche he nameth the concordaunce of histories, newly perused. And continued from the beginnyng of Kyng Henry the seuenth, to thende of Queene Mary,* London: Jhon Kyngston.

Feather, John (1981), 'John Nourse and his authors', *Studies in bibliography,* **34,** 205–26.

Feiling, Keith Grahame (1954), *Warren Hastings,* London: Macmillan.

Ferguson, W. Craig (1989), *Pica Roman type in Elizabethan England,* Aldershot, Surrey and Brookfield, VT: Scolar Press.

Ferriar, John (1788), *The prince of Angola: a tragedy, altered from the play of Oroonoko. And adapted to the circumstances of the present times,* Manchester: printed by J. Harrop.

Ferriar, John (1809), *The bibliomania,: an epistle, to Richard Heber, Esq,* London: T. Cadell, and W. Davies.

Ferriar, John (1816), *Medical histories and reflections,* Philadelphia: published by Thomas Dobson, at the Stone House, no. 41, South Second Street. William Fry, printer.

Ferriar, John (1996), *The bibliomania (1809),* Portico monograph no. 6, Introduction by David Thame & notes by John Walker, Manchester: Portico Library.

Ferriar, John & Dibdin, Thomas Frognall (2001), *The bibliomania by John Ferriar; Bibliography by Thomas Frognall Dibdin,* Marc Vaulbert de Chantilly (ed.), London: Vanity Press of Bethnal Green.

Fleming, John (1962), *Robert Adam and his circle, in Edinburgh & Rome,* London: J. Murray.

Fox, Charles James (1808), *A history of the early part of the reign of James II; with an introductory chapter to which is added an appendix,* London: William Miller.

Franklin, Benjamin & Heberden, William (1759), *Some account of the success of inoculation for the small-pox in England and America : together with Plain instructions by which any persons may be enabled to perform the operation and conduct the patient through the distemper,* London: W. Strahan.

Froissart, Jean (1513), *Croniques de France, Dangleterre, Descoce, Despaigne, de Bretaigne, de Gascongne, de Flandres, et lieux circunuoisins,* Paris: Guillaume Eustace.

Fuller, Thomas & Fuller, John (1662), *The history of the worthies of England,* London: Printed by J. G. W. L. and W. G.

Gesner, Konrad (1545), *Bibliotheca universalis: sive catalogus omnium scriptorum locupletissimus, in tribus linguis, Latina, Græca et Hebraica: extantium et non extantiu[m], veterum et recentiorum in hunc usq[ue] diem, doctorum et indoctorum, publicatorum et in bibliothecis latentium. Opus novum & no[n] bibliothecis tantum publicis privatisve instituendis necessarium, sed studiosis omnibus cuiuscunq[ue] artis aut scientiæ ad studia melius formanda utilissimum / authore Conrado Gesnero Tigurino doctore medico,* Zurich: apud Christophorum Froschouerum.

Gibbon, Edward (1814), *The miscellaneous works of Edward Gibbon, esq., with memoirs of his life and writings,* John Holroyd Sheffield (ed.), London: J. Murray.

Gildas (1525), *Opus nouum. Gildas Britannus monachus cui sapientis cognome[n]tu[m] est inditum, de calamitate excidio, & conquestu Britanniæ, quam Angliam nunc uocant, author uetustus a multis diu desyderatus, & nuper in gratiam D. Cuthberti Tonstalli, Londinen[sis] Episcopi formulis excusus: In hoc authore, preter multiplicem hic illic historiaru[m] interpositionem, uidere licet grauissimas illius temporis regu[m], pri[n]cipu[m], ducu[m], episcoporum... &c. correptio[n]es*, Polydore Vergil & R.Ridley (eds), Antwerp: printed by Christoffel van Ruremund.

Glaister, Geoffrey Ashall (1960), *Glossary of the book; terms used in paper-making, printing, bookbinding, and publishing*, London: G. Allen and Unwin.

Godwin, Francis (1601), *A catalogue of the bishops of England, since the first planting of Christian religion in this island: together with a briefe history of their liues and memorable actions, so neere as can be gathered out of antiquity*, London: impensis Geor. Bishop.

Goldast, Melchior (1674), *Philologicarum epistolarum centuria una diversorum a renatis literis doctissimorum virorum, in qua veterum theologorum, jurisconsultorum, medicorum, philosophorum, historicorum, poetarum, grammaticorum libri difficillimis locis vel emendantur vel illustrantur: insuper Richardi de Buri Episcopi Dunelmensis, &c. Philobiblion & Bessarionis... Epistola ad Senatum Venetum, omnia quondam edita ex bibliotheca Melchioris Haiminsfeldii Goldasti, cum duplici ... indice; addita nunc præfatione Hermanni Conringii*, Leipzig: impensis Joh. Bart. Oeleri.

Goldschmidt, E. P. (1955), *The first Cambridge Press in its European setting*, The Sandars lectures in bibliography 1953, Cambridge: Cambridge University Press.

Goldsmith, Oliver & Parnell, Thomas (1795), *Poems by Goldsmith and Parnell*, London: printed by W. Bulmer and Co..

Gosson, Stephen (1579), *The schoole of abuse: conteining a plesaunt inuectiue against poets, pipers, plaiers, jesters, and such like caterpillers of a comonwelth: Setting vp the flagge of defiance to their mischieuous exercise, & ouerthrowing their bulwarkes, by prophane writers, naturall reason, and common experience: a discourse as pleasaunt for gentlemen that fauour learning, as profitable for all that wyll follow virtue...* London: Thomas Woodcocke.

G. R & A. M. (1712), *The belief of witchcraft vindicated: proving, from scripture, there have been witches; and from reason, that there may be such still. In answer to a late pamphlet, intituled, The impossibility of witchcraft*, London: printed by J. Baker.

Granger, James (1769), *A biographical history of England, from Egbert the Great to the Revolution: consisting of characters disposed in different classes, and adapted to a methodical catalogue of engraved British heads. Intended as an essay towards reducing our biography to system, and a help to the knowledge of portraits. Interspersed with variety of anecdotes, and memoirs of a great number of persons*, London: T. Davies.

Gray, Thomas (1775), *The poems of Mr. Gray. To which are prefixed memoirs of his life and writings by W. Mason*, York: printed by A. Ward.

Grayling, A. C. (2003), 'Hazlitt's Tribute', *History Today*, 53 (4), p. 8.

Greene, Robert (1592), *Greenes, groats-vvorth of wittte, bought with a million of repentance. Describing the follie of youth, the falshood of makeshifte flatterers, the miserie of the negligent, and mischiefes of deceiuing courtezans. Written before his death, and published at his dyeing request,* London: imprinted [by J. Wolfe and J. Danter] for William Wright.

Greene, Robert (1620), *A quip for an upstart courtier; or, a quaint dispute between velvet breeches and cloth breeches,* London: printed by G. P[urslow].

Grose, Francis (1787), *A provincial glossary, with a collection of local proverbs, and popular superstitions,* London: printed for S. Hooper.

Grose, Francis (1792), *The olio: being a collection of essays, dialogues, letters,… epitaphs, &c. chiefly original,* London: printed for S. Hooper.

Grose, Francis (1772-87), *The antiquities of England and Wales : being a collection of views of the most remarkable ruins and antient buildings accurately drawn on the spot,* London: printed for S. Hooper, no. 25, Ludgate-Hill.

Hall, F. W (1913), *A companion to classical texts,* Oxford: Clarendon Press.

Hall, John N. (1991), *Trollope: a biography,* Oxford: Clarendon Press.

Hamilton, Anthony, Count (1730), *Les quatre Facardins, conte,* Paris: rue S. Jacques, chez Jean Fr. Josse… a la Fleur de Lys d'Or.

Hardison, O. B (1968), *English literary criticism: the Renaissance,* London: Owen.

Harley, Robert (1744-46), *The Harleian miscellany: or, a collection of scarce, curious, and entertaining pamphlets and tracts, as well in manuscript as in print found in the late Earl of Oxford's library. Interspersed with historical, political, and critical notes…* William Oldys ed., London: printed for T. Osborne.

Harling, Robert (1938), *The London miscellany: a nineteenth century scrapbook,* Oxford: Oxford University Press.

Haslewood, Joseph (1790), *The secret history of the green rooms: containing authentic and entertaining memoirs of the actors and actresses in the three Theatres Royal,* London: printed for J. Ridgway; J. Forbes; and H. D. Symmonds.

Haslewood, Joseph (1824), *Some account of the life and publications of the late Joseph Ritson, esq.,* London: R. Triphook.

Haslewood, Joseph (1833), *Catalogue of the curious and valuable library of the late Joseph Haslewood, esq. F. S. A,* London: printed by W. Nicol.

Hay, Denys (1952), *Polydore Vergil: Renaissance historian and man of letters,* Oxford: Clarendon Press.

Heberden, William (1802), *Commentarii de morborum historia et curatione,* London: apud T. Payne.

Heberden, William & Heberden, William, Jr (1802), *Commentaries on the history and cure of diseases,* London: T. Payne.

Hellinga, Lotte (1982), *Caxton in focus: the beginning of printing in Emgland,* London: British Library.

Hope, Thomas (1807), *Household furniture and interior decoration,* London: Longman, Hurst, Rees, and Orme.

Hope, Thomas (1809), *Costume of the ancients,* London: printed for William Miller, Albemarle-Street, by W. Bulmer and Co. Cleveland-Row, St. James's.

Hope, Thomas (1819), *Anastasius, or, memoirs of a Greek written at the close of the eighteenth century,* London: John Murray.

Howe, Ellic (1947), *The London compositor: documents relating to wages, working conditions and customs of the London printing trade 1785-1900,* London: The Bibliographical Society.

Howe, Ellic (1950), *A list of London bookbinders, 1648-1815,* London: The Bibliographical Society.

Howells, John G & Osborn, M. Livia (1984), *A reference companion to the history of abnormal psychology*, Westport, Conn: Greenwood Press.

Huizinga, J. (1952), *Erasmus of Rotterdam: with a selection from the letters of Erasmus*, F. Hopman & B. Flower (trans.), London: Phaidon Press.

Hulst, Samuel van (1730), *Bibliotheca Hulsiana, sive catalogus librorum quos collegit... Samuel Hulsius, etc*, The Hague: apud J. Swart & P. de Hondt.

Hunter, Michael Cyril William (1981), *Science and society in restoration England*, Cambridge: Cambridge University Press.

Jackson, L. (n.d.), *The Victorian dictionary*, http://www.victorianlondon.org

Jerdan, William (1866), *Men I have known*, London: George Routledge and Sons.

Juan, Jorge & Ulloa, Antonio de (1748), *Relacion historica del viage a la America meridional : hecho de orden de S. Mag. para medir algunos grados de meridiano terrestre y venir por ellos en conocimiento de la verdadera figura, y magnitud de la Tierra, con otras varias observaciones astronomicas, y physicas*, Madrid: por Antonio Marín.

Jurin, James (1734), *Geometry no friend to infidelity: or, a defence of Sir Isaac Newton and the British mathematicians, in a letter to the author of the Analyst. Wherein it is examined how far the conduct of such divines as intermix the interest of religion with their private disputes and passions, and allow neither learning nor reason to those they differ from, is of honour or service to Christianity, or agreeable to the example of our blessed Saviour and his apostles by Philalethes Cantabrigiensis* [James Jurin], London: printed for T. Cooper.

Juvenal & Persius (1867), *Decii Junii Juvenalis et A. Persii Flacci satiræ*, Arthur John Macleane (ed.), London: Whittaker; G. Bell.

Knight, Samuel (1724), *The life of Dr. John Colet, Dean of S. Paul's in the reigns of K. Henry VII. and Henry VIII. and founder of St. Paul's school with an appendix containing some account of the masters and more eminent scholars of that foundation; and several original papers relating to the said life*, London: printed by J. Downing.

La, Croix du Maine, François Grud, Du, Verdier, Antoine, Rigoley, de Juvigny, Jean Antoine, La, Monnoye, Bernard de, Bouhier, Jean, Falconet, Camille, et al. (1772–1773), *Les bibliothèques françoises de La Croix du Maine et de Du Verdier Nouvelle édition dédiée au roi, revue, corrigée & augmentée d'un Discours sur le progrès des lettres en France, & des remarques historiques, critiques & littéraires de M. de la Monnoye et de M. le Président Bouhier...; de M. Falconet... Par M. Rigoley de Juvigny*, Paris: Saillant & Nyon [etc.].

Laborde, Alexandre de (1806–20), *Voyage pittoresque et historique de l'Espagne*, Paris: impr. de P. Didot, l'aîné.

Lambarde, William (1568), *Archaionomia, siue de priscis anglorum legibus libri: sermone Anglico, vetustate antiquissimo, aliquot abhinc seculis conscripti, atq[ue] nunc demum, magno iurisperitorum, & amantium antiquitatis omnium commodo, Bre tenebris in lucem vocati. Gulielmo Lambardo interprete. Regum qui has leges scripserunt nomenclationem, & quid priȝterea accesserit, altera monstrabit pagina*, London: ex officina Ioannis Daij.

Lambarde, William (1576), *A perambulation of Kent: conteining the description, hystorie, and customes of that shyre. Collected and written (for the most part) in the yeare. 1570. by William Lambard of Lincolnes Inne Gent. and nowe increased by the addition of some things which the authour him selfe hath obserued since that time*, London: for Ralphe Nevvberie, dwelling in Fleetestreete a litle aboue the Conduit.

Lambarde, William (1962), *William Lambarde and Local Government. His 'Ephemeris' and twenty-nine charges to juries and commissions*, Conyers Read (ed.), Ithaca, N.Y.: published for the Folger Shakespeare Library by Cornell University Press.

Laneham, Robert (1575), *A letter: whearin, part of the entertainment vntoo the Queenz Maiesty, at Killingwoorth Castl, in Warwik Sheer in this soomerz progress 1575. iz signified: from a freend officer attendant in the Coourt, vntoo hiz freend a citizen and merchaunt of London*, London: Robert Alde.

Laneham, Robert (1907), *Robert Laneham's letter: describing a part of the entertainment unto Queen Elizabeth at the castle of Kenilworth in 1575*, F. J. Furnival (ed.), London: Chatto and Windus.

Lang, Andrew (1890), *Rhymes à la mode*, London: K. Paul, Trench, Trübner & co., ltd.

Lebeaux, Richard (1984), *Thoreau's Seasons*, Amherst, MA: University of Massachusetts Press.

Leland, John (1710–1712), *The itinerary of John Leland the antiquary publish'd... by T. Hearne. To which is prefix'd Mr Leland's New-Year's gift. (A discourse concerning some Antiquities lately found in Yorkshire. Nænia upon the death of Sir T. Wyatt. Dr Plot's account of his intended journey through England and Wales. Antoninus' Itinerary through Britain, with... Dr R. Talbot's annotations upon it. A tale of two swannes [in verse]... by W. Vallans, etc.)*, Oxford: printed at the Theater.

Lewis, C. S. (1954), *English Literature in the Sixteenth Century: Excluding Drama*, Oxford: Clarendon Press.

Lewis, Matthew Gregory (1796), *The monk: a romance*, London: J. Bell.

Lewis, Matthew Gregory (1808), *Romantic tales*, London: printed by D.N. Shury for Longman, Hurst, Rees, and Orme.

Lewis, Wilmarth Sheldon (1961), *Horace Walpole*, New York: Pantheon Books.

Locke, John (1976), *The correspondence of John Locke*, E. S. De Beer (ed.), Oxford: Clarendon Press.

Luttrell, Narcissus (1857), *A brief historical relation of state affairs from September 1678 to April 1714*, Oxford: at the University press.

Luttrell, Narcissus (1972), *The parliamentary diary of Narcissus Luttrell, 1691–1693*, Henry Horwitz (ed.), Oxford: Clarendon Press.

Lyly, John ([1589]), *Pappe with an hatchet : Alias, a figge for my God sonne. Or cracke me this nut. Or a countrie cuffe, that is, a sound boxe of the eare, for the idiot Martin to hold his peace, seeing the patch will take no warning. VVritten by one that dares call a dog, a dog, and made to preuent Martins dog daies*, London: imprinted by Iohn Anoke, and Iohn Astile [i.e. T. Orwin], for the Bayliue of Withernam, cum priuilegio perennitatis, and are to bee sold at the signe of the crab tree cudgell in thwack-coate lane.

Lysons, Daniel (1796), *The environs of London: being an historical account of the towns, villages, and hamlets, within twelve miles of that capital; interspersed with biographical anecdotes*, London: printed by A. Strahan, for T. Cadell, jun. and W. Davies.

Lysons, Daniel & Lysons, Samuel (1806), *Magna Britannia; being a concise topo-graphical account of the several counties of Great Britain*, London: T. Cadell and W. Davies.

Lysons, Samuel (1801–17), *Reliquiæ Britannico-Romanæ, containing figures of Ro-man antiquities discovered in England*, London: printed by T. Bensley, and sold by Messrs. Cadell and Davies, T. Payne, and White, Cochran, and Co..

MacCarthy Reagh, Justin comte de, Bure, Jean J. de & Bure, Marie, J. de (1815, 1817), *Catalogue de livres rares et précieux de la bibliothèque de feu M. le comte de Mac-Carthy*, Paris: chez de Bure frères.

Malone, Edmund (1800), *The critical and miscellaneous prose works of John Dryden : now first collected: with notes and illustrations ; an account of the life and writings of the author, grounded on original and authentick documents ; and a collection of his letters, the greater parts wich have never been published*, London: printed by H. Baldwin and Son, for T. Cadell, Jun. and W. Davies.

Mantello, Frank Anthony Carl & Rigg, A. G (1996), *Medieval Latin: an intro-duction and bibliographical guide*, Washington, D.C: Catholic University of America Press.

Mascall, Leonard (1590), *A booke of fishing with hooke & line, and of all other instru-ments thereunto belonging. Another of sundrie engines and trappes to take polcats, buzards, rattes, mice and all other kindes of vermine & beasts whatsoeuer, most profitable for all warriners, and such as delight in this kinde of sport and pastime*, London: printed by Iohn Wolfe, and are to be solde by Edwarde White dwell-ing at the little North doore of Paules at the signe of the Gunne.

Mascall, Leonard (1600), *A booke of fishing with hooke and line, and of all other instruments thereununto belonging : another of sundrije engines and traps, to take polcats, buzzards, rats, mice, and all other kinds of vermine and beasts whatsoeuer, most profitable for all warriners, and such as delight in this kind of sport and pas-time*, London: printed by Iohn Wolfe, and are to bee sold by Edward VVhite, dwelling at the little North dore of Paules at the signe of the Gun.

Masters, Robert (1753), *The history of the College of Corpus Christi and the B. Virgin Mary (commonly called Bene't) in the University of Cambridge, from its foun-dation to the present time. In two parts. I. Of its founders, benefactors and mas-ters. II. Of its other principal members*, Cambridge: printed for the author, by J. Bentham.

Masters, Robert (1784), *Memoirs of the life and writings of the late Rev. Thomas Baker, B. D., of St. John's college in Cambridge : from the papers of Dr. Zachary Grey, with a catalogue of his ms. collections*, Cambridge: printed by J. Archdeacon printer to the University; sold by J. & J. Merrill, and J. Deighton, Cambridge [etc.].

Maxted, Ian (n.d.), http://www.devon.gov.uk/library/locstudy/bookhist/.

Metzger, Bruce M. (1992), *The text of the New Testament: its transmission, corrup-tion, and restoration*, Oxford: Oxford University Press.

Middleton, Thomas (1950), *The witch*, W. W. Greg (ed.), London: printed for the Malone Society.

Montfaucon, Bernard de (1739), *Bibliotheca bibliothecarum manuscriptorum nova: ubi, quæ innumeris pene manuscriptorum bibliothecis continentur, ad quodvis lit-eraturæ genus spectantia & notatu digna, describuntur & indicantur*, Paris: apud Briasson.

Montfaucon, Bernard de, Komnenos, Joannes, Porphyrios & Bouhier, Jean (1708), *Palæographia Græca,* Paris: apud Ludovicum Guerin [etc.].

Moran, James (2003), *Wynkyn de Worde: father of Fleet Street, with a chronological bibliography of works on Wynkyn de Worde,* compiled by Lotte Helinga and Mary Erler and a preface by John Dreyfus, London: Wynkyn de Worde Society.

Mores, Edward Rowe (1778), *A dissertation upon English typographical founders and founderies,* London: privately printed by John Nichols.

Morhof, Daniel Georg (1747), *Danielis Georgi Morhofii Polyhistor, literarius, philosophicus et practicus* [etc.], Lübeck: sumptibus Petri Boeckmann.

Mukherjee, Neel (2000), 'Thomas Drant's rewriting of Horace', *Studies in English literature, 1500–1900,* **40** (1), pp. 1–20.

Nichols, John & Bentley, Samuel (1812), *Literary anecdotes of the eighteenth century; comprizing biographical memoirs of William Bowyer, printer, F. S. A,* London: printed for the author, by Nichols, son, and Bentley.

Noble, Mark (1804), *A history of the College of Arms: and the lives of all the kings, heralds, and pursuivants from the reign of Richard III, founder of the college, until the present time,* London: printed for J. Debrett and T. Egerton.

Noble, Mark (1806), *A biographical history of England, from the revolution to the end of George I's reign : being a continuation of the Rev. J. Granger's work; consisting of characters disposed in different classes; and adapted to a methodical catalogue of engraved British heads; interspersed with a variety of anecdotes, and memoirs of a great number of persons,* London: W. Richardson.

O'Dwyer, E. J. (1967), *Thomas Frognall Dibdin: bibliographer and bibliomaniac extraordinary,* Pinner: Private Libraries Association.

Oldys, William (1737), *The British librarian: exhibiting a compendious review or abstract of our most scarce, useful, and valuable books in all sciences, as well in manuscript as in print,* London: printed for Tho. Osborne.

Orlandi, Pellegrino Antonio (1722), *Origine e progressi della stampa o sia dell'arte impressoria e notizie dell'opere stampate dall'anno MCCCCLVII sino all'anno MD,* Bologna: Constantinus Pisarius.

Oswald, John Clyde (1928), *A history of printing; its development through five hundred years,* New York: Appleton and Company.

Palmer, Samuel (1732), *The general history of printing: from its first invention in the city of Mentz, to its first progress and propagation thro' the most celebrated cities in Europe. Particularly, its introduction, rise and progress here in England. The character of the most celebrated printers, from the first inventors of the art to the years 1520 and 1550. With an account of their works, and of the most considerable improvements which they made to it during that interval,* London: printed by the author.

Panzer, Georg Wolfgang (1788), *Annalen der altern Deutschen Litteratur : Anzeige und Beschreibung derjenigen Bucher welche von Erfindung der Buchdruckerkunst bis MDXX in deutscher Sprache gedruckt worden sind,* Nürnberg: Grattenauer.

Panzer, Georg Wolfgang (1793–1802), *Annales typographici ab artis inventæ origine ad annum MD [-MDXXXVI] post Maittairii Denisii aliorumque doctissimorum virorum curas in ordinem redacti emendati et aucti,* Nürnberg: impensis Joannis Eberhardi Zeh, bibliopolæ.

Parks, Stephen (1999), *The Luttrell file: Narcissus Luttrell's dates on contemporary pamphlets, 1679-1730,* New Haven, CT: Beinecke Library

Parsons, Robert (1580), *A brief discours contayning certayne reasons why Catholiques refuse to goe to church. Written by a learned and vertuous man, to a friend of his in England. And dedicated by I.H. to the Queenes most excellent Maiestie,* imprinted at Doway [i.e. East Ham]: by Iohn Lyon [i.e. Greenstreet House Press].

Pasquill of England (1589), *A countercuffe giuen to Martin Iunior by the venturous, hardie, and renowned Pasquill of England, Caualiero. Not of olde Martins making, which newlie knighted the saints in heauen, with rise vp Sir Peter and Sir Paule; but lately dubd for his seruice at home in the defence of his countrey, and for the cleane breaking of his staffe vppon Martins face,* London: printed, betweene the skye and the grounde, vvithin a myle of an oake, and not many fieldes of, from the vnpriuiledged presse of the assignes of Martin Iunior [i.e. John Charlewood].

Pasty, Caroline Petty (1800), *The mince Pye; an heroic epistle humbly addressed to the sovereign dainty of a British feast,* London: printed by Thomas Bensley.

Paterson, Samuel (1772), *Joineriana: or the book of scraps,* London: printed for Joseph Johnson.

Pearson, Thomas (1788), *Bibliotheca Pearsoniana. A catalogue of the library of T. Pearson, Esq. ... which will be sold by auction, by T. and J. Egerton... on the 14th of April, 1788.* London: T. and J. Egerton.

Peck, Dwight (1977), 'Government suppression of Elizabethan Catholic books: the case of Leicester's Commonwealth', *Library Quarterly,* **47** (2), pp. 163–77.

Peignot, Étienne Gabriel (1802), *Dictionnaire raisonné de bibliologie: contenant, 1. l'explication des principaux termes relatifs a la bibliographie... 2. des notices historiques detailleés sur les principales bibliothèques anciennes et modernes... 3. enfin, l'exposition des differents systèmes bibliographiques, etc...* Paris: Chez Villier.

Percy, Thomas, Smith, David Nichol & Brooks, Cleanth (1944), *The Percy letters,* Baton Rouge, LA: Louisiana State University Press.

Pettegree, Andrew (2002), *Europe in the sixteenth century,* Oxford: Blackwell Publishers.

Pfintzing, Melchior, Treitz-Saurwein, Marx & Schäufelein, Hans (1517), *Die geuerlicheiten vnd eins teils der Geschichten des loblichen Streytparen vnd hoschberümbten Helds vnd Ritters Herr Tewrdannckhs,* Nürnberg: durch den eltern Hannsen Schönsperger burger zu Augspurg.

Plomer, Henry R. (1925), *Wynkyn de Worde and his contemporaries from the death of Caxton to 1535: a chapter in English printing,* London: Grafton & Co.

Pope, Alexander (1824), *The works of Alexander Pope, esq. with notes and illustrations by himself and others. To which are added a new life of the author, an estimate of his poetical character and writings, and occasional remarks,* William Roscoe (ed.), London: printed for C. & J. Rivington [etc.].

Putnam, George Haven (1962), *Books and their makers during the middle ages; a study of the conditions of the production and distribution of literature from the fall of the Roman empire to the close of the seventeenth century,* New York: Hillary House Publishers.

Pybus, Charles Small (1800), *The sovereign. Addressed to His Imperial Majesty, Paul, Emperour of all the Russias,* London: T. Bensley.

Rabelais, François (1964), *Pantagruel,* Pierre Michel (ed.), Paris: Gallimard.

Reed, Talbot Baines (1952), *A history of the old English letter foundries; with notes, historical and bibliographical, on the rise and progress of English typography*, A. F. Johnson (ed.), London: Faber & Faber.

Renouard, Antoine-Augustin (1803), *Annales de l'imprimerie des Alde, ou, histoire des trois Manuce et de leurs éditions*, Paris: Chez Antoine-Augustin Renouard.

Renouard, Antoine-Augustin (1838), *Annales de l'imprimerie des Estienne, ou, histoire de la famille des Estienne et de ses éditions*, Paris: chez J. Renouard.

Reviczky, Károly Imre Sándor, Count (1794), *Bibliotheca Græca et Latina, complectens auctores fere omnes Græciæ et Latii veteris quorum opera, vel fragmenta ætatem tulerunt, exceptis tantum asceticis et theologicis Patrum noncupatorum scriptis; cum delectu editionum tam primariarum, principum et rarissimarum quam etiam optimarum splendidissimarum atque niti dissimarum, quas usui meo paravi Periergus Deltophilu...Editio altera cum emendationibus auctoris*, Berlin: typis Joannis Friderici Unger.

Richard de Bury (1996). *The love of books: the Philobiblon of Richard de Bury*, http://sailor.gutenberg.org/etext96/phlbb10.txt

Rickard, Peter (1989), *A history of the French language*, 2nd edn, London: Unwin Hyman.

Rogers, Samuel (1856), *Recollections of the table-talk of Samuel Rogers; to which is added Porsoniana*, Alexander Dyce (ed.), New York: D. Appleton and Company.

Roscoe, William (1795), *The life of Lorenzo de' Medici, called the Magnificent*, Liverpool: printed by J. M'Creery, and sold by J. Edwards, London.

Roscoe, William (1802), *An address, delivered before the proprietors of the Botanic Garden in Liverpool, previous to opening the Garden, May 3, 1802: to which are added the laws of the institution, and a list of the proprietors*, Liverpool: printed by M'Creery.

Roscoe, William (1805), *The life and pontificate of Leo the Tenth*, Liverpool: printed by J. McCreery.

Roscoe, William (1807), *The butterfly's ball, and the grasshopper's feast*, London: printed for J. Harris.

Roscoe, William (1819), *Observations on penal jurisprudence, and the reformation of criminals. With an appendix; containing the latest reports of the state-prisons or penitentiaries of Philadelphia, New-York, and Massachusetts; and other documents*, London: printed for T. Cadell and W. Davies, Strand, and John and Arthur Arch, Cornhill... J. M'Creery, Printer, Black-Horse-Court.

Roscoe, William (1827), *A brief statement of the causes which have led to the abandonment of the celebrated system of penitentiary discipline, in some of the United States of America*, Liverpool: printed by Harris and co. Sold by T. Cadell [etc.].

Roscoe, William & Hodgson, Isaac (1823), *An address from the Liverpool Society for the Abolition of Slavery on the safest and most efficacious means of promoting the gradual improvement of the negro slave in the British West India Islands preparatory to their becoming free labourers, and on the expected consequences of such change*, Liverpool: Smith.

Roxburghe, John Ker 3rd Duke of (1812), *A catalogue of the library of the late John, Duke of Roxburghe arranged by G. and W. Nicol... which will be sold by auction on Monday, 18th May, 1812, etc. by Robert H. Evans*, London: Robert H. Evans.

Ruzicka, Rudolph (1943), *Thomas Bewick, engraver*, New York: Typophiles.

Sainte-Maure, Charles de, Duke de Montausier (1784), *La guirlande de Julie, offerte à Mlle. de Rambouillet, Julie Lucine d'Angenes, par M. le Marquis de Montausier,* Paris: privately printed.

Saintsbury, George (1896), *A history of nineteenth century literature (1780-1895),* London: Macmillan and Co.

Savage, William (1822), *Practical hints on decorative printing, with illustrations engraved on wood and printed in colours,* London: published for the Proprietor, by Messrs. Longman, Hurst, Rees, Orme, and Brown,[etc.].

Savage, William (1832), *On the preparation of printing ink; both black and coloured,* London: printed for the Author, and sold by Longman, Rees, Orme, Brown, Green, and Longman.

Savage, William (1841), *A dictionary of the art of printing,* London: Longman, Brown, Green, and Longmans.

Schelhorn, Johann Georg (1725–1730), *Amoenitates literariæ, quibus variæ observationes, scripta item quædam anecdota & rariora opuscula exhibentur,* Frankfurt and Leipzig: apud Daniel Bartholomæi.

Schoeck, Richard J. (1990), *Erasmus of Europe,* Edinburgh: Edinburgh University Press.

Shakespeare, William (1807), *Mr. William Shakespeares comedies, histories, & tragedies: Published according to the true original copies,* London: J. Wright.

Shemek, Deanna (1998), *Ladies errant: wayward women and social order in early modern Italy,* Durham, NC: Duke University Press.

Smith, H. Maynard (1938), *Pre-Reformation England,* London: Macmillan.

Smith, John Stafford (1779), *A collection of English songs, in score for three and four voices composed about the year 1800 taken from the M.S.S. of the same age revised and digested by John Stafford Smith,* London: printed for J. Bland.

Smyth, Richard (1682), *Bibliotheca Smithiana: sive catalogus librorum... quos multo æræ [sic] sibi comparavit... Richardus Smith Londinensis. Horum auctio habebitur Londini, in area vulgo dicta Great St. Bartholomews Close, in angulum ejusdem septentrionalem, Maii die 15. 1682,* London: Richard Chiswell.

Smyth, Richard (1849), *The obituary of Richard Smyth: secondary of the Poultry compter, London: being a catalogue of all such persons as he knew in their life: extending from A.D. 1627 to A.D. 1674,* Sir Henry Ellis (ed.), London: printed for the Camden society.

Solomon, Harry M (1996), *The rise of Robert Dodsley: creating the new age of print,* Carbondale IL: Southern Illinois University Press.

Somers, John, first Baron (1748), *A collection of scarce and valuable tracts: on the most interesting and entertaining subjects: but chiefly such as relate to the history and constitution of these kingdoms selected from an infinite number... in the Royal, Cotton, Sion, and other publick, as well as private libraries; particularly that of the late Lord Sommers. Revised by eminent hands,* London: printed for F. Cogan.

Somers, John, first Baron (1809–15), *A collection of scarce and valuable tracts : on the most interesting and entertaining subjects, but chiefly such as relate to the history and constitution of these kingdoms: selected from an infinite number in print and manuscript, in the Royal, Cotton, Sion, and other public, as well as private libraries, particularly that of the late Lord Somers,* Walter Scott (ed.), London: printed for T. Cadell, W. Davies [etc.].

Somervile, William (1796), *The chase: a poem,* London: printed by W. Bulmer and Co.

Sophocles (1550), *Sophoclis Aiax Flagellifer, et Antigone. Eiusdem Electra,* Georgio Rotallero (trans), Lyon: apud Seb. Gryphium.

Southey, Robert (1805), *Madoc,* London; Edinburgh: Longman, Hurst, Rees, and Orme.

Southey, Robert (1807), *The remains of Henry Kirke White...with an account of his life,* London: Vernor, Hood, and Sharpe; Longman, Hurst, Rees, and Orme, [etc.].

Spencer, George John & Dibdin, Thomas Frognall (1814–15), *Bibliotheca Spenceriana: or, a descriptive catalogue of the books printed in the fifteenth century and of many valuable first editions in the library of George John Earl Spencer,* London: Longman, Hurst, Rees, & Co. [etc].

Spenser, Edmund (1579), *The shepheardes calender conteyning twelue æglogues proportionable to the twelue monethes. Entitled to the noble and vertuous gentleman most worthy of all titles both of learning and cheualrie M. Philip Sidney,* London: printed by Hugh Singleton, dwelling in Creede Lane neere vnto Ludgate at the signe of the gylden Tunne, and are there to be solde.

Spenser, Edmund (1805), *The shepheardes calender: in eight volumes, with the principal illustrations of various commentators to which are added, notes, some account of the life of Spenser, and a glossarial and other indexes,* Henry John Todd (ed.), London: F. C. & J. Rivington.

Stephen, Leslie (1878), *Samuel Johnson,* London: Macmillan.

Stephenson, Robert Louis (1899), *The letters of Robert Louis Stevenson to his family and friends,* Sidney Colvin (ed.), New York: Charles Scribner's Sons.

Sterne, Lawrence (1967), *The life and opinions of Tristram Shandy, gentleman,* Graham Petrie (ed.), Harmondsworth: Penguin Books.

Stewart, Charles (1809), *A descriptive catalogue of the oriental library of the late Tippoo Sultan of Mysore. To which are prefixed, memoirs of Hyder Aly Khan, and his son Tippoo Sultan,* London: sold by Longman, Hurst, Rees, and Orme.

Suidas (1705), *Suidæ lexicon, Græce et Latine. textum Græcum cum manuscriptis codicibus collatum a quamplurimis mendis purgavit, notisque perpetuis illustravit: versionem Latinam Æmilii Porti innumeris in locis correxit; indicesque auctorum et rerum adjecit Ludolphus Kusterus,* Cambridge: typis academicis.

Summerson, John (1945), *Georgian London,* London: Pleiades Books.

Sutherland, L. S. & Mitchell, L. G. (1986), *The history of the university of Oxford: the eighteenth century,* T. H. Aston (series ed.), Oxford: Clarendon Press.

Sweet, Rosemary (1997), *The writing of urban histories in eighteenth-century England,* Oxford: Clarendon Press.

Sydenham, Thomas (1809), *The works of Thomas Sydenham, M.D., on acute and chronic diseases; with their histories and modes of cure with notes, intended to accommodate them to the present state of medicine, and to the climate and diseases of the United States,* Benjamin Rush (ed.), Philadelphia: Benjamin & Thomas Kite.

Thackeray, William Makepeace (n.d.), *The Newcomes: memoirs of a most respectable family,* London: Walter Scott Ltd.

Thornton, Thomas (1804), *A sporting tour through the northern parts of England, and great part of the highlands of Scotland,* London: printed for Vernor and Hood.

Tomalin, Claire (2003), *Samuel Pepys: the unequalled self,* Harmondsworth: Penguin Books.

Toomer, G. J. (1996), *Eastern wisdome and learning: the study of Arabic in seventeenth-century England,* Oxford: Clarendon Press.

Tyacke, Nicholas (1997), *The history of the University of Oxford: Seventeenth-century Oxford,* T. H. Aston (series ed.), Oxford: Clarendon Press.

Updike, Daniel Berkeley (1922), *Printing types: their history, forms, and use,* 2nd edn, Cambridge, MA: Harvard University Press.

Valentia, George, Viscount (1809), *Voyages and travels to India, Ceylon, the Red Sea, Abyssinia, and Eqypt, in the years 1802, 1803, 1804, 1805, and 1806,* London: William Miller.

Verdier, Antoine du (1585), *La Bibliotheque d'Antoine du Verdier... contenant le catalogue de tous ceux qui ont escrit, ou traduict en françois, & autres dialectes de ce royaume, ensemble leurs oeuvres imprimees & non imprimees; l'argument de la matière y traictée; ... ou autre chose notable tiree d'aucunes d'icelles oeuvres. Aussi y sont contenus les livres dont les autheurs sont incertains. Avec un discours sur les bonnes lettres servant de preface. Et à la fin un supplement de l'epitome de la bibliotheque de Gesne,* Lyon: B. Honorat.

Vergil, Polydore (1534), *Polydori Vergilii Vrbinatis Anglicæ historiæ libri XXVI,* Basle: apud Io. Bebelium.

Verne, Jules (1995), *Around the world in eighty days,* Oxford: Oxford University Press.

Vervliet, Hendrick D. L. (2004), 'Robert Estienne's printing types', *The library,* 5 (2), pp. 107–75.

Virgil (1789), *Opera,* Richard François Philippe Brunck (ed.), Strasburg:

Virgil *The Æneid of Henry Howard, Earl of Surrey* (1963), University of California publications in English no. 26, Florence H. Ridley (ed.), Berkeley, CA: University of California Press.

Vogt, Johann (1753), *Catalogus historico-criticus librorum rariorum: jam curis quartis recognitus et copiosa accessione ex symbolis et collatione bibliophilorum per Germaniam doctissimorum adauctus,* Hamburg: sumtibus Christiani Heroldi.

Wagner, John A. (1999), *Historical dictionary of the Elizabethan world: Britain, Ireland, Europe, and America,* Phoenix, AZ: Oryx Press.

Wakefield, Robert (1524?), *Sacrarum literaru[m] professoris eximij oratio de laudibus & vtilitate triu[m] lingua[rum] Arabicæ Chaldaicæ & Hebraica, atq[ue]; idiomatibus hebraicis quæ in vtroq[ue]; testame[n]to i[n]ueniu[n]tur,* London: apud VVinandum de Vord.

Walpole, Horace (1791), *The castle of Otranto: a gothic story. Translated by William Marshal... from the original Italian of Onuphrio Muralto...,* Parma: printed by Bodoni, for J. Edwards, London.

Walpole, Horace (1806), *A catalogue of the royal and noble authors of England, Scotland, and Ireland; with lists of their works by the late Horatio Walpole, Earl of Orford. Enlarged and continued to the present time, by Thomas Par,* London: printed for John Scott.

Wanley, Humfrey (1705), *Antiquæ literaturæ septentrionalis libri duo quorum primus Georgii Hickesii... linguarum vett. septentrionalium thesaurum..., et Andreæ Fountaine... numismata Saxonica & Dano-Saxonica complectitur ; alter continet*

Humfredi Wanleii librorum vett. septentrionalium… catalogum [etc.], Oxford: e Theatro Sheldoniano.

Warner, J. Christopher (1998), *Henry VIII's divorce : literature and the politics of the printing press*, Woodbridge, Suffolk: Boydell Press.

Weston, David (2003), 'William Hunter: zodiac man', *Scottish book collector*, (7/8), pp. 17–23.

White, John (1788.), *A catalogue of the entire collection of… coins and medals … books, engravings… shells… &c., being the property of… J. White… which will be sold, etc.*, London.

Wiburn, Perceval (1581), *A checke or reproofe of M. Howlets vntimely shreeching in her Maiesties eares : with an answeare to the reasons alleadged in a discourse therunto annexed, why Catholikes (as they are called) refuse to goe to church: vvherein (among other things) the papists traiterous and treacherous doctrine and demeanour towardes our Soueraigne and the state, is somewhat at large vpon occasion vnfolded: their diuelish pretended conscience also examined, and the foundation thereof vndermined. And lastly shevved thatit [sic] is the duety of all true Christians and subiectes to haunt publike church assemblies*, London: at the three Cranes in the Vintree, by Thomas Dawson, for Toby Smyth.

Windle, John & Pippin, Karma (1999), *Thomas Frognall Dibdin 1776–1847: a bibliography*, New Castle, DE: Oak Knoll Press.

Winship, George Parker (1926), *Gutenberg to Plantin: an outline of the early history of printing*, Cambridge, MA: Harvard University Press.

Woodburn, Samuel (1816), *Woodburn's gallery of rare portraits; consisting of original plates, by Cecil, Delaram, Droeshout… &c., with facsimile copies from the rarest and most curious portraits, illustrative of Granger's Biographical history of England, Clarendon's History of the rebellion, Burnet's History of his own time, Pennant's London, &c… containing two hundred portraits, of persons celebrated for their diplomatic services, military or naval atchievements, literary acquirements, eccentric habits, or some peculiar feature in their lives deserving the notice of the historian and biographer; particularly the… equestrian set of plates in the illustrated Clarendon, belonging to the Right Hon. Earl Spencer, K.G., with others from the most remarkable and singular prints, in the possession of different noblemen and gentlemen, celebrated for their collection of rare portraits*, London: pub. for the proprietor, by G. Jones.

Woodhouse, John (1803), *A catalogue of the entire, elegant and valuable library of John Woodhouse, Esq., comprising… books, in antient and modern English history … which will be sold by auction… Dec. 12, 1803*, London: Leigh, Sotheby, and Son.

Wordsworth, William & Wordsworth, Dorothy (2000), *The letters of William and Dorothy Wordsworth*, Ernest de Selincourt (ed.), Oxford: Clarendon Press.

Workman, Leslie J. (1992), *Medievalism in England*, Cambridge: Boydell & Brewer.

Index

TIGER OF THE STRIPE

*Typeset by Tiger of the Stripe
in Adobe Caslon Pro for the text,
English Textura for the blackletter &
Victor Gaultney's Gentium for the Greek.
The cover is set in
Adobe Caslon Pro, Founder's Caslon
(for the fist) digitised by the late Justin Howes,
English Textura & Fell Roman,
the last two being from
Hoefler & Frere-Jones's
Historical Allsorts.*

Lightning Source UK Ltd.
Milton Keynes UK
UKOW051451010812

196910UK00001B/136/A